5

FILM SCORE

FILM SCORE

The View from the Podium

Edited and Introduced by
TONY THOMAS

South Brunswick and New York: A.S. Barnes and Company
London: Thomas Yoseloff Ltd

A.S. Barnes and Co., Inc.
Cranbury, New Jersey 08512

Thomas Yoseloff Ltd
Magdalen House
136-148 Tooley Street
London SE1 2TT, England

Library of Congress Cataloging in Publication Data

Main entry under title:

Film score.

    "Film music discography":
    Bibliography:
    Contains essays on "film music" by composers of film music introduced by short biographical sketches.
    1. Moving-picture music—Addresses, essays, lectures.
I. Thomas, Tony, 1927-
ML2075.F46   782.8'5   78-75341
ISBN 0-498-02358-3

Books by TONY THOMAS

The Films of Errol Flynn (with Rudy Behlmer and Clifford McCarty)
Ustinov in Focus
The Busby Berkeley Book
The Films of Kirk Douglas
Cads and Cavaliers
Music for the Movies
Sam Wood: Hollywood Professional
The Films of Marlon Brando
Song and Dance Man: The Films of Gene Kelly
The Films of the Forties
Harry Warren and the Hollywood Musical
Burt Lancaster
Hollywood's Hollywood: The Movies About the Movies (with Rudy Behlmer)
The Great Adventure Films
Gregory Peck

PRINTED IN THE UNITED STATES OF AMERICA

CONTENTS

	Preface	7
	Acknowledgments	11
1	Aaron Copland	15
2	Miklos Rozsa	26
3	David Raksin	39
4	Franz Waxman	49
5	Hugo Friedhofer	61
6	Max Steiner	71
7	Erich Wolfgang Korngold	83
8	Dimitri Tiomkin	91
9	Hans J. Salter	101
10	Bronislau Kaper	115
11	Alfred Newman	127
12	Bernard Herrmann	143
13	Elmer Bernstein	154
14	Henry Mancini	164
15	Fred Steiner	175
16	William Alwyn	187
17	John Addison	197
18	Jerry Fielding	209
19	Jerry Goldsmith	219
20	Leonard Rosenman	230
	Film Music Discography	245
	Motion Picture Music: A Select Bibliography	260

PREFACE

It is a peculiarity of film music that if it isn't just right, it can be very wrong. Appropriateness is the key concern and, in the happy circumstance where appropriateness is matched with inspiration, the film then gets a subtle added dimension. That, in a nutshell, is what film music is all about—the supplying of another dimension, the adding of something not conveyed by the script, the acting, the direction, or the photography. Marrying music to film is, like all forms of marriage, fraught with problems and pitfalls. But it also offers potent opportunities for composers of imagination and inventiveness. Perhaps the most fascinating thing about composing for films is the potential. In terms of quality and effectiveness, it has no boundaries. However, there is no need to belabor that point since the views expressed in this book by the composers themselves provide all kinds of variations on that theme.

There are some other peculiarities about the craft of writing music for films, many of which arise from the undeniable fact that artists are peculiar people, as are their problems and their aspirations. Those who are gifted with the talent to invent, create, and compose are, fortunately, beyond the norm. The film composer has, however, two rather negative forces working against him—snobbism and ignorance. The snobbism comes from outside the industry, from so-called serious critics and music lovers who have always tended to regard that which is written for films as being of less value than what is written for the concert hall, the opera, the ballet, or the theater. There seems to be an eagerness to judge film composition by its worst examples rather than its best. Most composers have come to terms with that narrow view, realizing that it makes as much sense as condemning the church for atrocities committed in its name. Of much greater concern to them is ignorance, because it comes mostly from within the industry and from the very people who hire composers—the producers.

The disparity between composers and producers is legend. In defense of producers, let it be said that theirs is the harder role because it requires them to be knowledgeable about every aspect of filmmaking, not the least of which is the task of raising the money and turning dreams into reality. A composer needs to be knowledgeable about only his own contribution, although it is a highly specialized contribution and has its own language—a language understood only by the musically educated. It therefore becomes difficult for producers and composers even to discuss what it is they aim to achieve. What a producer wants is quite simply a successful picture; he is a businessman and he is more often than not carrying the heavy burden of other people's investments. In terms of music, he would also like a tune that will become popular away from the picture and help promote it. It is sometimes difficult for a composer to argue that a score which subliminally enhances the film and helps meld all of its elements is really of greater value than a simple melody that can be immediately lifted off the main title and transferred to a recording.

The aim of music in films is to enlarge the emotional content, especially in scenes where the other elements have failed to reach their potential. But music has its limitations; it can help a picture but it can never save it; and both the composer and the producer have to realize the functions of the score. Producers sometimes fondly imagine that by laying an impressive score on a sound track, they will cover up the deficiencies of the visuals. It never does, just as excellent photography cannot help a bad performance by an actor. Obvious as this may seem, it is a point frequently overlooked, and composers sometimes fondly imagine that the film is a concert platform for them. It isn't.

Scoring films is perhaps the most difficult aspect of filmmaking because it is the least tangible—which also makes it a great challenge. Aside from the inescapable restrictions of timing and the requirements of scoring that preclude the development of material, such as in a concert compositon, there are few rules in writing music for films. It allows for all kinds of music, from the most grandly symphonic to the most austere instrumentation, touching on every style and school of composing, even electronic and whatever happens to be currently popular. The requirement is only that the music suits and serves the purposes of the picture, that it is effective, that it works.

Ralph Vaughan Williams, who did not come to film scoring until he was in his sixties, looked upon the cinema as a serious and important outlet for composers of great merit. He urged the best musicians of his day to realize their responsibility in helping to lift film scoring out of the realm of hackwork. He also looked upon film scoring as a fine discipline, "I recommend a course of it to all composition teachers whose pupils are apt to be dawdling in their ideas, or whose every bar is sacred and must not be cut or altered." Vaughan Williams admired the practical attitudes necessary for film composition and amused himself at the thought of tough-minded film producers bearing down on famous old masters who indulged themselves with repeated endings and drawn out codas. He considered scoring a fine art, albeit a specialized one, but he believed it would never reach its full potential until producers realized that all the components of filmmaking should come together from the very beginning of the production—not segregated and assembled at the last moment, as is still the case more often than not. "It is only when this is achieved that the film will come into its own as one of the finest of the art forms."

The purpose of this book is to state the case for the film composer and his craft. Only those unusually interested in film music will go to see movies because of the score, but even those of average musical receptivity will find a greater enjoyment of the total experience of filmgoing if they become aware of what a skilled composer can bring to that experience. It is hoped that the book may bring this point closer to the consideration of film producers, particularly those who currently look on music only as an afterthought, as an appendage. The late Bernard Herrmann often said he feared producers calling on him in somewhat the same manner they called upon a mortician—to come in and try to fix up the body. It is, of course, better that the composer be involved while the production is still alive.

A personal footnote: My own interest in film music goes back to my early years as a moviegoer and my good fortune in growing up in a musical milieu. Later, as a broadcaster and writer, I was able to expand that interest. I am grateful that it turned out that way. I found the composers to be, with few exceptions, well worth the knowing. Getting to learn about their craft expanded my appreciation not only of films, but of music as well.

                                                              Tony Thomas

ACKNOWLEDGMENTS

I received a great deal of help in putting this book together. In the case of the living composers I am, obviously, grateful to each one for his cooperation. In the case of the Franz Waxman chapter, I thank his son John. And I thank Mrs. Lee Steiner for allowing me to use the words of her husband Max. In preparing the Alfred Newman piece I thank his, and my, good friend Ken Darby. I also thank Rudy Behlmer and Clifford McCarty for their assistance, and in the job of typing the manuscript I thank Kathy Burns. She and her husband Bob were primary movers in the birth of the book.

Tony Thomas
Burbank, California
January, 1979

FILM SCORE

Aaron Copland.

1
AARON COPLAND

That only a small portion of Aaron Copland's output has been written for the screen is a point to ponder. It is not, as many people suppose, because of a lack of interest in film composition on his part. It is simply that he has seldom been invited by the major production houses of Hollywood. That the most successful and universally esteemed of American composers has not been more widely employed in films is easier to explain than to understand. It is an American conundrum, and it has much to do with distance—not simply the distance between New York and Los Angeles, but the spiritual and artistic gulf between the American East and West. The situation does not have any similarity elsewhere. British composers can write for the concert hall and the cinema without moving outside London. Paris and Moscow offer the same advantages. But most American feature films are scored in California, and for the most part, composers need to reside there in order to be employed. However, once they do that, once they *settle*, they become a part of the Hollywood environment, and they become somehow estranged from the so-called main body of serious American composition.

The problem is abetted by the tendency among almost all California filmmakers to lean more toward popular than serious art. They may admire a composer of the stature of a Copland, but they tend not to employ such a man.

What makes the Copland case even harder to understand is his great success in writing film music. Although he has written the scores for only six commercial features and two documentaries, each score is regarded as textbook study. The symphonic suite

from *The Red Pony* (1949) is the most popular concert presentation of any American film score, and it has been recorded several
times. His influence on the younger generations of American composers, including many who make their living writing film scores,
has been profound. He even received Hollywood's top prize, the
Oscar, for his score for *The Heiress* (1949) but he has not been
hired by a Hollywood studio since then. Copland's only subsequent film score was written in New York in 1961, for the not very
successful *Something Wild*. He later reworked much of the
material into his suit "Music for a Great City." The most ironic
aspect of Copland's adventures in Hollywood is that he won his
Oscar for *The Heiress* even though his title music for the film was
removed and replaced by an arrangement of "Plaisir d'Amour."
This is the only instance of a score winning an Oscar after having
been shorn of its overture, which is usually the part of a score that
makes the most impact.

Despite having been given something of a cold shoulder by
Hollywood, Copland does not denigrate the art of film scoring.
He still believes that the cinema is a serious outlet for composers
and a challenge to their talents and he feels that the whole level of
contemporary music could be raised if better music was written for
motion pictures.

Aaron Copland had long been established in the concert and
recital halls before he turned his attentions to film music. Born in
Brooklyn in 1900, he had been one of the students of the
celebrated teacher Nadia Boulanger in Paris in the twenties, and
by the following decade he was able to earn a living, as do few
composers, from his music. He had written several scores for the
New York theater; he had won wide approval with his ballet score
Billy the Kid; and he was intrigued by the possibilities of film. In
1939 Copland was hired to score *The City*, an impression of
American life for the New York World's Fair. He later used some
of the thematic material in his suite *Music for Movies*. Shortly
after doing the documentary, he was approached by Lewis
Milestone, who had produced and directed a film of John
Steinbeck's *Of Mice and Men* (1940) and who wanted something
beyond the then Hollywood norm in the way of a score. The picture was in itself something of a departure: it was an intelligent
treatment of a well-respected piece of American literature, and it
attempted to retain the realism of the material. Copland's score,

with its light textures and use of simple, quasi-folk themes, pointed to a possible new direction for American film music. The composer also extracted parts of it for a further two movements of his *Music for Movies*.

Of Mice and Men resulted in Copland being asked to write the score for another example of classic Americana, Thornton Wilder's *Our Town*. It remains a quintessential example of purely American sound, again lightly scored, with a main statement of only five notes. It is a tribute to Copland's skill that those five notes speak eloquently for the delicacy, poignancy, and past lifestyle of the story. Copland also employs this theme in his five-movement suite *Music for Movies*. It is a suite which should be studied by all who are interested in capturing the American ethos in music.

Despite the critical esteem Copland enjoyed for having scored *Of Mice and Men* and *Our Town*, he did not receive any major studio contracts. Both films were offbeat products, and neither did big business at the box office. However, the films benefited Copland by proving his ability in the medium and marked him as a composer for special occasions. Such an occasion came up three years later when Samuel Goldwyn made *The North Star* (1943), one of Hollywood's few salutes to Russia. It was an expensive production, and it kept the composer busy for several months, writing an extensive score utilizing songs and dance as well as symphonic material. Unfortunately, the film did not please the general public, and with the swiftly changing political tides, it was doomed to become a forgotten item within a few years.

Copland did not appear on the Hollywood scene for another six years, when he was brought back for *The Red Pony*, again an acclaimed piece of Steinbeck Americana and again a rather special production. It was a modest success with the public, but with time it has achieved prestige, particularly because of its score, which can rightly be regarded as Copland's magnum opus in film music. The subsequent suite, in six movements, is a virtual sound picture of the story, dealing as it does with life on a California ranch and a young boy's love for a horse and his friendship with a cowboy. This beautifully evocative music is a happy example of a score that perfectly serves the needs of a film and yet is able to live independently when later arranged in concert form. It also strengthens the argument that film provides such opportunities;

there is no reason to think that the suite from *The Red Pony* is of lesser musical quality because it was originally written for film rather than for a ballet.

Copland's only contract to score a major Hollywood production was *The Heiress*, produced by Paramount and directed by William Wyler. By 1949 Hollywood was less scared than before of making films of prestigious plays, and the hiring of Copland no doubt increased the prestige. His score aptly evokes the New York of 1850 and utilizes various dance tunes of the time. It is the most operatic of Copland's film scores and uses the device of motifs for the main characters, a device he avoids in his other scores. In this instance, he felt it appropriate to the story, which is focused on three main characters and their interplay. Despite the large amount of material in the score, Copland declined to adapt it later for a concert suite, feeling that the music did not lend itself to that form. When his title music was removed from the final print, after he had left Hollywood, Copland issued a press statement disclaiming responsibility. It doubtless altered the dramatic effect he had hoped to establish for the setting of the story. It did not prevent him from winning an Oscar, but Copland has not scored a Hollywood picture since. In 1961 he wrote the score for the New York-produced *Something Wild*.

Even if Aaron Copland does not write any more music for films, what little he has done is ample to serve as an inspiration and a guideline. His scores will continue to be examined by students, whose only confusion may come from not understanding why a composer of such obvious skill was employed so seldom by film producers. The following article, written by the composer for the *New York Times* in 1949*, proves that he also had a marked ability to describe the functions and purposes of film scoring.

Aaron Copeland on Film Music

The next time you settle yourself comfortably into a seat at the neighborhood picture house don't forget to take off your ear-muffs. Most people don't realize they are wearing any—at any

*©1949 by The New York Times Company. Reprinted by permission.

rate, that is the impression of composers who write for the movies. Millions of moviegoers take the musical accompaniment to a dramatic film so much for granted that five minutes after the termination of a picture they couldn't tell you whether they had heard music or not.

To ask whether they thought the score exciting or merely adequate or downright awful would be to give them a musical inferiority complex. But, on second thought, and possibly in self-protection, comes the query: "Isn't it true that one isn't supposed to be listening to the music? Isn't it supposed to work on you unconsciously without being listened to directly as you would listen at a concert?"

No discussion of movie music ever gets very far without having to face this problem: Should one hear a movie score? If you are a musician there is no problem because the chances are you can't help but listen. More than once I've had a good picture ruined for me by an inferior score. Have you had the same experience? Yes? Then you may congratulate yourself: you're definitely musical.

But it's the spectator, so absorbed in the dramatic action that he fails to take in the background music, who wants to know whether he is missing anything. The answer is bound up with the degree of your general musical perception. It is the degree to which you are aurally minded that will determine how much pleasure you may derive by absorbing the background musical accompaniment as an integral part of the combined impression made by the film.

One's appreciation of a work of art is partly determined by the amount of preparation one brings to it. The head of the family will probably be less sensitive to the beauty and appropriateness of the gowns worn by the feminine star than his wife will be. It's hopeless to expect the tone-deaf to listen to a musical score. But since the great majority of movie patrons are undoubtly musical to some degree, they should be encouraged not to ignore the music; on the contrary, I would hope to convince them that by taking it in they will be enriching both their musical and their cinema experience.

Recently I was asked rather timorously whether I liked to write movie music—the implication being that it was possibly degrading for a composer of symphonies to trifle with a commercial product. "Would you do it anyhow, even if it were less well paid?" I think I would, and, moreover, I think most composers would, principally because film music constitutes a new musical medium that exerts a fascination of its own. Actually, it is a new form of dramatic music—related to opera, ballet, incidental theatre music—in contradistinction to concert music of the symphonic or chamber music kind. As a new form it opens up unexplored possibilities, or should.

The main complaint about film music as written today in Hollywood is that so much of it is cut and dried, rigidly governed by conventions that have grown up with surprising rapidity in the short period of twenty-odd years since the talkies began. But, leaving the hack composer aside, there is no reason why a serious composer, cooperating with an intelligent producer on a picture of serious artistic pretensions, should not be able to have his movie scores judged by the same standards applied to his concert music. That is certainly the way William Walton in *Henry V,* Serge Prokofieff in *Alexander Nevsky* or Virgil Thomson in *Louisiana Story* would want to be judged. They did not have to lower thier standards because they were writing for a mass audience. Some day the term "movie music" will clearly define a specific musical genre and will not have, as it does nowadays, a pejorative meaning.

Most people are curious as to just how one goes about putting music to a film. Fortunately, the process is not so complex that it cannot be outlined here.

The first thing one must do, of course, is to see the picture. Almost all musical scores are composed after the film itself is completed. The only exception to this is when the script calls for realistic music—that is, music which is visually sung or played or danced to on the screen. In that case the music must be composed before the scene is photographed. It will then be recorded and the scene in question shot to a playback of the recording. Thus, when you see an actor singing or playing or dancing, he is only making believe as far as the sound goes, for the music had previously been put down on film.

The first run-through of the film for the composer is usually a solemn moment. After all, he must live with it for several weeks. The solemnity of the occasion is emphasized by the exclusive audience that views it with him: the producer, the director, the musical head of the studio, the picture editor, the music cutter, the conductor, the orchestrator—in fact, anyone involved in scoring the picture. At that showing it is difficult for the composer to view the photoplay coldly. There is an understandable compulsion to like everything, for he is looking at what must necessarily constitute the source of his future inspiration.

The purpose of the run-through is to decide how much music is needed and where it should be. (In technical jargon this is called "to spot" the picture.) Since no background score is continuous throughout the full length of a film (that would constitute a motion-picture opera, an unexploited cinema form), the score will normally consist of separate sequences, each lasting from a few seconds to several minutes in duration. A sequence as long as seven minutes would be exceptional. The entire score, made up of perhaps thirty or more such sequences, may add up to from forty to ninety minutes of music.

Much discussion, much give and take may be necessary before final decisions are reached regarding the "spotting" of the picture. In general my impression has been that composers are better able to gauge the over-all effect of a musical accompaniment than the average non-musician. Personally I like to make use of music's power sparingly, saving it for absolutely essential points. A composer knows how to play with silences; knows that to take music out can at times be more effective than any use of it might be.

The producer-director, on the other hand, is more prone to think of music in terms of its immediate functional usage. Sometimes he has ulterior motives: anything wrong with a scene—a poor bit of acting, a badly read line, an embarrassing pause—he secretly hopes will be covered up by a clever composer. Producers have been known to hope that an entire picture would be saved by a good score. But the composer is not a magician; he can hardly be expected to do more than to make potent through music the film's dramatic and emotional values.

When well contrived there is no question but that a musical score can be of enormous help to a picture. One can prove that point, laboratory fashion, by showing an audience a climactic scene with the sound turned off and then once again with the sound track turned on. Here briefly is listed a number of ways in which music serves the screen:

1. Creating a more convincing atmosphere of time and place. Not all Hollywood composers bother about this nicety. Too often, their scores are interchangeable; a thirteenth century Gothic drama and a hard-boiled modern battle of the sexes get similar

treatment. The lush symphonic texture of late nineteenth century music remains the dominating influence. But there are exceptions. Recently, the higher grade horse-opera has begun to have its own musical flavor, mostly a folksong derivative.

2. Underlining psychological refinements—the unspoken thoughts of a character or the unseen implications of a situation. Music can play upon the emotions of the spectator, sometimes counterpointing the thing seen with an aural image that implies the contrary of the thing seen. This is not as subtle as it sounds. A well-placed dissonant chord can stop an audience cold in the middle of a sentimental scene, or a calculated wood-wind passage can turn what appears to be a solemn moment into a belly-laugh.

3. Serving as a kind of neutral background filler. This is really the music one isn't supposed to hear, the sort that helps to fill the empty spots between pauses in a conversation. It's the movie composer's most ungrateful task. But at times, though no one else may notice, he will get private satisfaction from the thought that music of little intrinsic value, through professional manipulation, has enlivened and made more human the deathly pallor of a screen shadow. This is hardest to do, as any film composer will attest, when the neutral filler type of music must weave its way underneath dialogue.

4. Building a sense of continuity. The picture editor knows better than anyone how serviceable music can be in tying together a visual medium which is, by its very nature, continually in danger of falling apart. One sees this most obviously in montage scenes where the use of a unifying musical idea may save the quick flashes of disconnected scenes from seeming merely chaotic.

5. Underpinning the theatrical build-up of a scene, and rounding it off with a sense of finality. The first instance that comes to mind is the music that blares out at the end of a film. Certain producers have boasted their picture's lack of a musical score, but I never saw or heard of a picture that ended in silence.

We have merely skimmed the surface, without mentioning the innumerable examples of utilitarian music—offstage street bands, the barn dance, merry-go-rounds, circus music, cafe music, the neighbor's girl practicing her piano, etc. All these, and many others, introduced with apparent naturalistic intent, serve to vary subtly the aural interest of the sound track.

Perhaps it is only fair to mention that several of these uses come to the screen by way of the long tradition of incidental music in the legitimate theatre. Most workers in the theatre, and especially our playwrights, would agree that music enhances the glamour and atmosphere of a stage production, any stage production. Formerly it was considered indispensable. But nowadays only musical comedy can afford a considerable-sized orchestra in the pit.

With mounting costs of production it looks as if the serious drama would have to get along with a union minimum of four musicians for some time to come. If there is to be any combining of music and the spoken drama in any but the barest terms, it will have to happen in Hollywood, for the Broadway theatre is practically out of the running.

But now perhaps we had better return to our hypothetical composer. Having determined where the separate musical sequences will begin and end he turns the film over to the music cutter who prepares a so-called cue sheet. The cue sheet provides the composer with a detailed description of the physical action in each sequence, plus the exact timings in thirds of seconds of that action, thereby making it possible for a practiced composer to write an entire score without ever again referring to the picture. Personally I prefer to remain in daily contact with the picture itself, viewing again and again the sequence I happen to be working on.

The layman usually imagines that the most difficult part of the job in composing for the films has to do with the precise "fitting" of the music to the action. Doesn't that kind of timing straitjacket the composer? The answer is no, for two reasons: first, having to compose music to accompany specific action is a help rather than a hindrance, since the action itself induces music in a composer of theatrical imagination, whereas he has no such visual stimulus in writing absolute music. Secondly, the timing is mostly a matter of minor adjustments, since the over-all musical fabric is there.

For the composer of concert music, changing to the medium of celluloid does bring certain special pitfalls. For example, melodic invention, highly prized in the concert hall, may at times be distracting in certain film situations. Even phrasing in the concert manner, which would normally emphasize the independence of separate contrapuntal lines, may be distracting when applied to screen accompaniments. In orchestration there are many subtleties of timbre—distinctions meant to be listened to for their own expressive quality in an auditorium—which are completely wasted on sound track.

As compensation for these losses, the composer has other possibilities, some of them tricks, which are unobtainable in Carnegie Hall. In scoring one section of "The Heiress," for example, I was able to superimpose two orchestras, one upon another. Both recorded the same music at different times, one orchestra consisting of strings alone, the other constituted normally. Later these were combined by simultaneously re-recording the original tracks, thereby producing a highly expressive orchestral texture. Bernard Herrmann, one of the most ingenious of screen composers, called for (and got) eight celestas—an unheard-of combination of Fifty-seventh Street—to suggest a winter's sleigh ride. Miklos Rozsa's use of the "echo chamber"—a device to give normal tone a ghostlike aura—was widely remarked and subsequently done to death.

Unusual effects are obtainable through overlapping incoming and outgoing music tracks. Like two trains passing one another, it is possible to bring in and take out at the same time two different musics. *The Red Pony* gave me an opportunity to use this cinema specialty. When the day-dreaming imagination of a little boy turns white chickens into white circus horses the visual image is mirrored in an aural image by having the chicken music transform itself into circus music, a device only obtainable by means of the overlap.

Let us now assume that the musical score has been completed and is ready for recording. The scoring stage is a happy-making place for the composer. Hollywood has gathered to itself some of America's finest performers; the music will be beautifully played and recorded with a technical perfection not to be matched anywhere else.

Most composers like to invite their friends to be present at the recording session of important sequences. The reason is that neither the composer nor his friends are ever again likely to hear the music sound out in concert style. For when it is combined with the picture most of the dynamic levels will be changed. Otherwise the finished product might sound like a concert with pictures. In lowering dynamic levels niceties of shading, some inner voices and bass parts may be lost. Erich Korngold, one of Hollywood's top men, put it well when he said: "A movie composer's immortality lasts from the recording stage to the dubbing room."

The dubbing room is where all the tracks involving sound of any kind, including dialogue, are put through the machines to obtain one master sound track. This is a delicate process as far as the music is concerned, for it is only a hair's breadth that separates the "too loud" from the "too soft". Sound engineers, working the dials that control volume, are not always as musically sensitive as composers would like them to be. What is called for is a new species, a sound mixer who is half musician and half engineer: and even then, the mixing of dialogue, music and realistic sounds of all kinds must always remain problematical.

In view of these drawbacks to the full sounding out of his music, it is only natural that the composer often hopes to be able to extract a viable concert suite from his film score. There is a current tendency to believe that movie scores are not proper material for concert music. The argument is that separated from its visual justification the music falls flat.

Personally, I doubt very much that any hard and fast rule can be made that will cover all cases. Each score will have to be judged on its merits and, no doubt, stories that require a more continuous type of musical development in a unified atmosphere will lend themselves better than others to re-working for concert purposes. Rarely is it conceivable that the music of a film might be extracted without much reworking. But I fail to see why, if successful suites like Grieg's *Peer Gynt* can be made from nineteenth century incidental stage music, a twentieth century composer can't be expected to do as well with a film score.

As for the picture score, it is only in the motion picture theatre that the composer for the first time gets the full impact of what he has accomplished, tests the dramatic punch of his favorite musical spot, appreciates the curious importance and unimportance of detail, wishes that he had done certain things differently and is surprised that others came off better than he had hoped. For when all is said and done the art of combining moving pictures with musical tones is still a mysterious art. Not the least mysterious element is the theatregoers' reaction: Millons will be listening but one never knows how many will be really hearing, so the next time you go to the movies remember to be on the composer's side. Remove those ear-muffs.

2
MIKLOS ROZSA

Of all European composers who made California their home, the
only one who reached great success in film scoring while maintaining his identity and activity as a composer of absolute music is
Miklos Rozsa. He has been prolific in writing for the screen, and
his style is so distinct it requires little musical awareness to spot it.
It is a strong, richly colored style, and it is as evident in his film
scoring as in his concert works. Rozsa has never looked upon composing for films as a lesser art and his standards in this regard are
the same as for his other compositions. All that differs is the approach, inasmuch as film music is an adjunct of the visual and
must make direct attacks on the emotions. Only a light-headed
critic would suggest that Rozsa's chamber music and his symphonic works sound like "movie music," although there have
been critics who have not been able to avoid this fatuous view.
After a performance in England of his *Theme, Variations and
Finale,* Opus 13, a critic commented that it showed unmistakable
signs of the composer's involvement in films. It was written in
1933, four years before Rozsa began his association with motion
pictures!

Rozsa was born in Budapest in April of 1908, into a comfortable
atmosphere, which included an exposure to culture. The family
spent their summers on an estate in northern Hungary and Rozsa
became interested in the music of the local people, the gypsies and
the Magyars, all of which was to have a bearing on the composer's
style. He made notes but not to the same extent as Bartok or Koda-
ly, since he was not interested in becoming an authority on folk
music. What fascinated him was the color and vitality of this

Miklos Rozsa, with author Tony Thomas (left).

native music. He had started his study of the violin at the age of five and three years later made his first public appearance as a violinist, playing a movement from a Mozart concerto and actually dressed as Mozart! Not long after this he conducted a school orchestra in a performance of Haydn's *Toy Symphony*. In high school he was elected president of the Franz Liszt Society, organizing concerts and advocating recognition of contemporary music. Some of his views, condemning pseudo-Hungarian music and demanding respect for the works of Bartok, caused him to be frowned upon by the Budapest musical establishment, but his success in winning prizes with his compositions made it difficult to hold young Rosza in line.

Rozsa's father, an industrialist, was not in favor of his son following a career in music and insisted upon a sound general education. It was agreed that Rozsa should proceed to Leipzig to further his education, ostensibly as a chemist, but with the aid of the German musicologist Hermann Grabner, he enrolled at the Conservatory of Music, one of the most esteemed schools of music in Europe. Grabner later wrote to Rozsa senior to assure him that his son was a musician of exceptional gifts and that there was little need to worry about his future. Rozsa's chamber compositions came to the attention of the venerable publishing firm of Breitkopf and Hartel, who put him under contract—a contract which still exists.

Rozsa graduated from the Leipzig Conservatory with honors in 1929 and for a time stayed on as an assistant to Grabner. He settled in Paris in 1932 following a concert of his chamber works and began writting a series of compositions, several of which brought him considerable critical acclaim but not a great deal of money. In 1934 he presented a joint concert with French composer Arthur Honegger and again found that although the notices were good, there was barely enough profit to buy a good supper. Rozsa asked Honegger, even then one of the most highly regarded of composers, how he managed to make a living and was astounded by the Frenchman's answer—that he wrote scores for films. Rozsa was completely unaware that serious music was being written for the screen, assuming that it was merely an outlet for pop composers, but followed Honegger's advice and went to see a picture he had just scored, *Les Miserables.* It was a revelation to Rozsa, who then tried to break into the field, but could not persuade anyone to give him the opportunity.

Three years would pass before Rozsa wrote his first film score. He had written a successful ballet, *Hungaria,* which ran at the Duke of York's Theatre in London for two years. While in London in early 1937 Rozsa met director Jacques Feyder, whom he had known in Paris. Feyder was impressed by *Hungaria* and asked Rosza to write the score for a film he was making with Marlene Dietrich and Robert Donat called *Knight without Armor.* The film was a production of Hungarian-born Alexander Korda, who was not disposed toward hiring an untried film composer, but Feyder insisted, and even went so far as to tell Korda the composer was a close friend of Zoltan, the production manager brother of Korda. This was quite untrue but it helped tip the scales. The end result left no one in doubt about Rosza's talent for film composition, and Korda put him under contract. Most of Korda's films over the next four years were scored by Rosza.

In 1940 Rozsa was working on the score—a very large and elaborate score—for Korda's *The Thief of Bagdad* at the Denham Studios when the decision was made, because of wartime conditions, to finish the picture in Hollywood. Korda made another three films in Hollywood—*That Hamilton Woman, Lydia,* and *The Jungle Book*—and required Rozsa to write the scores. When Korda returned to England, the composer decided to remain in Hollywood and began what would become a long and profitable association with the film capital. In 1943 he signed a contract with Paramount and proceeded to write music of a quality far beyond anything ever produced for that studio, of which *Double Indemnity* (1944) and *The Lost Weekend* (1945) are the prime examples. They were not, however, written without some ruffling of executive feathers; it was not until praise started to flow that the Paramount brass agreed that the Rozsa scores were "exactly" what they had in mind.

Rozsa's career in Hollywood has somewhat strangely structured itself on four distinct stylistic layers. He refers to it as being a casualty of movie "type casting." With such pictures as *The Thief of Bagdad, The Jungle Book,* and *Sahara,* he acquired a reputation for writing exotic, subtropical music. Then came *The Lost Weekend* and a plunge into the world of mental disorder, followed by the similarly dark and psychologically troubled *Spellbound, The Strange Love of Martha Ivers, The Red House,* and *Time Out of Mind.* In 1947 Rozsa signed a contract with Universal and almost immediately became a commentator on American crime with his music for the searing *Brute Force, The Naked City, Criss Cross,* and *The Asphalt Jungle.* Two years later he accepted a contract with MGM and soon became the leading composer for epic historical subjects, especially those with biblical settings. It began with *Quo Vadis* in 1951 and continued with *Ivanhoe, Plymouth Adventure, Julius Caesar, Young Bess, Moonlight Moonfleet,* and *Diane.* This proved to be the firmest typecasting of all, so that when MGM remade *Ben-Hur* in 1959, there was little doubt as to whom they would choose to write the score. It brought Rosza his third Oscar; the previous ones were for *Spellbound* in 1945 and *A Double Life* (another classic in mental disorder!) in 1948. With *King of Kings* and *El Cid,* both composed in 1961, and *Sodom and Gomorrah* the following years, Rozsa's fourth period of typecasting progressed to a point where it became of concern to him.

The concern unfortunately coincided with the swift decline in the number of films produced by the Hollywood studios in the Sixties and the tendency of producers to look more and more to pop

music for their pictures. It is difficult to understand that a composer of Rozsa's prestige and experience scored no films for the
five-year period 1963-1968. Of the projects offered him since then,
very few have seemed to him to be worthwhile. A man of some af-
fluence, Rozsa has long been in a position to be selective.

Miklos Rozsa is among the few film composers who is also a
musicologist, having received his doctorate from the Conservatory
in Leipzig. From 1945 to 1965 Rozsa was on the faculty of the
University of Southern California as a professor of film music
theory and technique. The following article is a revision, with
some expansion, of one of his lectures, used here with his permission and guidance.

Miklos Rozsa on Film Music

More than a hundred years have passed since Richard Wagner
created the aesthetic definition of his artistic programme, calling it
Gesamtkunstwerk (the all comprising work of art), meaning the
perfect combination of music, drama and acting. In his works, the
music was the dominating and most important factor.

Today no art comes nearer the Wagnerian ideal than the most
vigorous and spontaneous art-form of the twentieth century, the
art of the cinema. It is a synthetic art, a *Gesamtkunstwerk* in the
best Wagnerian meaning, being again the combination of drama,
acting, and music. However, and this is the greatest difference between the cinema and the Wagnerian ideal, music plays a minor
part in it. On the other hand, the evolution of music in films over
the past forty years has been enormous, and the requirements have
grown steadily. It offers composers problems and possibilities such
as Wagner never knew, and it certainly helps defy the old tradition
that a composer of serious or even progressive music cannot make
a decent living by his art.

The kind of composer who a century ago would have composed
operas, dramatic theater music, or program symphonies, is the one
who can turn in our time to the cinema. Naturally there are
numerous new technicalities, which he has to learn, and from the

artistic point of view, the most important fact is that he has to con-
dense his musical writing to a given and unchangeable timing. But
even this, which may be the most difficult task for a young composer, who is accustomed to formulating his musical thoughts according to the rules of musical form and logical development of his
themes, can be learned with practice in a short time by a talented
man. He must possess, however, a gift for fast musical invention
and the ability for quick writing. He has to be an absolute master
of his craft; therefore, his college or conservatory training must be
the same as every composer undergoes.

As for the difference between writing music for the concert hall
and writing it for the cinema, it is basically one of intent. Style is
not the point. If I have a certain style, you can find it in my concert
music as in my film music. What the film composer has to keep in
mind is that his score must be understood immediately: there is no
second hearing; it has only one chance to do its job. The customer
goes to a concert solely for the purpose of hearing music; the
customer goes to the cinema to see—perhaps "experience" would
be a better word—a film. In writing music for films I therefore
compose along more simple lines. It must be direct. The music
should help complete a psychological effect. There is just so much
that an actor can express with his dialogue or his face and body,
but music can go beyond that point and convey much
more—provided, of course, that it is a film being made by people
who fully understand the impact of music. Sad to say, music is still
the Cinderella of the film arts.

The first use of music in motion pictures had a not-altogether-
artistic purpose. It was a sort of camouflage. The projection
machines of the early times were terribly noisy, and music had the
not too glorious role of distracting the audience's attention from
this monotonous and nerve-racking noise. Later, when pictures
became more pretentious in length and content, showing real life
on the silver screen but without the speech and noises of common
life, it was necessary to find an aural element to accompany the
strictly visual one. Music was a natural to break the silence of the
projection room. However, this music of the early days had little
connection with the picture itself. It had no more relationship with
the happenings on the screen than the music in a restaurant has
with the conversations at the tables. It had to create an agreeable
atmosphere, playing popular tunes, and thus satisfying the spec-

tator's ear, as the picture did his eye. Usually it was a simple piano which supplied the musical needs of the cinema patrons.

With the development of the pictures, the music of the cinema underwent a rapid development, too. The piano was soon augmented by a violin, then a cello and other instruments, and as the movie houses grew, so grew the orchestra in size and quality. Toward the end of the silent era, the orchestras, if picture houses attained the size of symphony orchestras, numbered sixty to eighty pieces. First-rate conductors and musicians supplied the music, which gained importance in this new and popular entertainment.

They soon found out, for instance, that the *William Tell* overture (a favorite piece of the silent days) doesn't fit a love scene, and Mendelssohn's *Spring Song* sounds comic when played to a funeral.

Therefore, the conductors started to select the music to the different parts of the photoplay. Every scene had its own rhythm, a rhythm of motion and action, and even a rhythm of the actual cutting of the scenes. The music had now the role of accentuating this rhythm with audible sounds, and the rhythm of the picture combined with the rhythm of the music, gave a remarkable and hitherto unknown effect: synchronization.

Another and no less important element was the accentuation of expression in the film. In the silent days, when no emotion could be expressed with the human voice, which is the most intense medium of expression, it could be replaced only by music. Besides creating the atmosphere of the action, it was only the music that made one really understand and feel what it was impossible to express with gestures. The disturbing titles, moreover, had the effect of stopping the tempo of the action. The music gave real pulsation, blood, color, and life to the silent pictures. Its importance was soon discovered, and through a long line, from adaptation of classical literature to the use of film music catalogues (consisting of characteristic pieces), the first musical scores began to be composed specifically for pictures toward the end of the twenties.

The silent pictures, lacking the quality of human speech and real noises, displayed a tendency to develop into an unrealistic art, and this tendency should have been helped and accentuated by the abstract and truly unrealistic art of the music, the two thus creating a homogeneous form of expression. However, the music of the film scores tried to replace the missing sound and degenerated very often into cheap imitations of realistic noises, destroying the aesthetic unity of the pictures.

Music has her own logically continuous form and is rhythmically organized. If we try to imitate the happenings, the naturalistic sounds and reactions of the picture, which follow each other without any coordination or logical rhythm, the music will completely lose its true significance and will sink into a disorganized, meaningless noise.

Once motion pictures introduced the actual sound of the speech and noises, they then became realistic and left the music with the task of carrying the irrational, unreal element. No longer did the music stand alone as the only aural expression. With the coming of sound, music not only had to share its role with the dramatic dialogue and naturalistic noises, but it had to subordinate itself to them. This all applies, naturally, to the atmospheric, descriptive, and emotionally expressive music that we call background scoring. This is something that most clearly should be understood by all composers who seek success in films: film music is an integral part of a collective effort of many artists and technicians. The composer who refuses to coordinate his music to the requirements of this collectivity refuses to serve the drama with his music and should therefore stay away from films.

The first sound films were mostly musicals. With the exception of the technical novelty, they didn't bring anything new to the screen. They were merely photographed operettas or musical comedies. The pictures seemed to lose for some time the aesthetics they had achieved in the last years of the silent era. The song hit became the most important element, and everything was built around it and sacrificed to it. Really artistic music seemed to disappear from the pictures, and the scarce background music satisfied itself with repeating again and again the musically and emotionally uninteresting theme songs.

My own earliest impressions came from this unfortunate decline in standards in film music. The few films I had seen by the mid-thirties did not lead me to imagine that it was a medium for serious composers, and when the French director Jacques Feyder asked me to write a score for him, I refused, saying that writing fox-trots was not in my line. I was amazed when he said he didn't want any fox-trots. I had much to learn.

It took some years before the motion picture art recovered from its decline during the early years of the sound era and found again its own and a new form, coming nearer and nearer to the Wagnerian ideal of the *Gesamtkunstwerk,* in which music of high quality is one of the components of the artistic expression.

Today the role of musical background in films is clear; the music serves the drama and creates in the subconscious an idealistic and sometimes irrational dimension against which the naturalistic components play. One could compare the music's function with the role of a Greek chorus, painting the drama and underlining and psychologically enhancing the action.

It is therefore natural that music need not accompany the entire length of the picture; scenes of objective realism without dramatic conflict and dialogue without emotional content don't need to be accentuated or brought nearer to our soul through the medium of music. In such scenes music is superfluous and therefore disturbing. There are, however, many parts in every picture whose aesthetic effect can be strengthened through music, which focuses the attention on dramatic highlights.

Another important function of film music is to bind together into a harmonious whole the short successions of pictures with different content—such as montage sequences, titles, or short cuts of pictorial happenings. Again, I stress the point that music should not closely illustrate every phase of this kaleidoscopic and entirely technical procedure, but only accentuate its rhythms and express the idea the director is trying to convey.

Should music be synchronized with the action? Yes and no. It should adopt the tempo, the rhythm, and the mood of the scene and form a homogeneous unity with it. It should be synchronized more with the dramatic content than with the actual pictures, movements, and irregular happenings. This technique, which is itself comic, works very well with cartoons or broadly comic scenes, in which the humorous element must be enhanced and expressed by the music. But I don't think it has any place in the scoring of human drama or everyday life. In my opinion it is most important that music should not illustrate the picture but complete its psychological effect.

Another problem arises when realistic music is required, music which is actually played on the screen. Here the composer must adapt himself faithfully to the period in which the music is played, as the realistic medium of the photography doesn't allow stylized interpretation. If you would film, for instance, the life of the Meistersingers of Nuremberg, their music played on the screen should be genuine sixteenth century music. Wagner's stylization (as magnificent as it is in opera) would be unthinkable as the real thing. For the music of primitive people, the composer has to study with the utmost care their scales, styles, and instruments to be able to create a sound that suggests reality on the screen.

I don't know who originated the idea that good film music is the kind that isn't heard, but I disagree entirely with this silly theory. Music should be heard, even if it is heard subconsciously, and it should join the drama and the acting, with everything together creating a work of art. This, of course, is the musician's dream and the practice in general is still far from realizing this ideal.

The system by which most film composers still work, even though it recognizes the importance of music, does not realize music's real importance in the creation of true cinematic art. Music is still considered as the salt that makes cinema meat taste better, but not as an equal ingredient which could be used with maximum efficiency in the kitchens of cinema cooks.

The composer's job starts when the picture is completely finished, with its final and unchangeable form, and therefore, the music has to content itself with filling out the spaces which the director's mercy has left for it, without any regard to the possibilities of musical form and development.

Real difficulties start when it comes time to mix the music with dialogue and natural noises. Here the music must play a very subordinate part, and it should stop entirely when unemotional dialogue begins. The blending of these two elements is mostly unhappy: either one understands the dialogue and doesn't hear the music, or one is able to follow the music, which distracts from the understanding of the dialogue. Therefore, music composed to accompany dramatic dialogue must be extremely simple, harmonically uncomplicated and homophonous. Stringed instruments blend better with human speech than woodwinds, and brass should be eliminated from the scoring of such scenes completely. Sound effects also should be taken into consideration, although the problem is not quite as delicate as with dialogue. If there is too much noise on the sound track, the music again fares better if it is not too involved. I once wrote a fugato for a battle scene, and the result was that the contrapuntal lines were completely swallowed up by the battle noises and one heard nothing of my brilliant counterpoint. A simpler, chordal music with a heavy brass instrumentation would have cut through and served the purpose considerably better.

The dreams of film composers are the silent scenes, where he is not hampered or limited in the possibilities of musical expression. In scoring *Lydia* (1941), I was able, in a dialogue sequence, to give an actual speaking part to the music; it became a sort of third person between the dialogue of the two actors, and it stopped each time their dialogue began. This had to be planned before the scene was shot, and it called for close cooperation between the director and the composer. Such opportunities are rare for composers in filmmaking.

I think that every artistic film has scenes in which the composer, by reading the script before the actual shooting starts, could develop certain ideas which would help the director in planning of the picture. For this purpose, the composer would need to be invited to the script conferences, but, unfortunately, this is seldom the case. The composer is usually called in after the others have done their work. And there always seem to be multitudes of reasons why the score should be completed in the shortest possible time. Either the release date has been set, or the producers have to leav town, or the financial backers want to see their product immediately and cannot understand why the music is not already on the sound track. The demands made upon composers and musicians in the film industry are of a kind that stagger belief. Seemingly only a composer knows that it takes time to write music. While directors, writers, actors and set designers may have worked on a film for half a year, it is not uncommon for a composer to be called in and asked to provide a score in a matter of weeks.

In spite of the conditions under which film composers most often work, much good music has been written for films, and the craft has developed into one of the most vital and interesting outlets for modern composers. Styles have changed, as they must, and we are now much closer to using the devices of contemporary composition, rather than being restricted by the musical language of the past. I am aware that this development has been slow. We cannot expect the musically uneducated audiences to appreciate the musical language of today when they were for so many years exposed to the post-Tchaikowsky and Rachmaninoff styles of yesterday, a style that was so fondly and strongly adopted in the early days of film scoring.

The real difficulty lies, however, not in the composer's ability, in his progressive tendency, or in the audience's receptivity, but mostly in the producer's musical taste, since it is the primary job of the composer to satisfy him. The final result is usually a compromise between the two—and so is the audibility of the music, after it has been dubbed with the dialogue and the sound effects. One usually asks for the best composer, one expects the best music, one rehearses and records with the utmost care, and then comes the dubbing session! Sometimes the music almost disappears, and more times than not its effectiveness is greatly diminished. Instead of allowing the music to merge with the action for an augmented effect, the engineers, at the command of the producers and directors, submerge the music, apparently because they feel it might distract attention. This could not be the case if the music is aptly composed for the picture.

Another vice of the picture makers is to cut the recorded music tracks without regard for their continuity. Very often, after having recorded the music, they find that the picture is too long, and then the music will be handled as merchandise sold by the yard, to be cut to the required length. Don't blame the poor composer should you hear sudden modulations, interrupted phrases, and meaningless continuity. You can imagine how surprised I was to hear a composition of mine after the sound cutter, in order to fit the music to the new length of the scene, had cut out every second bar. The effect was indeed astonishing.

If we follow the development of film music from the first classical adaptation, a style which fortunately seems to have disappeared entirely, to the elaborate scores of today, we must be aware that the role of music in films has become more and more important. The composers's task is great and his responsibility is enormous. Music in films reaches a wider potential audience than music in any other form. The quality of that music is something with which we should all be concerned.

David Raksin.

3
DAVID RAKSIN

David Raksin was among the first American composers to set out with the idea of becoming a film composer. In 1935, when he arrived in Hollywood, there were few musicians in the film industry who had actually made it their goal. Most of them had drifted into film work from the musical theater or other avenues of activity because the sound film had created demand for composers, arrangers, and musicians, while at the same time lessening the employment in those other avenues. The idea of music in films had fascinated Raksin even as a child. He had observed the accompaniment given silent pictures and became impressed by what music was able to do to an audience.

Raksin was born in Philadelphia on August 4, 1912. As an infant, he was taken by his father on Saturday mornings to Philadelphia's Metropolitan Opera House in the days when that huge edifice was used for silent movies instead of opera. Raksin's father conducted the orchestra that played while silent pictures were unreeled there, and on Saturday mornings he and the orchestra worked out their scores from that cue sheets sent with the films, which carried instructions as to what should be played when and where. Raksin senior also operated a music store, and his son worked in it while attending Central High School where he played in the school orchestra, taught himself to play the organ, and edited the school's literary magazine. He also organized a dance band (he was twelve at the time) and did well enough to receive his card from the Musicians Union. He studied the piano as a child, and with the aid of his father, whose instrument was the clarinet, he mastered woodwinds and percussion. In short, it was an ideal nurturing ground for a man who would become one of Hollywood's most distinctive composers.

Raksin earned his tuition at the University of Pennsylvania, and contributed to his family's support, by playing in dance bands and in the orchestra of the CBS station in Philadelphia (WCAU). At the university, he studied under the esteemed composer Harl McDonald, then head of the music department, and participated in practically all the university's musical activities. Raksin also had a strong interst in jazz and compiled an extensive glossary of jazz terminology.

At the age of 21, he went to New York and played in, and arranged for, various dance bands. For a very short while he was with Benny Goodman. Then he got a chance to do arranging for the reconstituted band of Roger Wolfe Kahn, who introduced him to Al Goodman, the radio and musical comedy conductor. Goodman bought from Raksin an arrangement of "I Got Rhythm," which Gershwin liked and which led to commissions for arrangements and eventually to a contract with Harms, Inc., the music publishers, whose staff, headed by Robert Russell Bennett, arranged the music of almost every Broadway musical.

In 1935, after Raksin had been at Harms for a year, two Hollywood orchestrators, Eddie Powell and Herb Spencer, thought he might be the right man to work with Charlie Chaplin on his music for *Modern Times*. They recommended him to Alfred Newman, who was the music director for the picture, and he was hired. Raksin's job was to make music out of the ideas, the whistling, and the humming of the great comedian, a man with no musical education but a keen sense of the value of music. After a week or so with Chaplin, Raksin began to argue with him about the score and was thereupon dismissed. Newman then examined the sketches and was so impressed with them that he persuaded Chaplin to rehire Raksin. The young composer made it understood that in resuming the job, he would continue to argue for what he considered the best results in the development of the comedian's ideas. Chaplin realized that Raksin was sincere in trying to make the best use of the music, and the two men remained friends from that point.

Raksin spent several months on *Modern Times,* and it bolstered his conviction that film scoring was the area of music in which he wanted to specialize. From 1936 to 1944 he was gainfully employed as an arranger, orchestrator, adaptor, and composer on a large number of features, shorts, cartoons, and documentaries, proving himself a versatile and prolific musician. In 1944 his score for *Laura* elevated him to a greater position of prominence in the industry; he not only composed an exceptionally effective score for a greatly popular picture, but invented a melody that continues to be among the most performed and recorded of all.

If there is a penalty in writing something as beautifully melodic as "Laura," it is only that producers use it as an example of what they expect from the same composer for the film at hand. Raksin, never a man to concur easily with views he considers misguided, has often had to argue that such an approach would be wrong. Composers of integrity sometimes pay a price for making a stand of this kind—and find the job has gone to someone more amenable to the producer's opinions. In Raksin's case, he was fortunate in several instances, as with his *Force of Evil* (1949), a score of great intensity and acerbity, and *The Bad and the Beautiful* (1952), a film whose music reflects all the lure and sting of its bittersweet Hollywood story. Many of Raksin's scores in this period were stylistically ahead of their time, using modernistic compositional structures, occasionally verging on the avant-garde. On occasion Raksin lost a few points, as in having his title music for *Separate Tables* (1958) and in *Carrie* (1952) rejected; in those cases a few musical sequences were beyond the comprehension of the producers. But both scores are highlights in the art of providing subtle musical comment on the visual. Sometimes there have been no problems at all, as with *Forever Amber* (1947), with its gloriously red-blooded romantic score, and *Too Late Blues* (1961), allowing for the full use of jazz textures. Raksin's wide scope includes comedies like *The Secret Life of Walter Mitty* (1947), westerns, like the superb *Will Penny* (1968), and grande guignol items, like *What's the Matter With Helen?* (1972), and such deft and witty cartoons as *Madeline (1952) and The Unicorn in the Garden* (1953).

David Raksin has been able to go far beyond the composing of music for films and has become the outstanding teacher in this sphere. In 1958 he began an association with the University of Southern California as a member of the faculty of theory and composition, and has conducted courses in film music theory and technique. Additionally, he has given courses on the same subject

at the University of California at Los Angeles appeared as a lec-
turer at colleges throughout the United States. Raksin has also
served his colleagues well by being, for eight years beginning in
1962, the president of the Composers and Lyricists Guild. Few
men in the Hollywood musical community have done more to
maintain high standards in film composition and establish fair
practices among those involved in this highly skilled and difficult
craft.

The following article is a blending of two pieces by Raksin—the
first written for *Daily Variety* in 1974 and used with their consent;
and the second a portion of the liner notes he wrote for his album
David Raksin Conducts His Great Film Scores (RCS ARL 1-1490).
The composer supervised the blending of his words.

David Raksin on Film Music

The new director turned out to be an amiable roughneck, about
my own age, bright and shrewd, talented, and still New Yorkish
enough to need to let me know that he was not about to have "any
of that Hollywood music" in his picture. What he wanted was
"something different, really powerful—like *Wozzeck.*" A string
of three-frame cuts of the aurora borealis flashed in my head. To
hear the magic name of Alban Berg's operatic masterpiece invoked
by the man with whom I would be working was to be invited to be
free! To hear it correctly pronounced was to doubt the evidence of
my own ears: here was a nonmusician who was not only aware that
Wozzeck existed, but actually thought of his film as one to which
so highly expressive a musical style might be appropriate. It was
too good to be true; but after all those years of struggling to be
honest with people who couldn't understand why I was reluctant
to compose pretty music for their violent and ugly movies, I was
ready to believe every word. I invited him out to my farm for dinner so that we could discuss the film, away from studio distrac-
tions.

So there we were in the living room, with drinks in hand, the
phonograph playing and the conversation taking its time to get
under way. I remember thinking that this was the way things ought
to be: I liked his script, I admired him, and I couldn't wait to hear
what he had to say and to get working on musical material for the

score. Suddenly irritable, he said "What's that crap you're playing?" "That crap," I replied, "is *Wozzeck!*" That was twenty-five years ago, and if there is a story that tells more about why film composers sometimes despair of their profession, I have yet to hear it.

So here we are, all these years later, and I am wondering what has changed. Having been invited to discuss the state of music in films, I find myself in the uncomfortable position of the tailor asked to give his opinion of the king's new clothes. If I am to be truthful, I have got to give up the neutralist, no-involvement copout that has enabled me thus far to avoid taking what is certain to be an unpopular stand. For there is no way to write about film music today without acknowledging the powerful current of revulsion toward many aspects of their own profession that is explicit in the words and attitudes of my most valued colleagues. I am not talking only of those who have been to some extent deprived of regular employment because of changing fashions in film scoring, and who might therefore be expected to look unfavorably upon present trends, but of leading figures who are as busy and successful today as they ever were and yet seem to find the situation unacceptable: their talk is of getting out, somehow. Why?

The answer is not simple. To begin with, there is the state of the industry; it should be news to no one that many people believe the industry has been plundered, ruined by incompetence, and left to twist slowly in the wind by men whose principal interests—whatever they be be—do not lie in filmmaking. The disastrous unemployment resulting from this circumstance has become worse as film companies have made more and more pictures abroad. American composers find it difficult to believe that the use of foreign composers is not related to the fact that they work for less money. As to the remaining available jobs, they are further curtailed by the relegation of the film sound track to the humiliating status of an adjunct to the recording industry. In too many cases, the appropriateness of the music to the film is secondary to getting an album, or a "single," and the voice of the artist-and-repertoire manager is heard in the land.

All this has become so much a part of the film music scene that anyone who challenges the propriety or, perish forbid, the artistic integrity of the process is sure to start heads shaking with concern for his sanity. Artist-and-repertoire tycoons sit in the control

rooms (how aptly named!) and freely render judgments upon the
viability of film scores as commodities on record racks: these opinions are as freely transferred to apply (as though they were perti-
nent!) to the function of the music in the picture, and nobody
seems to question the competence of these people to decide what is
right for a sequence or for a film. Where are the proud directors
and producers, formerly so zealous to ensure that all components
of their films interacted to fashion the synergistic marvel that is a
motion picture? I suspect that they are to be found standing in line
at Tiffany's to ask, "Where do you keep your chrome?"

There are times these days when I suspect that my students at
USC and UCLA are trying to provoke me into "putting down"
rock or pop film scores indiscriminately. And I feel absurdly pious
when I ask them whether they can imagine pictures like *Easy
Rider, The Last Picture Show,* or *American Graffiti* with any
other kind of music. The fact is that the music in those films was
just what it should have been. But I do not find this is to be equally
true of all films in which such music is used. For unless we are willing to concede that what is essentially the music of the young is appropriate of all the aspects of human experience with which films
are concerned, we must ask what it is doing on the sound tracks of
pictures that deal with other times and generations, other lives. It
is one thing to appreciate the freshness and naiveté of pop music
and quite another to accept it as inevitable no matter what the subject is at hand—and still another to realize that the choice is often
made for reasons that have little to do with film itself: one, to sell
recordings, and incidentally to garner publicity for the picture;
two, to appeal to the "demographically defined" audience, which
is a symbolic unit conceived as an object of condescension; and
three—and to my mind saddest of all—because so many directors
and producers, having acquired their skills and reputations at the
price of becoming elderly, suddenly find themselves aliens in the
land of the young, tormented by the fear of not being "with it,"
they are tragically susceptible to the brainwashing of music-biz
types. What is one to think of men of taste and experience who can
be persuaded that the difference between a good picture and a bad
one is a "now" score that is "where it's at?"

As though that were not bad enough, the situation has
deteriorated further because of an epidemic of "Griffithitis," a
term which I derive from D. W. Griffith's blunder when he threw

out the score originally composed for *The Birth of a Nation* and substituted a hodgepodge of mismatched pieces. My favorite boss, Alfred Newman, used to say that the trouble with Hollywood was that "everybody knows his own job—plus music!" These plus-music boys, as he called them, have never been more in evidence than they are today. Although I want to believe that an art of multiple components, such as film, should be guided by a single hand, and that that hand ought to be the director's, that belief has been sorely tried by the ignorance of music, as applied in films, and the uncontrollable willfulness which my colleagues and I so often encounter. When I first suggested that any composer who had not had at least one score thrown out was either a novice or a hack, or unbelievably lucky, even my friends thought I was merely setting up defences. Now that so many of the better composers have suffered the humiliation of seeing their talent and experience defeated by the tin ear with the power behind it, they are beginning to wonder about the validity of an art that is at the mercy of so many untutored minds.

It would be ridiculous for me to contend that only we, and not the men who make the films—and who know or ought to know what they require of the music—are always right. But it would be equally foolish to believe that the most talented and skillful composers who ever wrote music for films could possibly strike out as often as recent statistics appear to suggest. I think that what has happened is that we have fallen into the hands of some ungovernable men whose ability to comprehend the language of music and its function in films lags far, far behind their other, often substantial skills, and who are unable to see in this shortcoming a compelling reason for abstaining from judgment in an area in which their competence is minimal. Directors scream their pretty heads off about the imposition of raw power by insensitive men who alter the delicate balances and destroy the subtle rhythms of their precious footage; then they put on their Dracula hats and go to work on our music! What is especially disheartening about this phenomenon is the compulsion of such people to discredit what they cannot make subservient to their purposes. Here I must pause to acknowledge gratefully those who were themselves free enough to grant me the freedom to do my best, and that would include the director who had second thoughts about *Wozzeck*.

Composing for movies was, withal, a noble profession—by

which I do not mean to suggest that the present situation is all bad or that movie music as we know it is finished. For one thing, there are certain new, young composers in whose talents one can rejoice and to whose future careers one can look—and listen—with hope. Even if one did not admire the more reserved kinds of musical utterances affected by some of today's brightest new lights (and more often than not I do), it would be necessary to concede that they are generally as appropriate in style to present modes of filmmaking as some of the more florid kinds of music would be inappropriate. But consider the apparent paradox that people who buy recordings of film scores are buying music—by Korngold, Steiner, Newman, and others—that is the antithesis of what is for the most part heard on the sound tracks of current films. The smartest money seems to believe that it is more than nostalgia which impels new audiences to seek out films in the Hollywood tradition, with their concomitant musical lyricism, and to buy recordings of such music. Perhaps the audience is about to realize that it is not necessary to choose among different modes of filmic expression as though they were irreconcilable alternatives, that we are free to enjoy as much of the spectrum as the spirit can accommodate.

It seems to be the general opinion that for Hollywood the days of wine and roses are gone forever. How paradoxical, then, to have lived through that era of 24-carat gilt, to recognize that it has passed, and yet to find oneself caught up in the current revival of interest in the music of that period. How odd to observe this neglected art, for so long in eclipse, emerging at last from beneath the surface of the sound tract to be heard.

All the more curious because, in those years, my favorite colleagues and I thought of ourselves (when we stopped working long enough to think at all) as men doing a job—professionals expected to be equal to just about anything that improvident planning or obdurate administration might contrive to put before us. Not that we lacked, or failed to demand, respect for ourselves or one another, but it would have been thought "uncool" to boast too flagrantly of impossible deadlines impeccably met. Moreover, to have acknowledged that we had been obliged to extend ourselves to get the work done would have been to admit that we did not really understand the nature of the game, in which it appears to have been the function of the professionals to make sense, and reality, out of the fantasies of amateurs—and to add a few of our own.

For us, time was the fulcrum upon which careers and destinies balanced and seesawed. To miss a deadline—a recording scheduled according to a more or less educated guess as to when music as yet unwritten should (rather than could) be ready—was to cancel out one's reputation for "reliability," an attribute more highly prized in music departments than talent. My old boss, Al Newman, used to say, "They don't want it good, they want it Thursday!" Yet, by accepting this travesty of a professional's creed—to accomplish the impossible as though it were all in a day's work—we brought upon ourselves even greater demands, so that all too often the music had to be composed in spite of the pressures of circumstances rather than because of inspiration from the film itself.

We are often asked—sometimes by other composers—how we managed to produce so much music upon demand and, especially, to synchronize within such minimal increments of time. Put simply, composing is what a professional composer does—whether the need to write arises from impulses generated from within or from outside stimuli. In the world of concert music, a commission for a work would be the equivalent to the latter. As to synchronization, if the talent for dramatic composition is present the technique can be learned readily enough.

But from there on it was—and is—work and more work: 140-hour weeks, last-minute tournaments of skill and endurance in which we slept only when we keeled over from fatigue. Some of us think that to speak frankly about the crazy way in which we worked is to hint at apology for the quality of the music. One of my oldest friends, who has managed to sustain a dark view of nearly everything despite personal successes that might have tempted lesser men toward optimism, liked to refer to the studio music department in which we worked as "the sausage mill." That was in the 1930s; today, when a sausage is as likely to be found in an art gallery as in a delicatessen, is as good a time as any to begin that long overdue reappraisal of the products of the "assembly line" and to try to discern whether any of them have merit. The generalization that seeks to discredit the artifacts of any human system on the ground that they are "mass produced" must fail because it does not attempt to distinguish among things that may differ significantly.

The fact is that the best composers in Hollywood produced a body of work that includes music of substantial merit. But the issue remains unresolved: the matter of the intrinsic worth of film music is not likely to be settled for a long time. And, in any case, not without a lot of listening! Somehow it seems to take time to find out whether things are going to last.

Meanwhile, how do we explain the resurgence of film music in recordings apart from the movies for which it was originally composed? What can it be that has brought this reticent art out of the shadows and set it before a new audience, an audience of its own? To dismiss the phenomenon as mere nostalgia will not suffice. It may be that film music has at last taken a step toward a place of its own, where it will not be subjected to invidious and irrelevant comparisons with music composed for other reasons and purposes. And high time. For there are important areas of human experience that are no longer described by any other music of our time. With the exception of a few marvelously talented composers, the avant-garde has so far outrun the concert audience that it is on the verge of becomming a cult phenomenon—although things are definitely looking up. At the other end of the spectrum, pop music is still, for the most part, too close to the finger-painting stage. Both have their devotees: the former, small and rather inbred; the latter, enormous, amorphous, and wonderfully partisan. Blessings upon them: all are friends of music, which needs all the friends it can get. But where does that leave everybody else?

In the answer to that question lies the reason why, in this unlikely time, so many people hark back so eagerly to the music we composed for the great romantic movies of the thirties, forties, and fifties. For within that music remains the last unexplored treasure of real melody, as we have known it all our lives. And that time may have been the last time when composers dealt openly and affirmatively with the life-sustaining idea of love, in terms comprehensible to the great audience.

4
FRANZ WAXMAN

Franz Waxman was part of the ironic benefit bestowed on the American film industy by the Naxi regime. He was among the many Jewish artists who were able to leave Europe ahead of the holocaust and who settled in the United States. He was the most prominent of the German (as distinct from the Viennese) musicians to contribute to the advancement of film scoring in Hollywood. Waxman was also a splendid conductor and invested much of his time in creating and guiding the Los Angeles Music Festival, which began in 1947 and lasted until his death twenty years later. His main interest was serving the cause of serious music, and he deeply resented the attitudes of critics who sneered at the work of film composers. It was a puzzle to Waxman, a true European at heart, that certain scores written in Russia and England received critical approval while almost everything written in California went virtually unrecognized. He, Rozsa, Korngold, and the other émigrés eventually came to accept it as a fact of life.

Waxman was the only composer to win two Oscars in successive years: *Sunset Boulevard* (1950) and *A Place in the Sun*. He was possibly the only composer to have a score used as the basis for a whole genre of film scoring; his first dramatic score in Hollywood was *The Bride of Frankenstein* in 1935 for Universal, and the music was subsequently used, either in pieces or in imitation, for the dozens of cheap horror pictures made by that studio over a period of a dozen years.

Waxman was born in Upper Silesia in December of 1906. He was the youngest of seven children in a family with no professional interests in music. His father, a successful steel industry salesman,

Franz Waxman.

did not encourage the boy to be a musician, despite the fact that young Waxman had shown an affinity for the piano and a talent for composition. At the age of 16 he began his first job, as a bank teller, but after six months rebelled against his father's wishes and enrolled in the Dresden Music Academy. In 1923 Waxman went to Berlin to study composition and conducting at the conservatory and supported himself by playing popular music in cafes in the evenings. Despite his devotion to serious music, it was his skill with the lighter variety that sparked his career. He was offered, and accepted, a job as pianist with the Weintraub Syncopaters, then one of the most popular jazz bands in Europe. This brought him into contact with composer Friedrich Hollaender (who anglicized his name to Frederick Hollander when he too went to Hollywood) and the whole strata of Berlin musicians. Hollaender encouraged Waxman's interest in serious music and arranged for him to meet men with whom he could study, including Bruno Walter.

With the coming of sound, the German film industry began to turn out a string of musicals. In 1930 Hollaender, who was under contract to the Universum Film Company (UFA), persuaded producer Erich Pommer to bring in Waxman as an orchestrator and conductor. One of Waxman's first assignments was working on Hollaender's songs for *The Blue Angel*, songs which helped bring Marlene Dietrich to world prominence. Three years later, after a great amount of arranging the music of other composers, Waxman came up with his first dramatic score. This was for Fritz Lang's filming of Molnar's *Liliom*. Waxman's music, which was ahead of its time in employing electronic instruments and human voices, aroused attention in the industry, but his career in Germany was in jeopardy because of the rise of the Nazis. Early in 1934, soon after he had married, Waxman was beaten by Hitlerites on a Berlin street. As quickly as possible he and his wife moved to Paris. Waxman worked on one French picture and then received an invitation to go to Hollywood, where Erich Pommer was doing his version of Jerome Kern's *Music in the Air*. He hired Waxman as music director. Waxman found it easy to adapt to the Hollywood community, partly because so many of his former UFA colleagues were already there, men like Peter Lorre and Billy Wilder. Not long after his arrival, he met director James Whale, who had admired the score of *Liliom* and who asked Waxman if he would be interested in scoring the horror fantasy he was currently making, *The Bride of*

Frankenstein. The result was a score that is as yet unsurpassed of its kind; the music sets the atmosphere as firmly as the photography and the theme for the monster makes him as pathetic as he is menacing. It is a masterpiece of moods and movements.

The Bride of Frankenstein brought Waxman an immediate offer from Universal to become the head of their music department, which he accepted, although he was far more interested in writing music than in being an administrator. A year later he was hired by MGM purely as a composer, and he stayed with that studio for seven years, writing scores for every kind of picture. In 1940 he was lent to David O. Selznick to write the music for Rebecca, the success of which furthered his esteem with both the public and the industry. In 1943 he moved to Warners and joined Korngold and Steiner in what, under the astute direction of Leo Forbstein, was generally considered the apex of the Hollywood school of film composition. He enjoyed greater freedom at Warners than at previous studios and worked on a number of interesting films, among them *Edge of Darkness, Mr. Skeffington, Objective, Burma!, The Pride of the Marines*, and *Humoresque*, all of which allowed for rich, dramatic scoring.

In 1947 Waxman made two decisions in order to achieve a higher level of personal satisfaction: he decided to freelance and to accept only those offers he thought worthwhile; and he formed the Los Angeles Music Festival, to indulge his love of the classics and to promote the cause of good music in an area, which despite the residency of many great musicians, lagged far behind European cultural standards. His programs contained the famed works of the masters, but he also introduced Californians to the output of many contemporary composers.

Waxman's judgment in accepting assignments was not always good, but he lavished great care on everything he did. Two of his scores in 1954 serve as good examples: the comic strip adventure *Prince Valiant*, which has a sumptuously romantic score; and the dull religious epic *The Silver Chalice*, with its deeply spiritual music. They might well have been sloughed off by a less serious-mind musician. It did not seem to occur to Waxman that many of the films he scored barely deserved the effort he put into them. And despite his double life as a film composer and the conductor of concerts, the quality of Waxman's music grew rather than diminished. In fact, the last few years of his life produced some of his finest work: *The Spirit of St. Louis, Peyton Place, Sayonara,* and *The Nun's Story*, which is a triumph in the art of film scoring. *The Nun's Story* won Waxman an Academy Award nomination, but he lost to Rozsa's music for the commercial blockbuster *Ben-Hur*. It was characteristic of the modest Waxman that he did not resent this. In fact he went on record as saying that he considered Rozsa the best of all composers working in films and that *Ben-Hur* well deserved its Oscar.

Waxman also found time to write noncinematic music, including a "Sinfonietta for Strings and Timpani," and a large-scaled oratorio, "Joshua," written to commemorate the death of his wife in 1957. In his last years, he accepted commissions to write for television, since the number of feature pictures had greatly diminished. In the sixties he also found himself joining other distinguished composers in being passed over in favor of the newer and more commercial sounds sought by producers. He would observe, as did some of his colleagues, that in Hollywood virtue is not necessarily its own reward. His last major score was for the spectacular but trashy *Taras Bulba* in 1962, which is worthy of viewing only because of its score, especially the sequence in which masses of Cossack tribesmen swarm over the landscape and converge into a unified force prior to battle. Waxman was not heard from again until four years later when he scored the routine war adventure *Lost Command*. He would write only one other score, for a picture so dull that it was never released in the theatre, *The Longest Hundred Miles*, and finally dumped into television. And on the subject of television it should be noted that Waxman had many of his fees for assignments in that medium paid directly to the Los Angeles Music Festival to swell their needy coffers.

Franz Waxman died of cancer on February 24, 1967, at 60 years of age and at the peak of his creativity. It was a major loss to both the studios and the concertgoers of Los Angeles. He felt deeply about the value of film as an outlet for contemporary composers and left a wealth of evidence to corroborate his views. The following article was pieced together from a number of letters and lectures given by the composer, and it is presented here with the approval of his son, John W. Waxman.

Franz Waxman on Film Music

Music, the theatre, film, and television have become the great emotional links between most people of our civilization. The great

French author, Albert Camus, said "The theatre is the greatest of literary forms because it is the most difficult. The difficulty consists in putting lofty ideas to a wide audience, in which imbeciles sit side by side with intelligent people. It demands great art." This rather provocative, yet true statement, applies just as well, perhaps even more, to the art of music, where some of the most complicated ideas of expression have found their way to the most primitive as well as to the most intellectual of people. The reason for this seemingly paradoxical procedure is clear. It lies in our hearts!

The impact of film is obvious and requires no comment from me. But I believe that impact can be made even more potent by the addition of music. In the years that I have been associated with films I have witnessed a constant improvement in the quality of composition. New ideas and new techniques are always in development, and intelligent producers have become aware of the contribution of music to the strength and dramatic power of their films. This awareness has not been gained without effort, and it is still up to the composer to prove the value of music. The need for writing good music offers a constant challenge to us.

I believe the film composer has a responsibility to the public as well as to the film itself. His music should be of the highest possible quality because it can be a guide to those who rarely hear orchestral music or attend concerts. However, the composer who writes for the movies has to realize that he works within certain limitations. He does not enjoy absolute freedom. He has to ponder constantly the drama and the action and the characterizations. He has to consider emotional impact and dramatic shock. He must evaluate mood and pace, timing and tempo. He must invent melodic themes that complement dialogue and action, and those themes must never dominate because the sound film still depends first on the eye and only second on the ear, and these dependencies must be interwoven and embroidered by music. The composer has to consider time patterns and drama patterns, both of which demand flexibility in composing and smoothness in scoring.

As the art of film scoring progressed, music began to be used for its own value, rather than merely as something to punctuate dynamics or supplement action. There are instances in which the mood of a scene will be accomplished by underscoring it with a single instrument. The tone color alone of the instrument will determine the acquired mood. In *Pride of the Marines* (1945), in the scene in which John Garfield walks alone through Pennsylvania Station, as the camera booms high giving the vast space of the terminal and the awful sense of loneliness of the man, going to war without a soul to bid him farewell, I used a solo trumpet. There is nothing as sad or as lonely as the sound of a trumpet and it was right for that scene. That one single instrument colored the mood.

I believe that the first and foremost principle of good scoring is the color of orchestration. The melody is only secondary. Looking at a scene or a sequence, I may see a horn or I may see massed violins. For example, in the opening sequence of *God is my Co-Pilot* (1945), which has a deeply religious, emotional tone to it, I used massed violins playing in a high register to convey the feeling. In the field of choral music, film composers have made audiences aware of the use of choirs and their value in scoring. Two good examples are Steiner's *The Corn Is Green* (1945) and Newman's *How Green Was My Valley* (1941).

I also believe that original composition, not the adaptation of music from other sources, is the answer to effective film music. An original score can be fitted much better to the needs of the film, except in cases where a musical production is being transferred bodily to the screen. Had I, for example, tried to adapt Wagner's *The Flying Dutchman* to my score for *Captains Courageous* (1937), audiences with a knowledge of music would immediately associate the music with something other than the film. For *Mutiny on the Bounty* (1935), Herbert Stothart used adaptations of old English sea songs because the picture dealt with a particular period in English history and the songs were appropriate. But *Captains Courageous* dealt with no particular period or nationality; it was just a moving story of simple fishermen and their regeneration of a spoiled boy. Music must always fit the style of the picture. The inspiration of the music comes from the dynamic strength of the story. Werner Jannsen did this with his *The General Died at Dawn* (1936). He purposely avoided traditional Chinese music and instrumentation because it would have detracted from the feeling of the drama.

The ability to compose is not all a film composer needs. He particularly needs a sense of dramatic balance to know where music will help the visual and where it will not. A double climax is no good. Sometimes the music and the action can reach a climax together, but at other times, when an actor's great moment is reached in his dialogue, music would overload it.

When I write music for a film I try to imagine what the sound of that music will be in a theatre, what it will sound like in relation to the dialogue and the action. It is a matter of tone color, and in some cases you can make a decision simply by reading the script. In a film like *Objective, Burma!* (1945), you can tell immediately that the music will have to be military and epic, and that some orientalism will be required for the Burmese locale. But it is only when you see the actual film that you realize the possibilities for scoring certain sequences. Such an opportunity was the sequence in *Objective, Burma!* where the pa.atroopers jump from the plane to pursue their mission in Burma. The music must be descriptive in character. The zig-zag figurations in the violins more or less characterize the jerky, abrupt movements of a man who is jumping from a plane. The hundreds of bodies floating in the air, descending in different directions, gave the inspiration for this violin figuration. Later the main theme joins in unison, and after everybody is safely on the ground, this same thematic material is developed in fugato played ponticello pianissimo by the strings until the end of the sequence.

Objective, Burma! called for mostly an extroverted kind of music but there are films that need just the opposite. In a psychological drama like *Possessed* (1947), the problems are more subtle. There are no battles, fires, chases, and so on. There are very few external events to be illustrated. There are mostly states of mind, conditions of feeling. You might say that in *Objective, Burma!* the composer had only to watch the characters, while with *Possessed* the composer had to get inside the characters. Joan Crawford for example, played an emotionally unbalanced young woman. Her condition has a complicated history, but, to make a long story short, let's say that it is based on her unreciprocated love for an engineer, played by Van Heflin. A number of times during the picture Heflin plays the piano—a passage from Schumann's *Carnival*. Frequently in the underscoring, I used that piece as an expression of Miss Crawford's attachment to Heflin. Now, at the point in the film where she realizes that he really doesn't love her, which is the point at which she begins to crack up, Heflin plays the Schumann piece again. He is apparently playing it correctly, but what the audience hears this time is a distorted version, omitting all the sharps and flats, which suggests what Miss Crawford is hearing. Here the distortion of the music was meant to correspond to the distortion of normal emotions.

I admit that the use of musical distortions to convey mental illness has become a cliché in film scoring, but it is still effective if done with taste and imagination. I don't know who started it but there is plenty of precedent in concert music. Smetana, in his quartet *From My Life*, used a high harmonic to illustrate the ringing in his ears that was one of the symptoms of his deafness. Religious mystics like Joan of Arc and Bernadette often claimed to hear voices and heavenly choirs. So there is some basis in reality for doing this sort of thing in music. I think composers must take advantage of all these suggestive powers of music. It is a way of reaching audiences very directly.

Another example of mental anguish presenting an interesting musical problem was *Sunset Boulevard* (1950), in which Gloria Swanson played a demented former movie star. The story builds toward her killing of her young lover, played by William Holden, which then causes her to become insane. Most of the music for this sequence is rather closely woven to the action seen on the screen. The main theme is one of a tango character, which stems from an earlier scene in which Miss Swanson makes reference to the early days of Hollywood and the tango dancing of Rudolph Valentino. This is the atmosphere in which she still lives, and I took this little bit of characterization as inspiration for this musical theme. As we see the hero packing and just about to leave Miss Swanson's luxurious home, the music underneath is the same as in the main title, only much slower, much heavier, much more foreboding of the tragic things to come, and as he, much against her will, leaves the house, she runs frantically after him. At this time the tango theme repeats itself in twisted and tortured harmonies until the fatal shot is heard. The body plunges into the swimming pool, the butler comes running out, witnessing the scene, and as we discover her in the grotesque pose, her mind already half gone, we hear a faint oboe solo in a theme as disjointed as her mind is at this moment.

I have never felt that music as function and music as art are necessarily opposed to each other. But it is true that film music operates in a set of circumstances quite different from the circumstances in which music is most often heard. Film music is heard only once, not many times as in concert music, and it must therefore have the qualities of simplicity and directness. The emotional impact must come all at once. It's not like concert music, which is full of secrets that are learned from long acquaintance and many hearings. To be simple and direct, music must have strong melodic lines and simple accompaniments, and as I have said before, this includes the use of musical ideas expressed by solo instruments, even without accompaniment.

After a film composer has decided on his materials, he is then faced with an even bigger problem—how to use them. I regard a film score as essentially a set of variations. In concert music, variations are usually written around a single theme. But in film music, where there are many themes, the variations turn out to be variations on a group of themes. Another difference is that in film music the variations are not motivated by purely musical considerations, as they are in concert music. The motivations come from the screen action.

The leitmotif technique is common in film scoring, that is, the attaching of themes to characters and then varying them as the situations change, and I have found this very practical in writing film music. It is an aid to composition and an aid to listening. Motifs should be characteristically brief, with sharp profiles. If they are easily recognizable they permit repetition in varying forms and textures, and they help musical continuity. The danger here lies in becoming complicated in the use of counterpoint. This can be evaluated only by the final effect it makes. I have used the fugato, for instance, very frequently. Now I don't expect an audience to stop looking at the picture and say, "Ah, Waxman has writen a fugato." But I think an audience will notice that somehow the music is growing in tension and excitement—because the reiteration of a single short motif, in a contrapuntal style, is a fairly obvious way of driving toward a climax. The technique of a fugato is strictly my own business. The dramatic effect is the audience's business.

I have already mentioned the responsibility that composers must assume toward the art of film scoring and toward the audience, but I must also point out that film producers and directors have a responsibility—toward music and toward the public. They are the employers, and who they hire and what they allow to go before the public is greatly important.

An example of progressive cooperation between producer and musician is the case of Bernard Herrmann's *Hangover Square* (1945), for which he wrote a piano concerto for the final sequence. He actually completed the music before the picture was shot; the director, John Brahm, liked it and conceived camera movement and direction to suit the concerto. The result was magnificent. It showed unity of rhythm, action, and movement that has seldom been achieved on the screen. Such achievement would be more common if producers and directors better understood the value of music as a component in filmmaking.

We also need responsible music critics, and in my opinion, we are short of such people in America, particularly in regard to film music. There are still too many who look down their noses at anything written for films. This is a very silly attitude, and it does not exist in Europe, where critics have not condemned composers because they write for the screen.

No matter what medium you write for, it is the way you write and what you write that is important. You can have awfully bad music written for an opera, and you can have awfully good music in a film score. It is a tragic thing in our Western civilization today that the popular song, the whole field of lighter music, and the so-called serious school have gone entirely different directions. A century or more ago this was not the case; there was a close contact between folk music and the symphonies of men like Haydn and Mozart, with their minuets and gavottes. Today the song writer goes one way and the serious composer goes another, and neither has much regard for the other. I consider this most deplorable. We need people who can recognize this and bring music back into focus with sensible attitudes. We need critics who will recognize that music can be of the highest artistic standards and still be enjoyed by millions, that music is not necessarily good only if it can be understood by the few.

The medium of film music is, under ideal conditions, the medium in which opportunity and outlet to a wide audience exists as never before. It is an art which has developed quickly and it continues to develop. We need composers, producers, and critics who realize all this. There is always room for fresh musical ideas in writing for the screen. There is no danger of stagnation.

Hugo Friedhofer.

5

HUGO FRIEDHOFER

There is a disparity between Hugo Friedhofer's high standing in his profession and his somewhat limited fame. His name is not touted as loudly as those of Steiner, Tiomkin, and Herrmann, and yet among all film composers, he is considered to be the master. Friedhofer has never courted publicity and he has been uncompromising in maintaining what he considers to be right and proper about his craft. His friend, David Raksin, explains, "Virtue may be its own reward, but excellence seems to impose a penalty upon those who attain it. Composing something that isn't a repetition of what's been done before, cultivating differences from others, seeking out what is special, requires extra time and a little more indulgence from producers. Those who want scores 'not good by Thursday' often prefer to promote men whose qualification is that they deserve it less."

Friedhofer arrived in Hollywood in July of 1929 and has been a witness to the entire development of film scoring in sound films. He has composed more than seventy scores, but he has also been a collaborator, adapter, arranger, orchestrator, and utility composer on many others. It would be indiscreet to reveal the number of scores by famous composers which contain segments, even entire titles, actually written by Friedhofer. As an orchestrator, he had few peers; in fact he was so highly regarded in that capacity that it became necessary for him to close that area of his career in order to proceed as a composer. Fifteen of Erich Korngold's scores were orchestrated by Friedhofer, as were more than fifty by Max Steiner. With Friedhofer it was never a matter of employment, but one of priority.

Friedhofer won an Oscar for his score for *The Best Years of Our Lives* (1946). He was also nominated for *The Woman in the Window* (1944), *The Bishop's Wife* (1947), *Joan of Arc* (1948), *Above and Beyond* (1953), *Between Heaven and Hell* (1956), *An Affair to Remember* (1957), *Boy on a Dolphin* (1957), and *The Young Lions* (1958). Among the scores for which he should have been nominated are *The Bandit of Sherwood Forest* (1946), *Enchantment* (1948), *Broken Arrow* (1950), *Edge of Doom* (1950), *Ace in the Hole* (1951; this won the Venice International Film Festival Award, the Bronze Lion of St. Mark, as the best score of the year), *Vera Cruz* (1954), *The Rains of Ranchipur* (1955), *The Barbarian and the Geisha* (1958), and *One Eyed Jacks* (1961). All these scores are considered textbook examples in the art of film composition.

In recent years Friedhofer has been teaching film composition, not in classes but to select individuals who visit him in his home. Quite a few of them are practicing film musicians. His influence, which sometimes extends to downright imitation, is far reaching, although seldom fully acknowledged. That such a man has received few offers of employment over the past dozen years is a sad comment upon the industry. It also points to the hypocrisy of the industry, whose producers are divided between those who seemingly have never heard of Friedhofer and those who allow that he is indeed a giant in his craft, but prefer to use composers who may possibly come up with the more "popular" sound. Well known among his colleagues for his mordant wit, Friedhofer snorts, "Yes, I'm a false giant in a community of genuine pigmies."

Friedhofer was born in San Francisco in May of 1902, the son of a cellist who had received part of his education in Dresden, where he met his wife, who was also of a musical family. The father started his son on the cello at age of 13, but it wasn't until five years later that Friedhofer decided to take music seriously. At 16 he dropped out of school, where he had majored in art, and worked at various jobs. Thinking that he might follow a career as a commercial artist, he studied painting at the Mark Hopkins Institute, while supporting himself working in the designing department of a lithograph firm. Once he decided to give up art and make a living as a musician, he studied seriously and gradually picked up jobs as a cellist. He played for two years with the People's Orchestra, set up as a rival to the San Francisco Symphony

Orchestra, and then in 1925 received a position with the orchestra of an ornate movie theater, the Granada.

With time Friedhofer found his interest in being a musician declining in favor of arranging and orchestrating music. He studied with Domenico Brescia, an Italian teacher who had been a fellow student with Respighi at the Conservatory in Bologna. Eventually Friedhofer was able to secure jobs arranging for theater orchestra. By 1929 the situation with live orchestral accompaniment changed with the coming of the sound film, which caused a depression among the many musicians throughout America who made their living playing in movie palaces. It was not to worry Friedhofer for long. His violinist friend George Lipschultz had become a music director at the Fox Studios in Hollywood and offered Friedhofer a job as an arranger. Thus began, in July of that year, the longest career of any musician associated with film scoring in California. His first assignment was that of arranging for the musical *Sunny Side Up,* followed by a continual stream of Fox pictures of every kind over the next five years. When that studio merged with Twentienth Century in 1935, Friedhofer was dismissed with most of the other employees, but unemployment was brief. By this time he had won the respect of Alfred Newman, who would call on his services frequently, but he also received an offer from Leo Forbstein, the dynamic head of Warner Brothers Music Department.

The call from Forbstein would open up Friedhofer's reputation as an orchestrator and provide good employment over the next ten years. Erich Korngold had been brought from Vienna to arrange the score for *A Midsummer Night's Dream* and Friedhofer was assigned to do the orchestration. The rapport between the two men was instant and Friedhofer would be the man Korngold chose to work with him on most of the music he composed for Warners. In 1936 Forbstein also brought Max Steiner from RKO and gave him the job of scoring the mammoth *The Charge of the Light Brigade.* Again Friedhofer was assigned as orchestrator, and again it was a case of composer and orchestrator becoming fast and firm colleagues. Interesting and profitable though it was, it had a drawback. Friedhofer's primary interest had long been composition, but the astute Forbstein, knowing full well that Korngold and Steiner were delighted with their orchestrations, offered no composing jobs to Friedhofer in all the time he was at Warners. In

1937, thanks to Newman, Friedhofer was hired by Goldwyn to compose the extensive score for *The Adventures of Marco Polo,* but it still made no impression on Forbstein. Finally, Friedhofer decided that he had to make a decision and put aside the comfortable but limiting life of the orchestrator.

In 1943 Friedhofer was more or less rescued by Newman, who offered him a contract to compose for Twentieth Century-Fox. Occasionally, Friedhofer, between assignments, would slip back to Warners and orchestrate the Korngold scores; such was his respect for Korngold that he found it impossible to decline. His career gained momentum as it became apparent that Friedhofer was a film composer of exceptional skill and that he was capable of tackling every conceivable kind of picture. The decline in film production in the fifties, and especially in the sixties, hit Friedhofer hard. It was not simply a matter of fewer assignments; Friedhofer was always meticulous in composing his scores and sometimes took longer to write them than producers allowed. It was not a time for composers who were meticulous and who preferred to take their time doing what they considered to be an exact job.

It was Korngold who pointed out to Friedhofer that he had an affinity for Mahler, which clearly enabled him to supply the kind of orchestration that Korngold preferred. And yet others have pointed out that Friedhofer's music has something in common with the more linear style of Hindemith. Friedhofer smiles at such comparisons. He was schooled in the German masters, but he also grew up with a feeling for American jazz and he professes a great interest in Spanish and Mexican music. His musical interests are wide-ranging, and studying the Friedhofer scores makes it clear that he has, and can, supply music suitable to any genre or geography. The consensus among other film composers in Hollywood when they are advising students is invariably, "Study Friedhofer."

Hugo Friedhofer on Film Music

A film composer has a certain educational responsibility. Where else can a creative musician function, experiment, and reach so many people? Certain forms that would elicit a negative response from an uneducated audience in a concert hall can be attempted successfully in films. Insofar as we are allowed to innovate, we can temper the public so that they won't be quite so shocked when they go out to hear some music. However, I am not saying that the life of a film composer is not without its irritations. You can bleed to death in this business unless you build up a certain immunity to what goes on. But if you have one film in ten with which you can be reasonably happy, you can count yourself ahead of the game. You suffer a little but that's par for the course. Without that, you don't get anywhere.

The primary function of music scoring is to give the pictures another dimension and to do it not by duplicating the action. Music can hint at something not seen; it can give the audience ideas of the motivations of the characters. All the best film scoring has striven to do this. Originally we had the "Mickey Mouse" technique, which was a hangover from the silent era, when the orchestra had to supply everything. Aesthetically it was undisciplined and chaotic. But Korngold changed all that. Although he used motifs, he took a more sensible approach. He was instrumental in changing a lot of the concepts about film scoring in that he wrote in longer lines and resisted the tendency to change mood every time the camera angle changed. He was an influence on Alfred Newman, who was himself highly qualified to score films because of his extraordinary theatrical instinct. He seemed always to know the right thing to do.

I believe that a film composer should be as economical as possible. Producers, however, who often know very little about music and its functions, don't always see it that way. Jack Warner, for example, insisted that Max Steiner write "wall to wall" music in his pictures. Steiner's purposes were many times defeated by this. Warner liked his music loud. Steiner might have written something very subdued, tense, or mysterious, but Warner would always have the engineers turn up the volume. The disparity of purpose between producers and composers is one of the unfortunate facts of life in filmmaking. I have lost count of the many times I have sat in a projection booth with a producer or director only to have him nudge me and say, "You're going to have to help me out here, it's a weak scene. We're counting on you to save it." My impulse, which I diplomatically have to restrain, has always been to reply, "If that's a weak scene, why in hell did you shoot it in the first place? Why didn't you rewrite it?'' And so the composer is called upon to smooth out the rough spots and try to give the picture continuity.

In the mid-thirties, in the years when sound film scoring began to come into its own as a musical force, the movie producers had the idea that big, important pictures needed to have big, important scores. That was particularly the case with producers who grew up in the days of silent films and the presentations of the big movie palaces, with their large orchestras. These men were used to that kind of sound as accompaniment to films, and so there was for a long time a sort of hangover of that attitude. It was a pity because it did not take into consideration the contribution made by dialogue and sound effects. They wanted full scoring all the time, even in battle scenes, which rarely need music because of all the noise going on. But they wanted that big sound, something that sounded expensive. That is where a certain Hollywood style begot a bad name among highbrow composers, who rather contemptuously looked down their noses at the Hollywood scene.

So we took the money and ran. The thing to do seemed to be to give them what they wanted, and little by little to do a bit of cultural boring from within. And it was a slow, subtle process of musical indoctrination, a kind of stimulation of good taste by getting away from from hidebound musical practices. The character of scoring gradually changed. One of the men who most helped bring it about was Alfred Newman, partly because of his influence on Darryl F. Zanuck. When Zanuck began running his own production company, Twentieth Century (which later merged with Fox), he called upon Newman's services because they had worked well together on a number of pictures. But Zanuck's ideas about the use of music in films was rather narrow and typical of the time. He liked tunes he could tap his feet to, and he thought of screen situations as cues for popular songs. Alfred gradually broadened his musical horizons, and by the time I got to work at Twentieth Century-Fox in the early forties, Zanuck was willing to give composers a more or less free hand, provided one had the recommendation of Newman, which I fortunately had.

Zanuck's early attitudes were fairly general throughout the industry for many years. Samuel Goldwyn was different. Goldwyn was not a musician, but he seemed to have a sense of good taste, something confined to a mere handful of film producers. There were, of course, other schools of thought about music, even among directors and producers of genuine merit. Frank Capra, for example, was adverse to music; he felt that if a scene required music, he had somehow failed. To him, there was something unreal about the idea of underscoring. One could very well have pointed out to him that there is something unreal about a sixteen-foot close-up of a head. That isn't realism either.

But things did change and by the time we came to *The Best Years of Our Lives* it was possible to employ even a chamber music sound. As an ardent lover of chamber music, I had grown up with an economical approach to the orchestra. Not that I don't like a big, fat, healthy sound when it is called for, but I don't like it to be muddy. Even with a big sound in the orchestra, I like a certain transparency. I like the air to come through.

We have always had the problem in America of film music not being taken very seriously. This has not been the case elsewhere. The Russians, for example, looked upon film scoring intelligently right from the beginning. They always employed so-called name composers. Prokofiev and Shostakovitch wrote many outstanding scores. Even as far back as *Potemkin* in 1925, the producers had a legitimate score composed and sent out with the picture. The Europeans always regarded film composition more seriously than our producers in Hollywood. Somehow the advent of the name composer, one who is associated with the concert hall rather than the cinema was, and still is, very slow in coming to this country.

Aaron Copland is an exception to the rule, and yet his adventures in Hollywood have not been exactly encouraging. I am happy to admit that Copland has been an influence on my work, especially with the score for *Best Years*. I came to know Aaron very well and learned to admire his musical integrity and forthrightness. He wrote the way he felt. His influence helped me weed out the run-of-the-mine schmaltz and aim to do more straightforward and simple, even folklike scoring. I don't think I actually looked over Aaron's shoulder but I admired the harmonic texture of his music. But making changes in the texture of scoring was not easy for any of us in those days. During the preliminary conferences on *Best Years,* director William Wyler, a man of great talent but, truthfully, not a man with a good ear for music, told me that he wanted the score to be different and that he did not want the "Hollywood sound." Then, after he heard the score, he asked me why I had not given him something like *Wuthering Heights,* a very beautiful score of Newman's. I explained to him that such a score would have been highly inappropriate for *Best Years.* I had a similar experience with Billy Wilder when we did *Ace in the Hole* (1951), which was a very bleak look at journalistic opportunism. At the final recording session he told me that he thought it was a good score, but that it had no melodies in it. I said, "Look, Billy, you've portrayed a set of characters on the screen and hardly any of them are admirable people. Would you—did you—want me to soften the blow?" He grinned and shook his head. But being German and in spite of that post-World War I cynicism that infuses practically every picture he has ever made, Wilder is still a kind of Wagnerian pussycat at heart.

As for that tired old bromide about good film music being the kind which the audience doesn't hear, let me quote Max Steiner, who was not a man to let ridiculous opinions go unchallenged: "If they don't hear it, what the hell good is it?" It is not important for the audience to be aware of the techniques by which music affects them, but affect them it must. Film music is absorbed, you might say, through the pores. But the listener should be aware, even subliminally, of continuity, of a certain binder that winds through the film experience. Having been thoroughly indoctrinated in my student years with the value of the variation techniques, I tend to move along those lines, because it gives a certain solidity and continuity to the score, instead of being just a series of chopped up shorter things. Too often what we have today are scores written with the record album in mind, sometimes consisting of a number of songs that are not particularly relevant to the film itself. That, to my way of thinking, is a destruction of the true purpose of the film score. A score must relate, it must integrate.

I take encouragement from the interest of the young generation in the great film scores, many of which were written long before their time. Perhaps this is an indication of a return to better work being done in films, although naturally updated with contemporary techniques. Of course, film music depends so much on the content of the film. One certainly couldn't score a film like *American Graffiti* with a Korngold score. That was a picture that called for source music, as did *The Great Gatsby,* and both films were adroitly scored in that fashion. Our great problem today is the influence of the recording industry and their bearing on film producers, who can be persuaded—and not entirely unreasonably—that a hit record benefits everybody. Everybody, that is, except those who are interested in the real functions of film scoring. Anyone who doubts this trend need only reflect that the Oscar for the best dramatic film score in 1974 went to Isaac Hayes for *Shaft*. To which I can only reply, "What score?"

The dominance of pop music in current film scoring is a matter of great concern because for the most part it violates the purposes of incidental composition. The primary purpose of film music is to integrate with all the elements in the film. I have said many times that the composer who comes to films without this realization firmly fixed in his head is in for disappointment. Better that he wins himself a scholarship and writes the music he wants to write. It is a peculiar breed of cat that fits into the business of film scoring.

In scoring a film I try to determine which are the key scenes. That way you don't waste your ammunition in places that aren't as crucial as others. You have to figure out which are your peaks and save up for that. Unless you think of a film as an architectural whole, you defeat yourself. My method is to see the film several times and then make four- or five-line sketches of my ideas. Anything more elaborate can cause you heartache because you may later have to tear it up. This is why you can only start scoring seriously after the film is edited. Aside from coming up with a few themes and formulating an overall concept, it is difficult to do something really constructive until you have the film edited down to the last foot. Otherwise you might end up writing five minutes of music for a scene that may run forty-five seconds. And there are, of course, so many factors to consider: the tempo of the film, the pacing, the lighting, the editing, the way the dialogue is delivered, and the moods established by all these things. If a composer is to be good at his craft, he should know a lot more than just composition. He must be conscious of everything that is going on.

Regarding film music in general, one might say that it is not in the nature of a film score to be wholly autonomous. In this respect it differs from music written for concert hall presentation in much the same way that a design for a stage setting differs from an easel painting. For example, a score conceived with as much detail or as richly textured as the Fourth Symphony of Brahms (we should live so long) would not be a good film score, regardless of its supreme merits as music. Inherently self-sufficient, it would constantly draw attention to itself at the expense of the drama it was intended to enhance. I do not mean to imply that music for a film should be as consistently bland and unobtrusive as the so-called "mood music" that accompanies the rattle of dishes and the buzz of small talk in a coffee shop. To the contrary, it is my belief that the ideal film score is one which, while at all times maintaining its own integrity of line, manages at the same time to coalesce with all the other filmic elements involved—sometimes as a frame; at other times as a sort of connective tissue; and in still other (although naturally rarer) instances, as the chief factor in the drama. Other than this, it would be foolhardy to make any sort of sweeping statement as to what film music should or should not be. The problems confronting the film composer are never twice the same and require, in every instance, another solution. The first commercially successful sound film made its debut fifty years ago. Ever since that time, composers of film music all over the world have been working at these problems, and one might venture to say that the ever-increasing demand on the part of the record buying public for music drawn from the sound track of this or that film may safely be considered as a testimonial to the success of their collective effort.

6
MAX STEINER

Of all the names associated with Hollywood music, perhaps no
other has quite as much luster as that of Max Steiner. He was active throughout the whole golden age of sound movies and he is
the composer, more than any other, attributed with the pioneering
of original music in film scoring. He helped perfect the craft but he
also had the gift of melody. Steiner was, in fact, a master of appealing tunes—relatively simple tunes and rhythms that deftly accentuated the characters and the sequences in the hundreds of pictures he scored. His productivity was astounding; over a thirty-five
year period he worked on more than three hundred films. Some of
those films will keep his name alive far into the future, particularly
King Kong (1932) and *Gone With the Wind* (1939). And his almost
three decades with Warner Brothers, writing music for the films of
Bette Davis, Errol Flynn, Humphrey Bogart, and James Cagney,
assure Steiner a firm place in the history of Hollywood.

Max Steiner came from an almost fabled musical background.
He was born in Vienna on May 10, 1888, the son of one of that city's leading theatrical producers. His grandfather, after whom he
was named, managed the famous Theatre-an-der-Wien and was
responsible for persuading Johann Strauss, Jr., to turn to the field
of operetta. The family's involvement in the cultural life of Vienna
was considerable. Max Steiner's father built the Riesenrad, the
giant Ferris wheel in the Prater, and his mother was a well-known
restaurateur. Their only child had the luxury of growing up with
almost every renowned composer and musician in Vienna as a
friend of the family. It was of little surprise to anyone that the boy
should reveal remarkable musical talents at an early age. After

Max Steiner.

normal schooling, he was enrolled in the Imperial Academy of Music and quickly mastered the piano, the organ, and several other instruments. He studied composition and theory, first with Robert Fuchs and then with Herman Graedner, followed by instructions in conducting from Felix Weingartner.

At 15 Steiner received a gold medal from the academy for completing in one year a range of musical studies normally expected to be spread over a four-year period. After leaving the academy, Steiner worked for his impressario father and on one occasion conducted a performance of the operetta *The Belle of New York* by Gustave Kerker, which drew the approval of the composer. Young Steiner also wrote an operetta called *The Beautiful Greek Girl* and conducted it. His father had advised him that the show was not a good one and declined to stage it in any of his own theaters. The son then took it to a competitor, Carl Tuschl of the Orpheum Theatre, who was pleased to produce it and even more pleased when it ran for a year.

In 1906, 18-year-old Max Steiner went to Russia with a touring operatic company as its conductor. He generally enjoyed life until he returned to Vienna, where his father's complicated financial affairs had resulted in bankrupcy. After that it was not so easy for young Steiner to find work, and he decided to move to London, a move somewhat motivated by his feelings for an English show girl he had met in Vienna. It took him a while to find employment in England, but once launched as a conductor and arranger for stage musicals, he found one job after another, which took him right through to the outbreak of war in 1914. Steiner then found himself with a real problem: he was an enemy alien.

Friends in the London theater persuaded Steiner that it was best for him to go to New York and helped raise money to send him there. But he needed more than money to leave wartime England; he needed official sanction. Fortunately he was a friend of an influential gentleman, the Duke of Westminster, and through him received the necessary papers. He was allowed to take little with him, and he arrived in New York in December of 1914 with thirty-two dollars in his pocket. As with his arrival in London, it took a while to get established, and before he was able to work at his own profession, Steiner had to take a series of menial jobs. Eventually, he was offered a job as a copyist with Harms Music Publishing, which quickly led to assignments as an orchestrator of stage musicals. By 1916 Steiner was established as a conductor on Broadway and over the course of the next thirteen years worked on so many musicals he claimed he could not remember them all.

Despite the vast amount of theatrical music with which Steiner dealt in all these years in New York, he was involved in very little composition. His talent seemed to lie in arranging, conducting, and generally breathing life into other men's music. The only show for which he wrote music, *Peaches*, lasted only two weeks. Up to the time he left New York in late 1929 to go to Hollywood, there was little about Steiner's career to lead him, or anyone else, to imagine that he would in the next decade become the most productive of all film composers, as well as the most influential.

Steiner was 42 when he arrived in Hollywood. His entry into the picture business came about through his composer friend Harry Tierney, for whom he had orchestrated and conducted *Rio Rita* on Broadway. When RKO bought the property for the screen, Tierney insisted that Steiner be hired to provide the same services he had rendered for the stage version. Because of his reputation on Broadway, the studio offered Steiner a one-year contract, although with the almost immediate slump in movie musicals, they wished they had not done so. However, it remained for Steiner to realize something that none of the film producers, at any studio, had imagined—the use of original composition as background scoring.

A listing of Steiner's credits during his slightly more than five years with RKO would suggest that his every hour was spent in writing and conducting music. In 1934, for example, Steiner scored thirty-seven films . He was most certainly busy, but most of these films required only main and end titles. That does not lessen his contribution, however, because certain films in each of these years did indeed contain full scores, beginning with *Symphony of Six Million* in early 1932 and *Bird of Paradise* a few months later. *King Kong* the following year left no doubt in any producer's mind about the value of original music in filmmaking.

Even more impressive than Steiner's vast output at RKO was his track record at Warners, beginning with *The Charge of the Light Brigade* (1936). In the incredible ten years following that picture, Steiner scored an average of eight major films each year, all of them requiring as much as an hour of music. It was a wonder he was able to live through 1939! That was the year in which he wrote the better part of three hours of music for *Gone with the Wind*, as well as providing music for eleven other films. He claimed it was only possible by taking pills to keep him awake. It was the price he paid for being a genius at his trade and for having the gift of invention, and the strength, to produce so prodigiously. It also came about as the result of his determination not to disappoint the producers who were relying on him, very few of whom had much idea of the skill and labor involved in creating music.

Despite the huge volume, Steiner never wished to stop composing for the screen. The decline toward the end of his life came about with the decline in the productivity of Hollywood in general and with a shift in the tastes of the newer producers, many of whom were propelled by the notion of using music more for its promotional value than its dramatic content. Steiner was also gradually defeated by his declining health, especially his failing eyesight, which were factors he never wanted to admit. He scored his last film in 1965 but would gladly have worked on others had they been offered. Steiner was 77 that year and resentful about having to retire. He died on December 28, 1971, after a long illness. His death broke a link not only with the golden age of Hollywood, but with the last glorious years of the Vienna of Emperor Franz Josef on whose knee he had once sat as a boy.

The following article is taken from an autobiography Steiner worked on in his last years but never completed to his satisfaction. The article truncates sections of that autobiography and it is here presented with the gracious consent of his widow, Lee Steiner.

Max Steiner on Film Music

The last Broadway musical on which I worked before coming to Hollywood was called *Sons O'Guns,* starring Jack Donahue and Lili Damita. It was a great success, but three or four weeks after the opening on November 26, 1929, Harry Tierney called me to Hollywood with an offer to orchestrate for RKO. It was the year of the stockmarket crash and the next few years were to be depression years, but I started my Hollywood career in high spirits. My composer friend Tierney met me on my arrival and took me to meet the executive producer of RKO, William Le Baron and his assistant Pandro Berman. I had come to the coast purely as an orchestrator.

My first film was completed in about three months, and then the studio became very quiet. However, I was on a one-year contract, and they assigned me to score some of the Rod LaRocque pictures. Roy Webb and I arranged the music for these inexpensive features, and all they would allow us were a ten-man orchestra, using mostly printed music, and a three-hour session in which to record.

By this time Hollywood was beginning to feel the slump, and RKO decided they didn't want any music in their dramatic pictures. This was motivated not only by the economic factor, but because they had decided you could not have background music unless you showed the source. In other words, you had to have an orchestra on view, or a phonograph or performers, so that people would not wonder where the music was coming from. They felt, therefore, that they had no use for a full music department. Roy Webb was sent back to New York, and I was the only one to remain, but only because my contract still had four months left to run.

About a month or so after this musical housecleaning, I was called to the front office and told that they had no use for me either. What, they asked, would I take for a settlement of my contract? We finally agreed on six weeks. I was really in a pickle because business was just as bad in New York as in Hollywood. I called an agent in New York, Jennie Jacobs, told her of my plight, and asked if she could get me a job. She called back to say that Arthur Hammerstein was opening an operetta in Atlantic City and advised me to fly east at once. I asked RKO for my release and was told they would have to check the matter over. Instead of releasing me they offered me the job of head of the music department, on a month-to-month basis without a contract. I accepted and wired Jenny that I couldn't accept the Atlantic City job. I have always felt this was a crossroad in my life. The whole thing was 'touch and go.' If I had gone to Atlantic City, I may never have been in Hollywood again. Who knows? Those are the breaks in our business.

I brought Roy Webb back from New York to be my assistant, and our first assignment under the new deal was *Cimarron,* with Richard Dix and Irene Dunne. At this point I had done no composing for motion pictures. When the picture was finished the studio tried to hire a composer who wasn't available, then several others who were also occupied. This was the early 1930's and there were very few composers here. Finally the gentlemen in the Front Office said to me, "Knock out a score for us. Don't spend too much money on it, and if we don't like it, we'll get somebody else to do it over. Just give us something we can have for the preview." I scored the picture to the best of my ability with a fairly small orchestra. The preview was a great success, and the next day both of the trade papers, *Variety* and *The Hollywood Reporter,* wanted to know who wrote the music and why there was no credit. This was my real beginning in Hollywood.

I scored so many pictures at RKO in the next six years that I can barely remember them. My first complete score, and the one which opened up the art of underscoring, was *Symphony of Six Million* in 1932, produced by a brilliant young man named David O. Selznick, who was to become a close friend. *Symphony* was the story of a Jewish doctor who moved from the East Side of New York to Park Avenue and, for a time, forgot his heritage. I felt a complete score would help the picture, and as an experiment, Selznick asked me to score one reel, about ten minutes, to see whether music would interfere with the dialogue or help it. It was decided that music did indeed help. That was when my career as a film composer really started.

King Kong was the film that saved RKO from failure. But when it was finished the producers were skeptical about what kind of public reception they could expect. They thought that the gorilla looked unreal and that the animation was rather primitive. They told me that they were worried about it, but that they had spent so much money making the film there was nothing left over for the music score—and would I use some available tracks. I explained that we had nothing suitable. But the man who was most responsible for the picture, producer Merien C. Cooper, took me aside and said, "Maxie, go ahead and score the picture to the best of your ability and don't worry about the cost because I will pay for the orchestra or any extra charges." His confidence in the film was certainly justified.

The Informer won me my first Oscar. John Ford also won for direction and Victor McLaglen for his performance. When this picture was being made, our executive producer was not very happy about it and asked me, "Who wants to see a picture that's always in fog?'' The background was the trouble in Dublin in the early 1920's between the British and the Irish republicans. There was a sequence toward the end of the picture in which McLaglen is in a cell and water is dripping on him. This is just before he escapes and is killed. I had a certain music effect I wanted to use for this. I wanted to catch each of these drops musically. The property man and I worked for days trying to regulate the water tank so it dripped in tempo and so I could accompany it. This took a good deal of time and thought because a dripping faucet doesn't always drip in the same rhythm. We finally mastered it, and I believe it was one of the things that won me the award. People were fascinated trying to figure out how we managed to catch every drop.

In 1936 David O. Selznick set up his own production company and asked me to be his music director. He had always appreciated my work and offered me such a better contract than I had with RKO that I couldn't turn it down. My first score for the new job was *The Garden of Allah,* and it is worth mentioning musically because it was the first time that the "push-pull track" was used. This was far superior to the old system, producing about the same difference in sound as between mono and stereo. It allowed for a wider range, with lots of bass and lots of highs. On the opening night at Grauman's Chinese Theatre in Hollywood, people were amazed at the sound that came from the screen.

I did quite a number of pictures for Selznick, but despite his successes, things did not go too well for him and his production slowed down. He one day asked me if I could help the financial situation by going over to Warners on a loan-out. I said I would and went over there to score *The Charge of the Light Brigade,* with Errol Flynn. The situation with Selznick did not improve, so we ended the contract, and I accepted one with Warners. Leo Forbstein was the head of their music department, and he was responsible for bringing me in on very good terms. Little did I realize the vast amount of work ahead.

Many people have written to me over the years to ask about my procedure in scoring a film. For their benefit, I shall try to explain. But this is entirely my procedure; other composers may have their own techniques.

In the first place, I very seldom read a script—and for two reasons. Sometimes I've read a script and then been very disappointd when I saw the picture. On the other hand I have read scripts that I didn't like but that turned into fine films. I prefer, therefore, to approach the picture without any prejudice one way or another. So I simply do not read scripts unless it is absolutely necessary, such as when a song is required and it needs prerecording.

The first step, of course, is to run the picture as soon as it is finished. I run it first by myself. I don't want anybody around me at this time, neither the producer nor the director, because they might throw me off with their ideas before I form my own impressions. While I am running the picture, I sit back and decide what kind of a score it requires and make my plans. A few days later, when I have thought it over or, in some rare instances, when I have already thought of a few tunes or themes, I will run the picture with the director, if he so desires. He, and perhaps the producer, will then give me their ideas of what should be done. Their ideas do not always coincide with mine. In this event, I may try to swing them over to my point of view, or it may be that their ideas are better than mine. Eventually, we come to some meeting of minds.

After this I run the picture a third time, this time reel by reel. A reel is a thousand feet and takes about ten minutes. This is when I start writing and working with my music editor. We lay out the music together, deciding at which points to start a music cue and where to end it. Sometimes it takes two days to do this. Then the editor takes the print of the film and times it; he breaks it down into minutes and seconds. The cues are numbered on sheets and on the opposite side, on the right hand side, the editor marks the timing in minutes. For instance, let's say the actor walks into a scene; this is marked as "00." He sits down in 6 seconds, starts to talk at 10 seconds, gets up at 23 seconds, walks out of the house at 40 seconds, comes back in at 50 seconds, and so on. Against this timing of minutes and seconds, I also have the footage indicated. The reason for this is that to err is human, and mistakes in this business are costly. Either the editor or I may make a mistake, or it could be a typographical mistake.

When we record, I have three punches on the screen. I use three-inch punches, which are eighteen frames apart. On the third punch the cue should hit. This is what is known as three timing. I also use the click track. This track is timed in eight, nine, ten frames, up to twenty-four frames, which is the highest and equals one second. If it's any longer we use twelve frames, half-seconds, and so on, depending on the speed of the music which the particular scene might call for. Both the orchestra and I use earphones—in one ear. This way we have one ear free so we can play and stay in tune, while we listen for the click track with the other ear. Incidentally, these various tempos I have mentioned—eight, ten, fifteen frames, and so on—correspond to the metronome tempos of 8, 90, and 150.

I use a numbered click sheet, which is my own invention. On this my editor indicates the cues I want to catch. He then presents a film track with the corresponding parts punched in. When we record, this track is run parallel with the original sound track. For instance, let's say the click track starts at number 1 and the first cue hits at 12, which will give me three bars at 4/4 or four bars at 3/4, whatever the case may be. Sometimes these cues hit at 12½ or 15½. Then I write my music against this track. I even use it during love scenes because it makes us absolutely foolproof. My orchestra is used to following these click tracks, which sound something like a metronome. In fact, in some cases, they don't even need a conductor; the click track leads them. It also helps keep the orchestra together. This saves an awful lot of time. Without the click track, we might have to make three or four takes (or recordings) or even as many as ten before I, or any other conductor, could hit the cues accurately. The click track, however, is infallible. It enables us to have one rehearsal and one take. It has been in use for years, but I think I am perhaps one of the first conductors to adapt it to my own use.

The difficulty for a man not used to composing this way is, obviously, to make his compositions sound natural and, at the same time, to write against these clicks. It took me some time before I learned to do it. I used it most effectively for the first time in *Gone With the Wind*. Of course, I do not always use it. There are some sequences that just don't lend themselves to this kind of writing or composing.

I do not use anyone else's music in my scores unless there is a direct reference or if another composer's work is called for in the script. In *Rome Adventure* one of the characters says, "Listen to the beautiful music of Borodin." But I prefer not to have to use source music. I can illustrate one of my reasons: A few years ago I went with my wife to Grauman's Chinese Theatre, and in scoring this particular picture the composer had used "Tales from the Vienna Woods." At this point, two people in front of us started to argue about the identity of the music. One claimed it was "The Blue Danube," the other said it wasn't. This went on during the high-point of the action of the picture, and my wife and I became exasperated because it was spoiling the film for us. It taught me a lesson: Never use music people have heard before because it may detract from concentrating on the film.

People interested in composing for the screen sometimes write and ask for advice. It is a exacting profession, and no one should think of entering it unless he realizes that he will be part of a team. As I see it, the most important thing about screen composing is the judgment involved in knowing when and where to place music—the location of the music and when to start and stop. Underscoring helps the action, sometimes. Music can slow an action that should not be slowed, and vice versa. There is a tired old bromide in this business to the effect that a good film score is one you don't hear. What good is it if you don't notice it? However, you might say that the music should be heard and not seen. The danger is that the music can be so bad, or so good, that it distracts and takes away from the action. And beware of embellishments; it's hard enough to understand a melody behind dialogue, let alone complicated orchestrations. If it gets too decorative, it loses its emotional appeal. I've always tried to subordinate myself to the picture. A lot of composers make the mistake of thinking that the film is a platform for showing how clever they are. This is not the place for it.

Erich Wolfgang Korngold.

7
ERICH WOLFGANG KORNGOLD

Korngold's name is indelibly linked with the golden age—usually considered to be the period from the mid '30s to the late '40s—of movie music in Hollywood, but he worked on only twenty films in his dozen years in the business and withdrew from film scoring in 1946 largely because he was alarmed about becoming known as a film composer. He was in no way ashamed of what he had written for the screen—he put the same love and labor into scoring as he had devoted to his operas and concert works—but he had not counted on the snobbism and disdain of American critics. When he first went to Hollywood, he was excited about the possibilities of good music in films, feeling that it was an opportunity of reaching millons, but toward the end he said, "A film composer's immortality lasts from the recording stage to the dubbing room." By the time of his death, at the age of 60 in November of 1957, Korngold, for most of his life a jovial and witty man, was quite bitter. A series of strokes had robbed him of his physical vitality and his astonishing ability to play the piano, but he also felt that he had outlived his musical values. He had never embraced the avant-garde theories, and he believed in the power of absolute tonality in music.

But life is full of ironies, and it is perhaps ironic that twenty years after his death Korngold should have been proven wrong. He is not a forgotten man, and it is now possible to acquire a wide selection of his works in recordings. What makes it even more ironic is that the renewal of interest in him was largely brought about by his film music. His admirers collected tape recordings of his scores, mostly pirated from television showings. This served the purpose of proving to record companies that a market did exist for this kind of music. RCA Victor finally took a chance in 1972 and produced an album of Korngold film music. They were amazed by its success, and it launched what would become known as their Classic Film Scores series, performed by the National Philharmonic Orchestra of London, conducted by Charles Gerhardt, and produced by George Korngold, the younger of the composer's two sons. RCA Victor thereafter issued Korngold's *Symphony in F Sharp,* Opus 40, and in 1975 his most esteemed work, the opera *Die Tote Stadt* ("The Dead City"), which had been revived with great success by the New York City Opera Company.

Anyone living in Vienna in the years just prior to World War I, anyone at all interested in music, would certainly have heard about Erich Wolfgang Korngold. He was the *Wunderkind,* the musical child marvel of his time. There was even talk that he was a second Mozart. He was just eleven when his pantomime ballet *Der Schneemann* was staged at the Vienna Court Opera in a command performance for Emperor Franz Josef. It proved to be no flash in the musical pan. Everything he wrote was published and performed—chamber music, concert pieces, songs, operas. He was 16 when he wrote his first two operas, *The Ring of Polykrates* and *Violanta,* and 23 at the time of *The Dead City.*

In 1932 a Viennese newspaper, *Neue Wiener Tageblatt,* conducted a poll among the European musical cognoscenti to determine which of the contemporary composers were considered the most important and the most influential. The two composers who headed the list were Schönberg and Korngold. Ironically, both men would end their lives in California. Korngold, as a young man, was quite a controversial figure in Vienna. It happened that his father was the most powerful music critic in Europe. Dr. Julius Korngold succeeded Hanslick at *Neue Freie Presse* and held the post for more than thirty years; like Hanslick, he was without mercy in scalding composers and performers who fell short of what he considered to be the proper standards of music. Fate dealt him something of an embarrassment in the form of a son. Erich Wolfgang was picking out tunes on the piano at the age of 3. By 7 he could play fluently, and by 10 he was performing his own compositions in front of famous musicians. After the success of *Der Schneemann* in 1908 (he was then 11), there was a steady flow of compositions, and the two sides of the controversy over the child's merits were drawn from those Julius Korngold praised and those he panned. The more extreme detractors even suggested that the father was doing the actual composing, to which he irately replied that if he were capable of writing such music, he would not be making a living as a critic.

Erich Korngold always felt his most vital ability as a composer lay in the field of opera. He most certainly had a gift for the dramatic, and it lent itself readily to the theater. In 1919 he wrote his first score for a play, for a Viennese production of Shakespeare's *Much Ado About Nothing.* His success in this new medium clearly inspired confidence to pursue further opportunities. In 1923 he began a profitable and enjoyable association with the esteemed impresario Max Reinhardt, beginning with the operetta *A Night in Venice,* musically restructured and orchestrated by Korngold from pieces taken from other operettas of Johann Strauss, Jr. The composer and the producer put together several other operettas using Strauss music, including *The Great Waltz* and their most successful version of *Die Fledermaus,* which appeared in London and New York as *Rosalinda.* There were also similar treatments of musicals by Offenbach and Leo Fall, all of which was in tandem with Korngold's involvement with his more serious compositions. It was entirely reasonable that such a composer would eventually find his way to writing for the screen.

The opportunity came in 1934 when Max Reinhardt turned up in Los Angeles to stage his production of *A Midsummer Night's Dream* at the Hollywood Bowl. Warner Brothers seized upon this as an opportune moment to plunge into cultural cinema. They commissioned Reinhardt to make a movie of his production, which interested Reinhardt greatly because it allowed an indulgence in cinematic fantasy, complete with full musical accompaniment. Korngold was the only musician he considered for the job, and the two agreed that the Mendelssohn stage score would be ideal for the film. Korngold then rearranged that score, bringing snippets of other Mendelssohn pieces into play and finding that arranging a score for a film was something well suited to his leanings. He returned to Vienna but offers brought him back to Hollywood a year later. His first original score was written for

Paramount, for a musical starring Gladys Swarthout and Jan
Kiepura, with lyrics by Oscar Hammerstein, II—*Give Us This
Night.* Despite the impressive array of talent, it was a feeble picture, with a ludicrous script and limp acting by its stars. It was a
low period in Hammerstein's artistic life, and the experience produced nothing of lasting value from Korngold. He spoke little
English at this time and was quite confused by the logistics of
Hollywood film production. However, it was while he was working on this forgotten picture that Warner Brothers asked him to
write a large-scale score for what they believed would be an
impressive costume epic, *Captain Blood,* with Errol Flynn in his
first starring role. The results were beyond even Warner Brothers'
fondest hopes.

Korngold became the first composer of international stature to
accept a Hollywood contract. The political situation in Europe
had, of course, much to do with his decision, particularly when
Hitler banned the planned premiere of Korngold's opera *Die
Kathrin.* Over the next decade he composed sixteen scores for
Warner films and set a new standard in composition for the
screen, bringing to the medium an operatic concept of scoring.
The former boy wonder of Vienna became the fair-haired boy of
movie music, winning Oscars for his *Anthony Adverse* and *The
Adventures of Robin Hood,* and being treated with a deference ac-
corded no other musician in the making of films in Hollywood. He
was given carte blanche in his choice of vehicles and seldom wrote
more than two scores in a year. If it can be said that Korngold's
music for films was on a higher plane than most of that written in
those same years, it must also be said that it had every reason to be
so.

The great good fortune that had blessed Erich Korngold for
most of his life left him after the age of 50, about the time he
decided to have done with film scoring. He returned to Vienna
after the war but was not able to rekindle the once fervent interest
in his music. Times had changed, and changed greatly. In his last
years in his home in North Hollywood, he completed a number of
concert works, including a violin concerto and a symphony, in
both of which he utilized some of his themes for films. His father,
and others close to him, encouraged him not to waste all that
beautiful music on the tracks of films that were seemingly locked
up forever in storage vaults. This was before Warner Brothers sold

its vast library to television. Even after that it did not occur to Korngold that his film music would one day take on a new life in recorded form. He felt, and had been encouraged to feel by critics, that he had damaged his reputation by writing for the movies.

It now seems that having written those fine scores for some worthwhile pictures is what has helped save Erich Korngold from possible oblivion. What really matters in terms of the art of film scoring is that Korngold's contributions brought new dimensions and proved to other composers that the screen was indeed a viable outlet for serious composition.

The following article first appeared in 1940 in the book *Music and Dance in California* and seems to be Korngold's only treatise on film scoring.

Erich Wolfgang Korngold on Film Music

When I came to Hollywood about six years ago, I knew no more about films and their making than any other mortal who buys his ticket at the box office. It was not even known to me that music—which happens to be my particular field—is only in rare cases recorded together with the picture, that is to say at the same time the camera photographs a scene. But my very first assignment, Reinhardt's production of *Midsummer Night's Dream,* was to make me familiar with all three music techniques. For this production, I had to make preliminary recordings, the so-called playbacks, of Mendelssohn's scherzo and nocturne, which were relayed over huge loudspeakers during the actual filming. Further, I conducted an orchestra on the stage for complicated, simultaneous "takes," and lastly, after the film was cut, I conducted a number of music pieces which were inserted in the completed picture as background music. In addition, however, I had to invent another, *new* method which was a combination of all three techniques and which was for music accompanying the *spoken word.* I wrote the music in advance, conducted—without orchestra—the actor on the stage in order to make him speak his lines in the required rhythm, and then, sometimes weeks later, guided by earphones, I recorded the orchestral part.

The playback system, which is used mostly for songs and dances in the so-called musicals, is without doubt the most satisfactory method for the composer. It not only enables him to create freely and independently but it also leaves him undisturbed by all kinds of noises such as cannon shots, ship sirens, rain and thunder storms. No dialogue—the composer's most hated rival—not even the softest footsteps (let alone galloping horses, rattling automobiles or roaring railroad trains!) interfere with his music. I myself have made only one such happy musical. Since *Captain Blood* I have been busy exclusively with the third and last technique—that of scoring. And I must confess that, despite the definite advantages offered the composer by the playback, I consider the task of composing and recording music for the completed picture the most interesting and, for the composer, the most stimulating. When, in the projection room or through the operator's little window, I am watching the picture unroll, when I am sitting at the piano improvising or inventing themes and tunes, when I am facing the orchestra conducting my music, I have the feeling that I am giving my own and my best: Symphonically dramatic music which fits the picture, its action and its psychology, and which, nevertheless, will be able to hold its own in the concert hall. And if the picture inspires me, I don't even have to measure or count the seconds or feet. If I am really inspired, I simply have luck. And my friend, the cutter, helps my luck along.

However, I am fully aware of the fact that I seem to be working under much more favorable conditions than my Hollywood colleagues who quite often have to finish a score in a very short time and in conjunction with several other composers.

So far, I have successfully resisted the temptations of an all-year contract because, in my opinion, that would force me into factory-like mass production. I have refused to compose music for a picture in two or three weeks or in an even shorter period. I have limited myself to compositions for just two major pictures a year.

Further, I am told that my method of composing is entirely different from that employed by other Hollywood composers. I am not composing at a desk writing music mechanically, so to speak, for the lengths of film measured out by an assistant and accompanied with sketchy notes on the action of those sections, but I do my composing in the projection room *while the picture is unrolling before my eyes*. And I have it run off for me again and again, reel by reel, as often as I need to see it.

It is entirely up to me to decide where in the picture to put music. But I always consult thoroughly with the music-chief whose judgment, based on years of experience, I consider highly important. I also keep the producer well informed and always secure his consent for my musical intentions first. But in none of my assignments have I ever "played" my music first to either the music-chief, the director or the producer. And the studio heads never make the acquaintance of my music until the day of the sneak preview. The executive producer always calls me in for the running of the picture's final cut and I am invited to voice my opinion for or against proposed changes, and I may make suggestions myself.

The actual composing of the music is not begun until the final cut of the picture is ready. But most of my leading themes and general mood motifs suggest themselves to me on reading the manuscript. Only when the picture has reached the stage of the final cut can I proceed to compose the exact lengths needed for the different music spots. Changes after the preview are often painful although, fortunately, I have not suffered any particularly smarting musical losses.

I have often been asked whether, in composing film music, I have to consider the public's taste and present understanding of music. I can answer that question calmly in the negative. Never have I differentiated between my music for the films and that for the operas and concert pieces. Just as I do for the operatic stage, I try to invent for the motion picture dramatically melodious music with symphonic development and variation of the themes.

The toughest problem in film music production is and remains the *dupe* system, i.e., the combining of dialogue, sound and music. It is difficult from the beginning to strike the right balance between dialogue and music, but it is achieved fairly accurately in the small intimate dupe room which is acoustically ideal. However, when the film reaches the theatres which are large, noisy, acoustically uneven, often poorly equipped, this delicate balance is easily upset, and even distorted.

But I am convinced that in time better solutions will be found. Motion pictures are young and neither the public nor those who are making them have a right to be impatient or ungrateful for what has already been achieved.

Dimitri Tiomkin.

8
DIMITRI TIOMKIN

It is often thought that Tchaikowsky and Rimsky-Korsakov would
have done well for themselves had they been alive and functioning
in the era of the sound film. Less kind observations have it that the
art of picture scoring has done well by them anyway. The color
and emotion inherent in Russian music lends itself to the needs of
the cinema. Splendid film scores have been written in Russia, but
only one Russian managed to carve a place for himself in
Hollywood—Dimitri Tiomkin. Whatever the faults of Tiomkin,
and many critics like to allude to his tendency to be loud and asser-
tive, his is a distinctive touch and his scores can be mistaken for
those of no other composer.

Tiomkin has always had the ability to compose music which
pulses and surges, and he has attempted whenever possible to be
involved in his films while they were being made, rather than wait
until they were completed before writing his music. His
characteristic of writing powerfully accented rhythms in the bass
clef is virtually a trade mark, and what is also characteristic of
Tiomkin is his love of being a film celebrity. No other composer
has so clearly enjoyed public appproval; with his Gregory Ratoff-
type accent and his sly humor, he has become an almost Hit-
chcockian figure. If nothing else, it has helped bring attention to
the otherwise somewhat neglected role of being a film composer.

Tiomkin was Hollywood's major link with the old school of
Russian composition. He was born at the turn of the century and
left his native Ukraine to receive his education in St. Petersburg
(Leiningrad). He spent seven years in the renowned conservatory
of that great Russian city, at the time Alexander Glazounov was its

God-like director. Tiomkin recalls that Glazounov pretended to be more stern than he actually was by nature and that musically he was conservative and cared little for the growing vogue of impressionism. Tiomkin studied composition as part of the general course given at the conservatory, but his chief interest was the piano, at which he had been started by his mother when he was a child. His teacher was Felix Blumenthal, whose many successful pupils included Vladimir Horowitz. To earn money, Tiomkin played piano in movie theaters as accompaniment to silent films, inventing music on the spot and little realizing that it would one day become an occupation at which he would excel.

The Russian revolution changed life in St. Petersburg drastically, bringing with it fewer opportunities for employment as a pianist. In 1919 Tiomkin left and went to Berlin where his doctor father had a successful practice. Tiomkin senior, with whom the boy had never been close, had remarried, and nothing came of their meeting. The young Russian then made the acquaintance of another pianist and moved in with him. Later they formed a two-piano team and toured various cities in Europe. Tiomkin was in Berlin for three years, during which time he studied with the greatly acclaimed pianist-composer-teacher Ferruccio Busoni, who was a master in giving his pupils a sense of harmonic form. Tiomkin believes that this influence, plus Glazounov's guidance in the romantic spirit of music, were invaluable in his later career as a composer for films.

Tiomkin decided to try Paris next; many Russian exiles, including Stravinsky and Diaghilev, were making names for themselves in various artistic outlets there. He did well enough as a concert pianist to get an American offer in 1925, and this allowed him to see several cities on tour and whetted his appetite for the burgeoning new music of America. Tiomkin, ever shrewd, sensed that it was the right time and the right place to make progress. He was abetted in these views by the enterprising young choreographer Albertina Rasch, whom he married. The bride was a spirited lady who clearly had bearing upon her husband's career. In 1928 he went to Paris to give the European premiere of George Gershwin's Piano Concerto in F. Returning to America with increased prestige, he performed in Carnegie Hall and on sundry tours in recital. The stock market crash in 1929 hit the pianist and his choreographer wife rather hard; there was little demand for their services in a time of financial depression. However, this was also the time when the sound film was presenting other opportunities, and Mrs. Tiomkin wisely realized that there would be room in Hollywood for those who knew about choreography. She had the idea of doing short, modern ballet sequences in musicals. She found a customer in MGM.

Albertina soon brought it to the attention of her employers that her pianist husband, then giving occasional recitals in Los Angeles, was also a composer. He had in fact written pieces for his recitals and for his wife's ballet company. Tiomkin's film career began in 1930, writing ballet pieces for three MGM pictures, one of which was the acclaimed *The Rogue Song,* starring Lawrence Tibbett. The decline of movie musicals shortly thereafter—a result of the glut of them—made it difficult for Tiomkin to pursue his new-found fascination in writing for the screen, but he was not a man to be deterred. He took what opportunities came his way, although it was not until *Lost Horizon* in 1937 that his career as a film composer was really launched. *Lost Horizon,* the score of which was conducted by Max Steiner, was a composer's dream project, presenting a richly romantic, exotic story of adventure and inspiration in the paradise of Shangri-La. Tiomkin's score called for the largest orchestra ever assembled at Columbia studios, causing director Frank Capra to hold his breath and studio chieftain Harry Cohn to rant and rave at the expense. But the results were worth the extra effort. It put Tiomkin on the map, and it began an interesting association between Capra and the composer, resulting in the scores for *You Can't Take It With You, Mr. Smith Goes to Washington,* and *Meet Mr. John Doe.*

Capra helped Tiomkin in his eagerness to learn about American music, supplying him with books of American folk songs, hymns, negro spirituals, cowboy ballads, and work songs. In 1940 Tiomkin wrote the score for *The Westerner* and discovered a flair for writing about the American West. Often asked to explain why he has done so well with westerns, Tiomkin points out that the steppes of Russia and the plains of America have much in common, as do the people who live in those remote, spacious landscapes. With Selznick's *Duel in the Sun* in 1947, Tiomkin also proved he had a definite talent for providing large-scaled epics with large and loud scores, something that would bring him a certain amount of disdain from the critics over the years. But while there are many examples of Tiomkin's penchant for the big symphonic sound, there are also examples of his being quiet and subtle, as in *The Moon and Sixpence* (1942), *The Men* (1950), *I Confess* (1953), and *36 Hours* (1965). He has on many occasions been pleasingly bombastic, almost always with pictures which required that kind of music, but he has surprised even his critics at times, as with Howard Hawks' splendid and sprawling western *The Big Sky* (1952), which contains a beautifully subdued and delicate score.

Tiomkin's fortunes improved rapidly with *High Noon* in 1952, for which he won two Oscars, one for the score and one for the song, with lyrics by Ned Washington. The film was originally issued with almost no music, but it was greeted with little enthusiasm at its first showings. It was then decided to have it scored by Tiomkin, whose music gave the picture tension and anguish. It also resulted, somewhat sadly, in a wave of title-songs being supplied for all manner of films by all manner of composers, but seldom with the effectiveness of *High Noon*. Not even Tiomkin himself was quite able to match that triumph, although his title song for *Gunfight at the OK Corral* (1957) comes close.

Tiomkin also won Oscars for *The High and The Mighty* (1954) and *The Old Man and the Sea* (1958), plus nominations for twenty other scores. By the end of the fifties he had become the highest paid composer in the history of the movies and, with the help of an expert publicist, a well known figure. His humor, his amusing accent, his general love of life, and his success helped to make Dimitri Tiomkin what is possibly the best known of all film composers—and helped bring attention to a trade that was largely unknown to most moviegoers. After his composing assignments declined toward the end of the sixties, Tiomkin became a producer of *McKenna's Gold,* an elaborate but dreary western that lost most of its investment and ended up, after two years of drawn-out production problems, being scored by Quincy Jones. He then tried to realize a life's dream and made a film about Tchaikowsky, filming it in Russia and running into continual troubles. It played well in Russia, but the English-language version swiftly sank from sight. The death of Albertina in 1968 seemed to signal the end of Tiomkin's career in films, certainly in Hollywood, which he left in order to live in Paris and London. Now, with his second wife, he lives in comfortable retirement.

The following article was written for *Films in Review* in 1951 and is here used by permission.

Dimitri Tiomkin on Film Music

In the years that I have been composing and conducting motion picture scores, the importance and value of background music have been increasingly recognized. Only a few years ago, music was considered a pleasant, unobtrusive reinforcement of a sequence's tempo and mood. Today it is far more.

Screen music is still unobtrusive, for being so is the primary characteristic of any movie score that is good. But screen music is now so artfully and effectively integrated with script, direction and the actors themselves, that it has come to be one of the means of story-telling. It is easy to prove this. Just try to transplant any picture's musical score to similar scenes in another picture. You will find that the transplantation doesn't live.

It is of incalculable value to the composer to be able to sit in on story conferences from the beginning. He will not only better comprehend the total trend, mood or purpose of the story, but he will be able to make suggestions that will enable the music to strengthen and fulfill the story.

For example, at random: consider the point in a story at which a man suddenly, without warning, slaps a woman. Let us say the writers conceived the scene to be with two characters standing together talking by a window. Now sudden violence like a slap in the face has more impact if *something unobtrusive* prepares the audience a second or two in advance. If this split-second preparation is not provided, the mind will resent being taken by surprise. The best "something," it has been found, is music.

When this slapping sequence is discussed in a story conference I might say to the writers, or the director: "I will have to have a few seconds in there just before the slap in order to prepare for it." And we would talk it over and conclude that the man will have to take a few steps in order to slap the woman. This will give me the time I need to presage the violent change of mood.

I have found that a composer will get full cooperation unless his requests alter the story line. Directors and writers know a composer's technical problems. They also know the importance of his contribution.

Not a few writers, and even some directors, have asked me whether a retentive and facile memory of what others have written, or one's own musical inventiveness, is more valuable in scoring a motion picture. I cannot remember ever deliberately cribbing music from others, except when it was intentional, legitimate, and acknowledged, as in my arrangements of Debussy's music for David Selznick's *Portrait of Jennie.*

Possibly even the most conscientious composer now and then inadvertently uses a fragment of melody that has stuck in his subconscious. But deliberately lifting phrases from the compositions of others is not only musical bankruptcy but incompetent craftmanship.

Maybe I am fortunately equipped. I was born into a family of concert musicians, and have studied music since I was five years old. When you have thought in terms of music as long as I have it is *easier* to write original music than to bother recalling appropriate bars of music written in the past. After all, scenes and even sequences change so swiftly on the screen that very often there isn't time for more than a couple of measures. It is really simpler and more effective to compose than to rummage around in classical music to find something that expresses the idea.

My first scoring of background music, if it can be called that, was when I was accompanist for the great European comedian, Max Linder. I sat at the piano and improvised all through his act. He was brilliant and unpredictable, and ad libbed freely and frequently. It was impossible for me to arrange and follow a definite score because he never did his act the same way twice. Consequently I watched him and listened to him and learned to divine intuitively what he would do, and thus to improvise what was actually pure mood music. I would even throw in sound effects, such as laughter, at what I thought were the right times.

Linder was one of the truly great comedians of our time. He worked dumb, in the inelegant show business phrase, but his pantomine and his appeal were eloquent. The only comparable artists today are Chaplin, Jimmy Savo, and possibly Cantinflas, the great Mexican clown.

Some gifted comics are so because of blind and blessed instinct, uninhibited by cerebral processes. Not Linder. He had an inspired comedy sense, of course, but he also had an analytical, ingenious mind. Except for Chaplin, I have never known another comedian who had such an objective view of his own art. Linder was sensitive and responsive to any audience, and could talk audience psychology with the intellectual perspective of a professor. On stage he would introduce a new bit suddenly and without previous thought, but later he could give a profound and opposite reason for having done what he did spontaneously.

My first contact with Linder was typical. A few months before World War I began he was making a triumphant tour that brought him to Petrograd. He arrived in the city by train, but flew from the station to the Astoria Hotel by plane. The effect of such an arrival, especially in 1914, was spectacular. History is beginning to distort Linder as an eccentric given to flashy public appearances and *outré* living. But it wasn't self indulgence, merely good business. Like Houdini, he was a showman off-stage, too.

Probably because movies were a nearly perfect vehicle for his pantomime, Linder was enormously enthusiastic over the future of films. Also impatient, because their technological advance seemed to him so slow.

All that now seems to me a far cry from scoring a motion picture, but is was my first step. After that experience I learned that it was easier, for me, to improvise than to recall and use bits of music from the classics or other sources.

After some years of composing symphony and concert music, I became interested in the ballet. It had always been one of my favorite arts, but at that time in my life I became fascinated by the astonishing correlation of sound and sight, or music and movement, that is the essence of ballet. It was also in this period of my life that I realized, for the first time, how much music contributed to story-telling, or more accurately, to the transmission of mood to the audience. I wrote considerably for the ballet. My numbers met with varying success. I found this my introduction to the composition of "background music."

After composing for several Broadway shows I fell under the spell of the motion picture camera. There is a much closer affinity between ballet and movies than casual thought suggests. The story becomes more involved in ballet, for the screen is a more plastic medium, and its story-telling is therefore simpler. Nevertheless, the eloquence of music is as indispensable to film as to the ballet. Sometimes I think a good picture is really just ballet with dialogue.

Dialogue, of course, is of primary importance in determining the genre of background music. It entails problems that must be overcome, and can be overcome only by certain musical techniques. It is difficult for a layman to realize that speaking voices have astonishing variation in pitch and timbre. It may seem incredible, but many actor's voices, however pleasant in themselves, and regardless of pitch, are incompatible with certain instruments. Clarinets, for instance, get in the way of some voices and magnificently complement others. Further, clarinets may be alien to the spirit of a play, or the characterization of a part.

Some actors have voices that are easy to write for. Actors like John Wayne impose almost no burdens on the composer. Wayne's voice happily happens to have a pitch and timbre that fits almost any instrumentation. Jimmie Stewart is another actor for whom it is a delight to write music. Paradoxically, his speaking voice is not "musical." But it has a slightly nasal quality and occasionally "cracks" in a way that is easy to complement. Jean Arthur's voice is somewhat similar.

Just why this type of voice should be easy to write for, I don't know. One might speculate that since these voices have little color in themselves, the complementary musical backdrop doesn't bump into or fall over the dialogue. The mere fact that such voices are unmusical gives them an additional definition.

Imagine an actress whose voice has the right harmonics and overtones of a low register clarinet statement. Assume a voice of incredible pure, round tones. It might be nice to listen to unaccompanied, but it would be a damned nuisance to write for. You'd have to breach the thirteen-tone chromatic scale and even abandon standard pitch before you got a congenial musical background.

The "crack" in Miss Arthur's and Mr. Stewart's voices is one of those strangely appealing imperfections, like a single strand of rebellious hair on an otherwise impeccable moonlit coiffure. But don't pursue this appeal of imperfect voices too far, or you'll run into Andy Devine.

Jean Arthur and James Stewart also illustrate another point: utilizing music to "soften" a face or to give it qualities it does not have inherently. This is not necessary with Stewart or Arthur because both have faces that reflect great sincerity. (Frank Capra, with whom I have had the pleasure of working on a number of pictures, once pointed out to me that unless a player has the sort of face that bespeaks sincerity he is not likely ever to beome a great star).

The camera is a merciless, analytical instrument. Even after every artifice of lighting and make-up, the close-up can be cruelly revealing. The composer, by providing pleasant melodic music, can direct attention from what the make-up artist could not hide. And in doing so the composer is surprisingly successful.

To comprehend fully what music does for movies, one should see a picture before the music is added, and again after it has been scored. Not only are all the dramatic effects heightened, but in many instances the faces, voices, and even the personalities of the players are altered by the music.

Because music can add to a personality and even to a player's physical appearance, I paid particular attention to Mala Powers as Roxanne in *Cyrano De Bergerac*, for which I composed and conducted the music. Miss Powers has a lovely, interesting face, but somehow it just didn't look French enough for me. In real life, of course, there are hundreds of thousands of pure-blooded Frenchmen who wouldn't look French. But on the screen a French woman should look like one. Consequently, I used French thematic music for all her appearances in *Cyrano De Bergerac*. By doing so, I like to think, I helped Miss Powers to project the effect of a daughter of France.

While on the subject of typically French music, I would like to point out that much of the music that is accepted as typical of certain races, nationalities and locales, is wholly arbitrary. Audiences have been conditioned to associate certain musical styles with certain backgrounds and peoples, regardless of whether the music is authentic.

For instance, all audiences think a certain type of steady beat of tom-tom or tympani drum, and a high, wailing wind instrument performing in a simple four or five-tone scale, connotes one thing: Indians. I have conducted no exhaustive research into the American Indian's music, but I suspect that this particular stylization of "Indian music" has very little similarity with the genuine article. In the past some composer freely adapted some possibly authentic Indian song, changed and altered it, and come up with the tom-tom effect we all know.

This "conditioned reflex" music, of course, is wholly arbitrary, but it is so effective that sometimes its use is compulsory. I have employed it in any number of Westerns, including Howard Hawks' *Red River*, which, in my opinion, is a classic movie. I have used the "Indian music" that everyone knows not because I am not resourceful enough to originate other music, but because it is a telegraphic code that audiences recognize. If while the white set-

tlers are resting or enjoying themselves, the background music
suddenly takes on that tympani beat, the effect on the audience is
electrifying. All know the Redmen are on the warpath even before
the camera pans to the smoke signals on a distant hilltop. If I introduced genuine, absolutely authentic Indian tribal music, it probably wouldn't have any effect at all.

This musical conditioning underlies much screen composing.
But it must not be hackneyed if it is to be effective. In the Indian
music mentioned above I never used standard bars and phrases. I
simply employed their mood. The idea is to avoid the usual and the
trite, and at the same time to retain the basic ingredients of the
musical "codes."

The screen composer, like every artist, must work within limitations. No matter how inventive and resourceful he is, he must also
be disciplined. He must, to some extent, compromise. For a motion picture is a collective art, and the composer's contribution
must enhance, not dominate.

9
HANS J. SALTER

In *Frankenstein Meets the Wolf Man* (1943), Larry Talbot (Lon Chaney, Jr.) lies in his hospital bed asleep. As moonlight creeps toward him, we hear a mysterious theme for strings, woodwinds,and celeste, interwoven with the three-note motif for the Wolf Man. When Talbot awakens and recoils from the moonlight, the strings play a sorrowful melody. But soon Talbot begins to turn into a werewolf, and the music builds with forceful use of the Wolf Man motif.

In *The Mummy's Hand* (1940), in the sequence showing the burial of Ananka and Kharis, in the Egypt of three thousand years ago, a choir intones a funeral chant in an ancient dialect, acccompanied by ominous chordal progressions.

In *The Ghost of Frankenstein* (1942), angry villagers storm Frankenstein's castle, as pulsating orchestral music seems to urge them onwards. Part of the melody in the sequence stems from the shepherd's horn theme for the monster's crazed friend Ygor (Bela Lugosi). Ygor's motif takes many guises throughout the film, sometimes dominating the score, at other times slyly insinuating itself into other themes.

These are just three examples of Hans J. Salter's impressive contribution to the art of scoring horror films. It is no exaggeration to claim that this particular facet of film scoring would not be quite the same had it not been for his profilic output at Universal Studios, starting in the late thirties and going right through the forties. The mere listing of his titles indicates not only that Salter turned out an incredible volume of work, but that Salter and his confrere Frank Skinner were the principle authors in a whole

Hans J. Salter.

subgenre of film scoring. Between them they did almost all of Universal's Frankenstein, Dracula, Wolf Man, Invisible Man, Sherlock Holmes, and sundry ghoulish items. This is not to say that Salter and Skinner made this kind of score their exclusive province. While writing music for these pictures, they also scored every other kind of film produced by Universal, westerns, romances, comedies, dramas, and musicals. Under the command first of Charles Previn, the uncle of André, and then under Joseph Gershenson, Hans J. Salter and Frank Skinner were the two principal composers at Universal, turning out a vast amount of product and seldom getting much recognition for their efforts. Universal, the well-tooled factory for programme pictures, was overshadowed by the likes of MGM, Twentieth Century-Fox, and Warner Brothers. So too was its music department, although in terms of productivity and high-speed professionalism it deserves full recognition.

Hans Julius Salter was born in Vienna in 1896, in what he fondly remembers as the last years of Franz Josef's empire, with its great interest in music and all the arts. He confirms that it was then a city with a touch of magic and that the magic went "with the wind" of World War I. He was enchanted with music from an early age, but he came from a nonmusical family, and his father, an office manager for a brewing company, was not in favor of him following a career as a musician. Instead he was encouraged to study medicine and enrolled at the University of Vienna to do so. He gave this up after two years, partly due to the death of his father and the need, as the eldest son, to support his family. There had never been any question in his own mind that he would devote his life to music—a resolve made as a child following military bands in the streets and listening to operetta music being played in coffee houses. At the age of 17 he began to take piano lessons, earning money to do so by tutoring fellow students at high school in whatever subjects they needed help. To earn the money to be a breadwinner, Salter gave piano lessons to children and eventually picked up assignments as a conductor in the many small musical theaters in Vienna and the suburbs—theaters which presented a continual stream of plays, operettas, and musicals.

While working as a theater conductor, Salter also found time and money to take tuition in conducting from the esteemed Felix Weingartner and, for half a year, lessons in composition from

Alban Berg. Salter remembers Berg as a charming gentleman—he was at the time in the process of writing *Wozzeck*—but felt that he was not a very good teacher. He learned much more from studying with Franz Schreker, who was an operatic composer with a genius for colorful orchestration. Salter made a living in what he calls the "musical minor league" of Vienna for three years and gaining a valuable range of experience before discovering the world of films. At the age of 23, he was hired by a film company in Vienna to conduct the performances of so-called film operetta music, which was played to silent film versions of operettas. This was a unique experience for its day and an important step toward the eventual blending of film and sound.

There was an ensemble of four singers, two ladies and two gentlemen, who sang with the orchestra to a silent picture. In order to achieve a semblance of synchronization, the lead line to the songs ran at the bottom of the screen. There were about eight to ten songs in each film, interrupted by silent film with titles. The conductor had to keep it in sync by watching the lead line and the actors on the screen. "With a little luck," says Salter, "we succeeded."

When this kind of work lost popularity, Salter decided to try his luck in Berlin, the center of the growing German film industry. He found the going tough, and the only job he could get was as a rehearsal pianist in an operetta house. After a lean period, he got a job as an organist in one of the big Berlin film palaces, which soon led to his becoming the conductor of the orchestra and quickly picking up a knowledge of conducting film music accompaniment. His success in this endeavor also opened up offers to conduct operas and concerts. The coming of sound made a vast difference to the German industry and created more jobs for conductors and arrangers in the wave of movie musicals produced in Berlin. He was hired by UFA and was gainfully occupied until 1933 and the rise of the Nazis.

Salter returned to Vienna, using it as his base to take jobs as a film music director in Austria, Hungary, Czeckoslovakia, and France. He had a strong sense of impending political disaster, which was not shared by all his colleagues, and began to make plans to move to America. This proved difficult, as it did for most Europeans with similar ideas, but with the aid of a friend who vouched for him, Salter arrived in New York in 1937. It was apparent to him that the only opportunities for him would be in Hollywood, and he quickly travelled there. He found colleagues from the German movies who had preceded him, among them Billy Wilder and composers like Franz Waxman, Bronislaw Kaper, and Frederick Hollander, who did their best to make the right introductions.

Work opportunities were not abundant, but with the help of three old friends from Vienna, writer Felix Jackson, director Henry Koster, and producer Joe Pasternak (who had established themselves by making the greatly profitable *Three Smart Girls)*, Salter was able to get his foot inside the doors at Universal. He began by doing unofficial jobs for Charles Previn, the head of the music department, and in early 1938 was given one sequence of *The Rage of Paris* to score. The approval with which the sequence was met led to a contract and a long association with Universal.

When Salter joined Universal, the studio was turning out an average of seventy films a year, most of them of program nature—films running sixty to seventy minutes and designed mostly as second features. The music department consisted of Previn, composers Frank Skinner and Charles Henderson, a few orchestrators hired part time, and an orchestra of some thirty players. The budgets and schedules at this time, from the late thirties to the late forties, were meager and, by today's standards, difficult to believe. Suffice to say that in 1942, for example, Salter was responsible for supplying music for thirty films. Few composers have ever had quite as much responsibility.

The large body of work would probably be largely forgotten today were it not for the Universal horror pictures, which have enjoyed a nostalgic, almost cultlike revival, but Salter was equally adept in the lighter and more romantic material, such as the scores for the Deanna Durbin musicals. His opportunities for scoring expensive, ambitious projects were limited because he was contracted to a studio largely involved in the production of program pictures, but there were occasional chances, such as Fritz Lang's *Scarlet Street* (1944), Frank Borzage's *The Magnificent Doll* (1946), Anthony Mann's *Bend in the River* (1952), and the Errol Flynn swashbuckler *Against All Flags* (1952), all of which contain music that is clearly the work of a composer of education and taste.

The following article is an edited transcript of material derived from tape recordings made by Preston Jones with the composer.

Hans J. Salter on Film Music

Like so many of the composers who came to Hollywood in the early years of the sound film, I did not set out with the idea of writing for films. It was a matter of circumstances. Originally I wanted to be a serious composer, but in order to make a living I became a conductor, which eventually led me into the film business. My love for opera and concert music gradually got pushed into the background as film scoring became my life's work, although it had great bearing upon what I did in films.

In my early days in Vienna, Richard Strauss and Gustav Mahler had enormous influence on all budding composers, and theirs were the styles everyone tried to emulate. Later we became aware of the French school, of men like Debussy and Ravel, followed by the great impact of Stravinsky. And of course Beethoven, Mozart, and Brahms were all basic to us. We sort of inhaled them as we grew up. Every composer is the product of a certain time and place. I was lucky to have my roots in Vienna in the early part of this century and it naturally affected my work in writing for films.

I have enjoyed my career in film music. I had more than my share of routine assignments, but there were many moments when I felt I had been able to not only make a valuable contribution to the effectiveness of the film, but when I was able to write music that gave me satisfaction. These were moments in which the music affected me deeply and gave me a thrill—a thrill of a kind you cannot get with any other kind of endeavor. It's a wonderful feeling of having created something really fine. One of them was the score for the Deanna Durbin picture *His Butler's Sister*, which is one of my favorites. Another one is *Thunder on the Hill*, starring Claudette Colbert as a nun. Of the many westerns on which I worked, I think fondly of *Bend in the River* with James Stewart and *Wichita* with Joel McCrea, which was well directed by Jacques Tourneur. Of the romantic scores, I particularly like *Come September*, with Rock Hudson and Gina Lollobrigida. Of the more dramatic films, I am proud of *The Magnificent Doll*, which starred Ginger Rogers as Dolly Madison. It was not a successful picture, but that is often the lot of the film composer, to write his best work for projects that fail with the public. To work in films, you have to realize this. The composer's satisfaction comes with his own honest evaluation of what he has done.

Despite all my experience in scoring, I was never able to realize my pet project, which was to write music for certain important scenes, prerecord it, and have the director play the music while he was actually shooting, as a stimulant to the actors. Some of them liked the idea, but for economic reasons it was never feasible. I still feel it would have had a good effect on the scene. It would have been similar to the prescoring we do in musicals, where the singers mouth their lines to the playback. This way we could have timed the scene to fit the moves and the dialogue, with the actors hopefully reacting to the highs and lows in the music. The nearest I ever came to this was in working with director Henry Koster on some of the Durbin films. In those we would take her songs, break them down into sections of so many bars each, and work out the camera movements to correspond with them. Let's say it would start on a long shot with the first six bars; Koster then knew he would cut at this point to a medium close shot and then a few bars later to a two-shot. This way he cut the picture to the score. He would shoot his scenes according to this blueprint, and there were seldom any problems. That was the nearest I came to scoring films the way I thought they should be scored, that is, with the composer as a member of the construction team and an important person in the shaping of the product. But it was always a matter of not enough time and not enough money. These days they seem to have more money, but time is still short and so is the willingness of most producers and directors to confer with or consult composers.

It was always my endeavor to write music that made sense as music and, within the flow of the music, to accentuate certain things in the film. It has been my talent to be able to write the kind of music that lends itself to film scoring. There is no describing this, other than to say that it requires a dramatic instinct and the ability to be able to write descriptively. There have been many fine composers who have tried film scoring and who found that the techniques were beyond their grasp, that they simply could not adapt themselves to it. Scoring requires more than the ability to invent music. Perhaps I can enlarge upon this opinion by discussing some of my own experiences.

The Universal horror pictures were a great challenge to me, as they would have been to any composer, because it was apparent when we looked at these things in their naked form that music would have to play a great part in their effectiveness. To be candid about it, a lot of these films were really not good—the scenes were disjointed, there was little cohesion, and they were not even scary. You had to create the horror with the music, to create the tension that was otherwise not there on the screen. It was such an obvious challenge that I became more and more interested in doing this kind of film. It wasn't that I had any interest in the macabre. These films gave me no thrill. It was just that they were so much in need of music, and for reasons that I have never been able to fully explain, I was able to devise a technique in dealing with them. I became known as "The Master of Terror and Suspense," and people could never understand how a nice, mild-mannered fellow from Vienna could become a specialist in such material. Neither could I, except to say that perhaps I had a certain affinity with fantasy stories. Other than that, it was simply a matter of applied technique. The musical devices at my command were evidently right, and I must admit it was a satisfaction to know that whenever other studios set out to make horror pictures, they usually showed the composers some of ours to give them an idea of what it was all about.

In those days, particularly in the early forties, we had no idea that these pictures would be studied and appreciated years later. There were no thoughts about writing for posterity. We were just trying to keep up with the frantic pace of one picture after the other. For example, a producer would show you his picture on a Monday. You then had one week to write a score, orchestrate it, and be ready to rehearse and record the following Monday. It was like a factory, where you had to turn out, say, so many dozens of red socks and so many dozens of green socks. And, of course, we must not forget that, in the order of importance, music was at the very bottom of the heap. It probably still is. Sound effects were always favored over music. It took a gradual education of the producers until they began to realize that in certain scenes the emotional impact of the music did more for their picture than the static sound effects. It was a constant hassle, and once I was even "asked" to stay away from the dubbing room so they could finish their picture without any interference. "Keep that God-damned music down" was a popular battle cry. I had to speak up for myself, because nobody else did. And no matter how well you did the job, the producers rarely made any comment. Perhaps they were afraid that if they paid us a compliment, we would ask for a raise. They were hectic days, and none of us thought that years later people would be studying our work.

My basic approach to film scoring has always been the same. I ask myself, What did the director want to tell the audience with this scene? Where does the picture need help? Where can it carry itself without any help? Often I told producers that they didn't need any music for a certain scene, and they usually argued that it did. There was a producer, who shall be nameless, who showed me his picture, *Phantom Lady*, directed by Robert Siodmak, and he said he wanted a lot of music in it. I told him that all it needed was music for the main and end titles, that the picture played well the way it was. He disagreed, but since he was the boss, I did as he wished. When the picture came to be dubbed, he started extracting the music for first one scene and then another, until finally all that was left was the main and end titles. Less than a year later, I had another experience with the same producer. He had made another picture with Robert Siodmak, *Uncle Harry*, and this time he informed me that the picture would not need any music. I looked at the film and told him I thought it needed music all the way through: it was structurally weak, and the story was limp. He said he would show it to a preview audience and get their reaction. The reaction was just what I had expected—the picture laid an egg. The next day the producer lost no time in telling me that the film needed a 100-percent score. That, of course, would have been too much. But I did score about 60-percent of the running time, and it did help save the film from being a disaster. I know it is often said that music, no matter how good, cannot save a bad picture, but I think most of those who say it never worked at Universal in my day.

Those people who feel that composers should do their own orchestrations should have been at Universal in those days. There simply was no time for such luxuries. I began at Universal as an orchestrator for Frank Skinner. Frank had been the studio's top orchestrator for several years, but when he was assigned his first score as a composer, *Son of Frankenstein* in 1939, I was asked to do his orchestrations. It was the beginning of a long friendship and a great working partnership. We worked on many pictures together, and it was a matter of close teamwork. I recall one stretch in scoring *Son of Frankenstein* in which we didn't leave the studio for two solid days. Frank would sit at the piano, compose a sequence,

and then hand it to me, and I would orchestrate it. While I was doing that, he would take a nap. Then I would wake him up so he
could write some more, and I would take a nap. This went on for
forty-eight hours. We had no choice because the recording date
was set. Frank had been given two weeks to write the score, which
was par for the course in those days, and Charlie Previn, the head
of the music department, would aggravate the situation with his
great enthusiasm for showing how well he ran the department. He
would say, "They want this picture by Thursday. Let's show 'em.
We'll give it to them by Wednesday." Charlie was a bachelor, and
he couldn't understand why some of us with wives and children actually had a life away from the studio.

Sometimes we would get a film that was clearly above the
average and for which we would try to make a special effort.
Tower of London was one of these, and we did it not long after
Son of Frankenstein. Frank and I decided to do something different. We recorded music of the period, by English composers
like Dowland, Byrd, and Purcell, laid it behind the film, with
regard for scenes but as a kind of mood. We used flutes, harpsichord, viola da gambas, and other old instruments. It was a good
idea, but it didn't work. The preview audience didn't respond to it,
and the studio executives were puzzled by the sound. Our score
was dumped and replaced by previously used material, some of
which was from *Son of Frankenstein*. It taught us to stay in line.
Perhaps today we would be praised for our concept, but not in
1939.

A great deal of music was used and reused at Universal in those
years. We were always fighting time, and it was a matter of
necessity. I would use bits and pieces of scores from the library, including my own, and Charlie Previn used to call this process
"Salterizing." I would try to create something that would be of
equal quality and value as a new score, but I'm sure that very few
people, inside or outside the studio, knew the difference. The
studio was turning out seventy or eighty pictures a year, and we
were a small music department. Even Charlie Previn would occasionally write a sequence. When Frank Skinner and I wrote a score
together, we would write themes for major sequences and then ex-
change them, in order for each of us to understand what the other
was doing and so we could maintain a cohesion of style. In musical
terms, we stayed within the bounds of tonality and did not try to

write anything too complicated. I was somewhat ahead of Frank in terms of harmony and melodic development, having had a formal musical education, which he had not, but I held back a little while he progressed. He was a fine musician and a dependable, hard-working friend. He had come from the field of dance band music, as a musician and arranger, and it was wonderful to see his ability grow with the job of arranging and writing for films. I can't speak too highly of Frank Skinner. He often did more than he needed to do, such as coming to my rescue when I couldn't finish a sequence on time. He could step in and help me write it.

In scoring horror pictures, the main element is that of creating atmosphere—the apprehensive mood, which keeps the viewer on the edge of his seat. For example, in *Frankenstein Meets the Wolf Man*, in the opening sequence where the ghouls approach the Talbot crypt, it was necessary to give the scene a sense of impending dreadfulness. I used a novachord playing a melody over string chords. These chords are based on fourths, which have a strange quality. Usually, chords are based on thirds but these are based on fourths—there's a fourth interval between the voices. When you move these chords back and forth, it gives a strange and mysterious feeling. And then, if you put on top of it an eerie-sounding melody line with the novachord, the poor man's moog synthesizer, it really adds up to something quite strong. In the same sequence, after the robbers open the Talbot coffin and the moonlight filters into the crypt, I placed the theme which accompanies every instance of Talbot turning into the Wolf Man. There is a celesta in that theme, with high strings and high woodwinds, and it is the interplay between those elements that creates the scary effect. The music in all these horrific moments must, of course, be chilling. When strange, ugly hands reach out, the music is usually lowpitched and builds on slow chords. Often this involves the use of the novachord, but in a low register, which is rarely used for normal occasions. Most people use the instrument for melody and high chords. But the low register has an ominous quality. Perhaps the best thing about working with the limited budgets at Universal—we rarely had more than a thirty-piece orchestra—was that it taught us to be ingenius in the use of instruments and in recording techniques.

We thought little about the horror pictures when we were scoring them, but time has given them a kind of distinction. It seems to me that those horror items of that era may survive better than most of the other films made at the time. It's a valid piece of Americana, and it is a unique body of work, with a certain style that cannot be duplicated. I think film music is an art form and so is the horror film, and the wedding between the two is necessary. And the scoring of these films gives composers more opportunity than people may imagine. I was often able to write musical sequences that were quite complete in form, with a beginning, a middle, and an end. In *Man-Made Monster*, for example, there is a sequence in which Lon Chaney plays with a dog. For this I wrote a scherzo. It stands up itself when heard away from the picture, but it also works well with the visual. It is always pleasing when you can do this because most of the time in scoring you cannot, and neither can you expect to. It's the wedding between the music and the picture that matters.

Some of my scores I look back on simply as routine assignments, but there are others that have given me a great deal of pleasure, and which have even affected me emotionally. There is a thrill that comes with film scoring that I have not felt with many other endeavors. The laws that govern the flow of a scene, visually, and the laws that govern music, aurally, are diametrically opposed. And to bring these two things into unison is not easy. Sometimes it almost made me cry to see how well the music fit the scene, how much it did for it, how it lifted the scene to a dimension not even the writer or the director had imagined. I sometimes could hardly believe the effect the music had. It's a unique feeling to get back what you have put in. Even in some of the horror scores, some of the sequences affected me deeply.

I would have to say that a great many of the directors and producers at Universal in the factory days were not men who showed much interest in music. There were exceptions of course. Val Lewton was one of them. He was a highly literate man, with a fine sense of humor. I wish I had been able to work on the horror films he did at RKO, but I was able to work on only two pictures with him, the light comedy *Please Believe Me* at MGM in 1950 and then *Apache Drums* back at Universal a year later. He asked me to do it and allowed me to do it in a manner different from most westerns. I thought the title music should consist of only drums, running against each other in counterpoint. I recorded them on five different tracks and then combined them into one. Lewton was all in favor of this, whereas the routine producers would surely not have been. I also had the idea of using genuine Indians to prerecord the war chants, except that my Indians turned out to be of the Hollywood tribe and knew nothing of their native languages. I studied different dialects and wrote Indian words to go along with the chants and dances, and then taught these Indians how to sing the words, which is quite an achievement for a Viennese composer. But if there is any rule in writing film music it is only that one should be prepared for—and capable of—anything.

One of the films I most enjoyed scoring was *Scarlet Street* in 1945 because it brought me together again with Fritz Lang. It is interesting to work with someone of that calibre because they usually have ideas about music which can help the composer, as it did in this case. Lang was a sophisticated, intelligent man, and he had strong feelings about the use of music in films. He had started out with the idea of being a painter, and he truly had an eye for all the arts. I remember this film because it was one of the first Hollywood pictures to end in a downbeat manner, in a realistic fashion with Edward G. Robinson trudging off into the night, haunted by the voices of Joan Bennett and Dan Duryea, the people whose deaths he had brought about. I had talked a great deal with Lang about the ending and disagreed with his concept that it should be totally bleak and despairing. I felt the music should lift the scene up a little and suggest some hope for the poor man. Musically it seemed natural to develop the thematic material and end on a rise, a kind of redemption. Lang wouldn't buy that. He said, "If we did that, it would defy the whole idea of my picture. This has to be downbeat, all the way to the last frame." He convinced me that he was right, and that's the way it was scored—somber to the end, with just a few finishing chords. This is one of the few occasions on which I have taken advice from a director or producer and felt that he was absolutely right. Mostly we are left to our own devices, and there have been times when a little inspired advice would have been welcome.

We film composers like to sit around and swap stories about producers, and of course we exaggerate. Mostly they are men with no musical education, and it is therefore difficult to communicate with them. It is my hope that future film courses given at universities for filmmakers will include a study of the function of music in film. Those who set out to make pictures may then come to realize that music is a kind of cohesion and that it can help bind a film together. It can give pictures a better flow and a certain tempo, and it can sometimes help clear up psychological misunderstandings within the film. In short, it can help steer the picture. If nothing else—and this I know from all those Universal horror pictures—it can certainly help cover up a lot of cinematic sins!

10
BRONISLAU KAPER

MGM's contribution to the history of music in Hollywood is a large one, and the composer most identified with it is Bronislau Kaper. His twenty-eight years at Metro began in 1936, and his output covers almost every kind of composition, although his forte has always been the writing of good humored, sophisticated music. This is as it should be because Kaper himself is a good humored, sophisticated gentleman, a cultured European noted in the Los Angeles artistic community for his wit and charm as well as for his efforts toward supporting that community. Kaper is a product of *mittel Europa* of what now seems like a millenium ago—the Europe of pre-Hitler times. He was born in Warsaw in 1902 and discovered music at the age of 7 when a piano was added to the Kaper home. He discovered an affinity for the instrument, even though it was not a musical family and his businessman father preferred that his son follow a career in law. Kaper did indeed study law, but also the piano and composition. His talent for music was so obvious that his family could not object to his choosing it as a career.

Kaper is still an exceptional pianist, possibly the most gifted pianist of any composer working in films. And he might well have made his name playing as a concert pianist had it not been for nervousness. He graduated from the Chopin Music School in Warsaw, a circumstance that required a public appearance—and the discovery that being a pianist requires more than talent. Kaper recalls that he was so scared while taking the street car to the school, where his major piece was to be the Chopin F Minor Concerto, that he was praying that the car might be involved in an acci-

Bronislau Kaper.

dent. It was not, and Kaper managed to get through his recital, but it convinced him that he did not possess the aplomb to be a performing artist. Shortly after this he went to Berlin to further his musical education and took a job writing songs for a cabaret in order to support himself. It was a time of burgeoning theatrical activity, and he was soon swept into the cauldron of German stage musicals and movies. He spent all of the twenties in Berlin, adapting and arranging material, accompanying artists, and gradually discovering his ability as a composer. By the early thirties some of his songs were being sung and recorded by the major singers of the day, including Richard Tauber.

The happy bustle of activity was curtailed by the rise of the Nazis, and in 1933 Kaper, then married, moved to Paris, where he became a part of the French film industry. In the summer of 1935, Louis B. Mayer happened to be vacationing in France, and everywhere he went he heard the song "Ninon," which Kaper had written for tenor Jan Kiepura. Mayer found out who wrote it, asked Kaper to come to his hotel in Paris, and with an hour signed him to an MGM contract. Arriving in early 1936, Kaper began his long sojourn as a Metro musician. And had there been any doubts in Mayer's mind about bringing a European song writer into his midst, it would have faded fast with Kaper's melody for the title song of *San Francisco*, written in collaboration with Walter Jurman. It was Kaper's great good fortune to be able to come up with what would soon become, and stay, a quintessential American city song. It was the perfect start to his life in Hollywood, and Mayer thereafter looked upon Kaper as his resident song writer. The only problem was that Kaper considered himself in more ambitious terms. Inventing tunes for songs was pleasurable, but there was even more satisfaction to be had in composing orchestral music. It took Kaper about four years to convince Mayer. In 1940 he wrote the score for *I Take This Woman*, starring Spencer Tracy, and from then on he averaged four or five scores each year. He proved himself adept at supplying music for light comedic pictures, but at the same time seized every opportunity to score the more dramatic vehicles. He had to fight, as did most artists, the straight jacket of type casting.

In 1941 Kaper added a song to the Metro treatment of *The Chocolate Soldier*, starring Nelson Eddy, and it soon became one of the songs most requested by that popular baritone's fans—"While My Lady Sleeps." For the darkly mysterious

Gaslight (1944), Kaper wrote one of his most subtle and serious scores. John Green, who later became head of music for MGM and worked closely with Kaper for several years, claims that Kaper is a master of the craft of underscoring dialogue, which is one of the most difficult and least appreciated aspects of film composition. Green recalls that he would at first be concerned about the complicated scoring supplied by the composer for these passages, but that once he began to play them with the picture the music fit perfectly the timing and flow of the visual.

Among the most popular of Kaper themes is *Green Dolphin Street*, a romantic costume epic scored in 1947. It took on a life of its own when Miles Davis recorded it in a jazz setting. Its cadences lent themselves to the peculiar modes of jazz. In 1952 the soap opera *Invitation* needed a poignant theme and from Kaper received something far beyond the quality of the picture. The minorish tones of the *Invitation* resulted in many recordings, although not nearly as many as the Kaper hit of the following year, the score for *Lili*, which brought him an Oscar. It has an essentially European flavor, as does the whole score of *The Glass Slipper* (1955), a Cinderella vehicle, whose score Kaper later adapted into a concert suite, and *The Swan* (1956), starring Grace Kelly in the delicate puritanian fable by Molnar. Such stories seem to bring out the gentle romantic in Kaper. He is devoted to classic literature, which is the reason he was determined to score *The Brothers Karamazov* (1958), a film that benefits greatly from his dark and soulful music.

Writing for romantic fiction has been something of a trap for Kaper, since it is a genre that appeals to his imagination, and because of it he has deliberately sought different projects. His talent for comedy is clearly demonstrated with *Auntie Mame* (1958) and *A Flea in Her Ear* (1969), the one American in character and the other French. Like most of his colleagues, Kaper has invested some of his best composition in films that did poorly at the box office. The *Red Badge of Courage* is a case in point. This 1951 John Huston version of the classic Civil War story was butchered by MGM when they felt the public would not pay to see an adult and philosophical study of young men in warfare. *Home from the Hill* (1960), a rather murky tale of family problems in the South, contains one of Kaper's most subtle scores. Less subtle, but highly effective on the sensuous level, is his music for *Butterfield 8*, which helped Elizabeth Taylor to win an Oscar.

Marlon Brando's *Mutiny on the Bounty* (1962) met with a mixed reaction, but in terms of photography and scoring it was far superior to the famous Gable-Laughton version. It is Kaper's most symphonic score, fully capturing the nautical adventures and particularly helpful in the Tahitian interludes, for which Kaper studied source music. Its principle theme, "Follow Me," became a favorite with the public. Kaper wrote another large score in 1956 for Richard Brooks' unsuccessful attempt to make an epic out of Joseph Conrad's *Lord Jim*. In this instance Kaper incorporated actual Balinese material and wrote what he considers one of his best melodies. Later attached to lyrics by Bob Russell, it was recorded as "The Color of Love." The fact that it did not become popular does not alter the composer's opinion. Indeed, as is often the case, what a composer hears in his own work are qualities beyond the average ear.

Like that of all the veteran Hollywood composers, Bronislau Kaper's output declined sharply with the sixties, due partly to the decrease in the number of feature films produced and partly to the inroads of pop music in the scoring trade. His theme for the long running *FBI* television series helped keep the wolf a long way from the door of his Beverly Hills mansion. Not kept from his door is a continual stream of friends and visitors from the music fraternity of Los Angeles, many of whom encourage Kaper to play his piano. He is the kind of musician who carries in his head a vast repertory, ranging from Clementi to Szymanowski, with digressions to such points as Polish folk music and Viennese operetta. A man of great vitality and with a keen interest in sports (he still practices fencing), Kaper is among the most social individuals in Los Angeles. His friend Miklos Rozsa claims, "No matter where I go in the world, whenever people hear that I live in Los Angeles, they ask 'Do you know Kaper?' "

The following article was put together from material given by the composer in the course of his extensive interview with Irene Kahn Atkins as an oral history for the American Film Institute. It is here used with the permission of Mrs. Atkins and the Institute.

Bronislau Kaper on Film Music

The first thing the film composer has to realize is that he is not his own boss. The second thing he has to realize, and this can be painful, is that the people for whom he works know a lot less about

music than he does. Sometimes they know so little it can almost
reduce a composer to tears. My boss at MGM for many years was
the great Louis B. Mayer, and I use the word "great" with respect,
because he ran the best film factory in the world, and ran it
beautifully. But his musical taste was limited. Mr. Mayer loved the
works of the operetta composers, and that was the kind of music
he wanted in his pictures. He has little sympathy with classical
works. He once astonished André Previn by saying, "André, do
you know why Heifetz is not a success?" He truly believed that if
Heifetz had played gypsy music he would have been famous. The
point of this story is not so much that Louis B. Mayer had a
limited appreciation of music, but that he had a fantastic
understanding of public taste. And if a composer wants to work in
films, he had best come to a similar understanding. This does not
mean he has to write down to them—only that he must be able to
communicate with people in a language they understand. This is
not the place to be avant garde, but on the other hand neither do
you have to write rubbish. I heard a score recently which I consider
to be brilliant, *The Outlaw Josey Wales* by Jerry Fielding. It was
not arrogant, and it had no cliches. It was distinguished dramatic
composition. That's how good film music can be.

It is a sad fact of life in the film business that a composer is at
the mercy of the film itself. Marvelous scores have been written for
movies which sank like rocks, which does not help the composer to
get his next job. But it can also work in reverse. I was hired to do
Auntie Mame because of my score for *Don't Go Near the Water*, a
navy comedy which made a lot of money for MGM. I wrote what I
think is a conventional score for it—a nice little theme here and
there, and some variations on "Anchors Aweigh." It was nothing
I would list among my greatest achievements, but because the picture did so well at the box office, the word got around that I had
written a superb score. Warners then arranged with MGM to hire
me, and it probably cost them twice as much as hiring someone
who was not under contract to a studio. It is possible that the
bosses at Warners had not even heard the score for *Don't Go Near
the Water*; all they knew was that it was a smash comedy and that
Kaper had written the score. It so happens that several of the films
with which I have made the most success have been lightly comedic
or romantic, and it has tended to give me a reputation as a composer of comedy scores. I don't agree, but I do know from long ex-

perience that a composer becomes identified with his best films. That is one of the problems of this business, and the business is full of them. Let's consider a few of them.

The trouble with writing music for movies is that you don't actually write it to the movie; you write it to a cue sheet. Usually you sit at home, removed from the emotional contact of the film and its people. When you watch a movie for the first time, you begin to think of music, and it seems fairly easy because your feelings are being stimulated by what you see and hear. Then you go home and you have to reproduce those feelings. You have to recall your responses. For me the most intriguing thing about scoring is writing music for dialogue, especially if certain actors have unusual tones in their speaking voices. Ingrid Bergman in *Gaslight*, for example. Hers has a strange, singing quality. Then there are others who mumble and you must be careful not to drown them. But most important, what you write must make musical sense. You cannot write music that will effect people emotionally unless it is good music. With that in mind, you next have to think of volume. If there is emotion in a scene, the music can be loud because the emotion will support it. If your music is loud in a scene which contains little dramatic feeling, then it will do more harm than good.

When I am assigned to a film, I like to look at it several times before I meet with the producer and director. Otherwise I am at a disadvantage because they know their material thoroughly, and I don't. My next decision concerns the amount of music the picture might need and which are the areas that need scoring. But you never know if your decisions are correct until you finally put the music to the picture. Sometimes ideas that look beautiful on paper do not work out well because you find that in some subtle way a scene does not take music. There is a general opinion that if you provide a weak scene with music, you will strengthen it. This is not always the case; sometimes you find it only makes it weaker.

Dialogue presents a composer with a challenge, but sound effects are, stated simply, a big problem. Composers are invariably men with a fair amount of ego, and they don't like playing a losing game with the sound department. My solution when dealing with a film I know will contain a lot of sound effects is to ask for a cue sheet giving me the information about the kind of effects that will be used and where. Sometimes they might even have the sound strips ready, and I can then listen to them and guage my music accordingly. Otherwise, you could write elaborate music for fantastic action sequences, music which might take you weeks to write, and then have it swamped by the sound effects. Those who create sound effects have their egos too, and they don't want a composer swamping what they do. Ideally a film should be scored after all the sound effects have been laid in, but there is never enough time to do that. The next best thing is to be aware of where the sound is to be used.

The effect on the ears of audiences in these scenes involving a great deal of action and noise can be very strange. I have received many compliments for the earthquake music in *San Francisco* and the earthquake music in *Green Dolphin Street*, except that there was no music in either sequence, only sound effects. There was a wild storm and flood sequence in *The Wild North*, and people have told me how well I scored it. Again, there was no music. The trick is simply that I led up to those sequences with music and then dropped it for the sounds to take over, and picked up again with music after the sounds died down.

It is difficult to advise young composers today on ways of perfecting their ambitions because the studio system under which I spent most of my career no longer exists. It was my luck to be a part of a major studio for twenty-eight years. It had its limitations, such as arguing with studio policy—MGM for example always liked its music scoring dubbed lower than most of the other studios—but there were great advantages, not the least of which was continuous employment. We also had the luxury of working with first class people, such as the music editors, all of whom were thoroughly educated in music and could speak to composers in musical language. We also had the best orchestrators, who could give you precisely what you asked for—and quickly.

I have had a great deal to do with scoring comedies and yet, to tell the truth, I really don't like comedy scores. To me the old-fashioned comedy scores sound like cartoons, with little jokes for solo instruments and the music trying to duplicate what is happening on the screen, which is ridiculous. Music can create funny effects, but not by trying to sound funny. It must do it by making comment. The biggest mistake is to play comedy music against funny dialogue. It just eats itself up. It's a waste of effort. You can accentuate something by calling attention to the fact that it is funny, and you can sometimes play straight music against comedy.

Because of this reputation for scoring comedies—like my reputation for writing earthquake music—I was called to Warners to do *Auntie Mame*, and I consider that one of the highlights of my experiences. I loved the picture, and I thought Rosalind Russell was the finest choice for that part that could possibly be made. And it gave me the opportunity to work with Ray Heindorf, an absolute giant in the art of film scoring. He had been with Warners since the early thirties, but he succeeded Leo Forbstein as head of the music department in 1948. Korngold referred to Heindorf as an enormous talent and he was right. Heindorf could work as fast as lightning and still turn in inspired arrangements and orchestrations, and conduct them with perfection. Working with him was a revelation. His timings were split-second perfect, and yet he left nothing to chance. An amazing man, he made it look so easy, and he seemed always to be in good humor. I have always been a bundle of nerves when working on a picture, but Heindorf was calm.

What interested me about *Auntie Mame* was not so much the fact that she was funny, but that she had a great soul. She acts frivolously and theatrically, but underneath it is her great love and compassion for people. This is what I tried to capture, the fact that she has suffered in life, but hasn't been crushed by it. With *Mame*, the first temptation was to comment on her gay, vivacious manner, but that would have been a mistake because Roz Russell conveyed all that magnificently—visually and spiritually. When something is effective on the screen, there is no need to add to it with obvious music. To have scored *Mame* comically would have cheapened the film.

Scoring *Mame* also gave me the opportunity to work with the great sound department at Warners, since that studio had always been foremost in pioneering good sound and always sympathetic toward the musical problems. In dubbing pictures at Warners, you had the feeling that they were helping you and not working against you. At MGM there was almost a fetish about dialogue, in making it clear and prominent. This was fine when important things were being said, but it often resulted in a rather stiff, naked sound, with the dialogue out in front and out of proportion with the rest of the sound. I didn't like the dubbing at MGM because it was so very cautious, as if people with hearing problems might be rushing up to theater managers all over the world and complaining that they couldn't understand what was being said. In making a film, if you really want to have a feeling that you're in touch with life, you should try to create a combination of sounds the way they exist in life.

But there were many fine things about being a musician at MGM, particularly after John Green became head of the music department in 1950. Dore Schary, at that time the head of the studio, was conscious of the fact that despite Metro being the greatest film factory in the world, its music department, especially its orchestra, was not regarded as the best in the industry. He told John he wanted the best that money could buy. When John replied that it would take a lot of money, all Schary said was, "Well, we've got a lot of money." We had always had some marvelous musicians at the studio, but now we got even more. And it must be said that Hollywood studio musicians are superb. First of all, many of them are key figures in the Los Angeles Philharmonic, and the others are those who specialize in film scoring, which can be more difficult than the usual task of playing in symphony orchestras. The balance of a studio orchestra is, for example, different from that of a standard orchestra. There are less strings, but lots of woodwinds and brass. The engineers are responsible for the way the orchestra sounds, and they compensate for the lack of strings with their microphone positioning. Therefore, the string players must be exceptionally good. There is no allowance for anyone who is less than good. It's all too expensive, and the producers cannot run the risk of multiple takes by using musicians who cannot perform perfectly. These musicians think fast and interpret fast.

The average musician in a symphony orchestra probably knows all the symphonies of Brahms and Beethoven, and he has the luxury of hearing those works in performances by other orchestras. With standard repertory there are standards and traditions, and even if a new composition is performed, there is plenty of time for rehearsals. This is not the case in the film situation, where musicians have to read music they have never seen or heard before, and record it within hours. Also, they must play music which, unlike classical music, is mostly formless, because of the fragmentary demands of the film. There is no tradition: it has to be read and played and fitted to the picture. These musicians are required to be extremely capable, and I have great respect for them.

Opinions vary as to the use of music in films, and that's a good thing. In any art there must always be room for new ideas. The only opinion to which I object is the one that claims there should not be any music in films. I think this is wrong. Films not only need music, they need it badly. Music is the simplest and most direct way of making a statement, even though it is subconscious. The interplay between the visual experience and the aural can be fascinating. The general public may not be aware of how they have been affected by the composer's work, but he knows, and so do his peers. Sometimes he even gets a pat on the back. After we had made *The Stranger*, Edward G. Robinson, a very cultured gentleman, came up to me and said, "Bronny, you made my acting better." A moment like that suddenly makes this difficult and often frustrating business seem very gratifying.

Alfred Newman (right) with Tony Thomas at the scoring of Flower Drum Song at Universal in December, 1960.

11
ALFRED NEWMAN

The most influential and powerful musician in the history of Hollywood music is Alfred Newman. He operated on three levels—as a composer, as a conductor, and as an executive—and he was superb on each. His association with films is in itself an interesting study since it covers the whole Golden Age of American movies, from the first years of the sound era through to the decline of the major studio systems. By the time of his death in 1970, Newman had spent forty years dealing with film music, and he had acquired more honors than any other man in the business. He won nine Oscars, and he was nominated for the Academy Award forty-five times. Newman once said, "In the recording of music for motion pictures, it is possible to achieve total perfection of performance. Don't settle for anything less!" Anyone who ever worked with him can attest that he was a man of his word.

Newman, who was born in New Haven, Connecticut, in March of 1901, was a prodigy. He was also the eldest of ten children, which had considerable bearing on the course of his career. Had it been a more affluent family, he would probably have indulged his talents and entered into a long period of study and development, first as a pianist and then as a conductor of serious music. With the encouragement of his mother, a lady with a passion for music, Newman began piano lessons at the age of 6, but since the family was short of money, the boy had to walk ten miles to the teacher, who charged twenty-five cents a lesson. However, the boy's talents were so obvious that friends brought him to the attention of a respected musician, Edward A. Parsons, who gave Newman a scholarship. A year later the boy was playing classical pieces at recitals Parsons held for advanced pupils. A group of local music lovers then decided to raise money to send him to New York, where he became a student of the eminent Polish composer-pianist Sigismond Stojowski. The twice weekly trip to New York by rail was made possible only by the kindness of a railroad conductor who never, throughout a two-year period, punched the boy's ticket.

Newman advanced swiftly under Stojowski's tutelage and won a Silver Medal in 1914 and a Gold Medal the following year in competitions at the Don Ende School of Music in New York. Stojowski then expanded Newman's education with studies in composition, but the economics of the Newman family made it hard for the boy to fully devote himself to music. It was necessary for him, at the age of 14, to find employment in order to help support his family. He was fortunate in having as one of his supporters, Mrs. Simon Baruch (mother of Bernard), who arranged for the boy to be hired as a pianist with the Strand Theater on Broadway. The theatre maintained an orchestra, which played between films, and Newman was presented as a boy-wonder pianist. Some months later he was hired by vaudeville star Grace La Rue as her accompanist on the Keith Circuit, which also required him to play solos during her change. It was while involved in this somewhat sleazy occupation that Newman appeared in New York's Town Hall in a recital sponsored by the great Paderewski.

Newman's work with Grace La Rue eventually led him to become interested in conducting for the theater. His ally in this ambition was Broadway music director William Daly, who taught Newman the rudiments of the craft and allowed him to conduct matinee performances. Newman was 15 at the time. Two years later he was working full time as a conductor of musicals, with his income going up and down with the relative success of the various projects. It was invaluable experience, but it deflected Newman from the world of serious music. He became prominent when he was hired as conductor of *The George White Scandals of 1920*, with a score by George Gershwin, which led to one musical after another all through the twenties in New York. It allowed him to work with all the prominent composers of the time, and it was while conducting Jerome Kern's *Criss Cross* in 1926 that he received his first offer to guest conduct a symphony orchestra, the Cincinnati, which came about through the admiration of Fritz Reiner.

Early in 1930, Irving Berlin contracted Newman to be the music director of the film *Reaching for the Moon*. He left New York somewhat reluctantly, having no interest in films, but accepted the job because it paid well and would last only three months. As soon as it was completed, Samuel Goldwyn asked Newman to stay and arrange the music for several of his pictures. In agreeing to do so, Newman set what would be the course of his life's work. So deeply and continuously busy in film work did Newman become that he was never able to return to Broadway or to his ambition of becoming a symphonic conductor. Goldwyn came to rely entirely on Newman for all musical matters. And Newman found himself challenged and intrigued by the possibilities for music opened up by the coming of sound on film. He had, as his colleagues testify, a keen ear for sound and thought in terms of high fidelity recording long before it became standard practice. In recording scores, he instructed his engineers where he wanted microphones placed.

Newman had written a few pieces of music during his years on Broadway, although he had never thought of himself as a composer. The opportunities presented by films caused him to discover his own talent for creating original music. He wrote his first score in 1931, *Street Scene*, the main theme of which soon achieved, and held, popularity. He used it several times in his scores at Twentieth Century-Fox. His association with that studio came about through Darryl F. Zanuck, who called upon Newman's services when he joined Twentieth Century Films, which merged with Fox in 1935. Goldwyn allowed Newman to work for Zanuck, and in 1939 he became general music director for Twentieth Century-Fox, although whenever Goldwyn had a musical problem he continued to call upon his ex-music director.

Newman was head of music for Twentieth Century-Fox for twenty years and managed it with authority and firm control. Zanuck trusted him without question and gave Newman a high budget with which to operate his department. It enabled him to maintain a first class orchestra and to hire those whom he considered to be the best arrangers, orchestrators, and composers. He defied the general belief that those who are greatly gifted as composers and interpretors are usually not good administrators. Newman knew how to use power. Says David Raksin, "He was an incredibly demanding boss, but if he figured you knew what you were doing—and you wouldn't be working with him if you didn't—the sky was the limit."

Newman worked on a total of 255 films and toward the end admitted that it was too much to have done. As a conductor, he was probably the finest ever to work in films. It was what he most loved to do, and the many who played under his baton claim that had circumstances been different, he would most likely have been an outstanding symphonic conductor. Despite his talent as a composer, he did not enjoy the work of sitting and inventing music. A most gregarious man by nature, the loneliness of composing disturbed him, and he admitted he often sat for hours looking at blank music paper before being able to write a note. Nevertheless, he was proud of what he considered to be his best scores: *Wuthering Heights* (1939), *The Song of Bernadette* (1943), and *Captain from Castile* (1947).

Of his nine Oscars only one was for dramatic composition, *Bernadette*. The others were for music direction, for a combination of conducting, arranging, and composing, and he made it no secret that these awards came to him as the head of a team: *Alexander's Ragtime Band* (1938), *Tin Pan Alley* (1940), *Mother Wore Tights* (1947), *With a Song in My Heart* (1952), *Call Me Madam* (1953), *Love is a Many Splendored Thing* (1955), *The King and I* (1956), and *Camelot* (1967). It should be noted that although the title song of *Love is a Many Splendored Thing* was written by Sammy Fain and Paul Francis Webster, the film contained a great deal of original scoring by Newman. Newman was also the only musician to win four Oscar nominations in the same year; in 1939 he was nominated for *The Hunchback of Notre Dame*, *They Shall Have Music*, *The Rains Came*, and *Wuthering Heights*. The abundance was just too much, and the award went elsewhere—rather surprisingly to the team of four composers who wrote the score for John Ford's *Stagecoach*, a classic film but not a particularly remarkable score. Newman felt, as did many, that the music Oscar that year should have gone to Max Steiner for *Gone With the Wind*.

Newman resigned from his post as head of music for Twentieth Century-Fox in January of 1960. He thereafter composed and conducted on a free-lance basis and also found time to do more recording. Much of 1964 and 1965 was spent writing the lengthy score for George Steven's *The Greatest Story Ever Told*, which, apart from the sheer labor of a long and difficult job, resulted in bitterness for Newman when Stevens deleted the "Hallelujah" ending of his score and substituted the celebrated one by Handel. It was an embarrassment and did nothing to help Newman's declining health. Addicted to work, he was also a chronic smoker, which contributed to his death at sixty-nine.

Newman's closest associate in his last years was choral director Ken Darby. They had known each other since Darby appeared as a singer in *The Cowboy and the Lady*, which Newman scored for Goldwyn in 1938. Says Darby, "He had the marvelous gift of innate and acquired good taste . . . a swift, analytical mind . . . and a pair of fantastically accurate ears." Thanks largely to the efforts of Ken Darby, who piloted the project and helped raise the necessary funds in cooperation with Martha Newman, the composer's widow, there now exists at the University of Southern California, Los Angeles, the Alfred Newman Memorial Library. It contains the bound film scores, sound-track albums, taped interviews, manuscripts, writings, and career memorabilia. The material is available for study on the premises.

The following article, made available by the Alfred Newman Memorial Library, is the script of a lecture given on October 15, 1968, in Los Angeles, in which Newman dealt with the problems involved in adapting stage musicals to the screen. As such, it is an especially valuable contribution to this book.

Alfred Newman on Film Music

In my early career, I was music director for many shows written for the stage by George and Ira Gershwin, Rodgers and Hart, Cole Porter, Jerome Kern, Vincent Youmans, and Sigmund Romberg, among others, and I found an exhilaration in their work which was very exciting indeed. It would be fair to say that I had gained considerable understanding in this area before coming to Hollywood in the thirties where I have acted in the same general capacity for innumerable musical films.

The screen is deeply indebted to the stage. The musical theater has been, and continues to be, a lively and generous spawning ground for excited and picturesque material so necessary and useful to the creation of musical films.

I once asked the late and beloved Oscar Hammerstein why he and Richard Rogers adapted so many of their musical shows from earlier plays and novels. He said, "It's much easier, safer, and more objective to second-guess somebody else's mistakes than to drown ignominiously in our own precious ideas."

Adapting a successful stage musical to the screen also has this advantage; to second-guess the weaknesses of the stage and to build upon the strong points. Unfortunately, sometimes, the opposite effect transpires, and the movie version of a great stage musical becomes "A ten-ton technicolor marshmallow!"

We are inclined, perhaps, to forget the great forward movement from the musical comedies of the twenties culminating—through the gradual growth of sophistication and maturity—in a work like *Pal Joey*, for example. *Oklahoma* was the great forerunner of the musical plays. It introduced a first rate ballet, happily replacing the naive chorus-girl routines of the earlier typical format. Then came *Carousel, South Pacific, Westside Story, Sound of Music, My Fair Lady, Camelot, Man from La Mancha* and *Fiddler on the Roof*, just to name a very few. They were really quite magnificent on the stage, and most of them were adapted to make films of quality. Taken altogether, the present scene is a far cry from a show I conducted called *Hold Everything* in which our Senator George Murphy did a rather bland ballroom dance with his wife, Julie, long before he teamed up with "would-be-senator" Shirley Temple Black!

The orchestra plays a vital, pivotal part in both stage and screen musicals. Since I am not at all chauvinistic about the screen, I should like for a moment to assume the role of the Devil's advocate.

The theater's pit orchestra is a tradition to all audiences of all ages. Whether it is in the best tradition is a moot point, but it is both seen and heard. Audiences, and I include myself, always get a kick of expectancy at the sight of the musicians slowly, almost reluctantly entering the pit carrying their instruments. Often as not, the trombone player has a bottle neatly camouflaged in his case from which he may covertly take a swig during some long tacet scene between numbers—to keep his lip in condition, of course! I know these things as a conductor. I've caught many of them at it—and not all trombone players—and, I might add, on occasion I was slightly envious! Excitement mounts as the oboe player sounds his A for the tune-up. Bedlam follows, flutes flutter, strings run scales, trumpets toot, and even the drummer gets into the act, testing his drums, a truly marvelous and heady sound.

Finally, the conductor taps for quiet, raises his baton, and the first notes of the overture blare forth. This seems to be a cue for the audience to chatter even louder than before, because this sound is stimulating—and always has been!

Upon conclusion of the overture, the house lights dim and the spotlights flood the prescenium. The introduction to the opening number brings a hush to the audience. The curtains part swiftly, and the show, which has been so eagerly awaited, is now on the road. This is the theatergoer's finest moment. There is a thrilling immediacy about a living performance. The actors, singers, dancers, and orchestra provide a chain of contact between themselves and the audience. They react to one another. Even if the show is only so-so, there exists a pervading human contact in which spontaneous applause or laughter can inspire the actors to a new and better performance. These are distinct advantages, which we in films are denied.

Now I resign as the Devil's advocate, the better to examine the obverse side of the coin.

The theater orchestra is, in general, rather small. There are several reasons for this. The most important from the producer's view is simple economics. More often than not, after two weeks of the New York run, the orchestra is further cut in size to effect even greater economies. Another limiting factor to the size of the orchestra is the dimension of the pit. There simply is not room down there for a larger group of musicians.

Let me hastily add that size alone should not be equated with quality. Many most effective and beautiful works have been composed for small combinations of musicians. But the theater orchestra must, of necessity, be a utility orchestra—a poor man's symphony, an acceptable dance band, a string ensemble, and a novelty combo, all rolled into one collaginous unit. Thus, the results are often inadequate and disappointing.

For example: a musical stage show may have a poignant love story requiring a large string section for mood and color. It may also employ a full-scale ballet, which should be accompanied by a symphonic complement. There might be a wild and eccentric dance number with overtones of comedy in which a novelty group of musicians is integrated with a modern jazz band.

Obviously, it is totally impossible for the pit orchestra to embody all these elements. Therefore, of necessity, a compromise must be made. I might add that this compromise is made very adroitly sometimes, but the total effect, for show after show, is a sameness of sound, which cannot be avoided even by the most skillful orchestrators and arrangements.

It is in this area that the film studio orchestra enjoys a distinct advantage. Each number to be translated to the screen can have its own hand-tailored instrumentation, sometimes a lute and Spanish guitar, sometimes the full symphony. And each song or dance is recorded separately, to be tied together later during the period of postscoring the entire film.

Now let me examine some of the problems of adaptation. On the stage, all the actors sing, or dance, or both. Yul Brynner and Gertrude Lawrence had no trouble projecting across the footlights the songs of *The King and I*. The voices of Mary Martin and Ezio Pinza rolled beautifully over the orchestra pit to the last row of the balcony in *South Pacific*. Julie Andrews, Richard Burton, and Robert Goulet vocalized memorable performances in *Camelot*. But, what happened when these great stage musicals were acquired by the film studios?

The late and talented Gertrude Lawrence was replaced by the equally beautiful and gifted Deborah Kerr, a fine actress, but a nonsinger. Mitzi Gaynor was cast in *South Pacific* opposite Rosanno Brazzi. Mitzi could sing, but poor Rosanno sounded much like a lost nanny goat. Most incredible of all, with Robert Goulet riding the crest of popularity among admirers of all ages, he was bypassed for the role of Lancelot in favor of unknown Franco Nero, an energetic and not unlikeable Italian actor who spoke broken English and sang not at all. Can you imagine the enormous task of teaching him to speak Arthurian English with a French accent?

Vanessa Redgrave, with a vast minimum of vocal equipment and control, replaced Julie Andrews as Guinevere in *Camelot,* and Richard Harris, who had never sung outside his gold-plated shower, became King Arthur. These, dear people, are problems.

My friend and associate, Ken Darby, has always maintained a sizeable stable of fine singers. He found a voice double for Deborah Kerr in Miss Marni Nixon. She and Deborah worked, sang, read lines, studied, and practically lived together for six weeks before we recorded a note of *The King and I*. By that time, Deborah could sing, Marni could act, and both of them knew every nuance of the dramatic values involved. One would start a speech, the other would pick it up, go into a song, and nobody could tell where one left off and the other began.

Another problem which Ken and I had to untangle in *The King and I* was exactly how to handle the complexities of Jerome Robbins' exquisite ballet, "The Small House of Uncle Thomas." The orchestral limitations in the stage version imposed by the small orchestra robbed it of much of its abstract charm and Siamese flavor. In the screen version, I suggested to Jerry Robbins that we eliminate the legitimate orchestral instruments altogether.

At any rate, there were sixteen percussionists playing a variety of tuned gongs, a series of triangles, vibraphones, marimbas, bass marimba, various drums, and an array of tuned gas pipes. Mr. Robbins was delighted, and, I must confess, the treatment was highly effective, retaining all the abstract sound and the indigenous qualities which comprised the dynamic heart of the ballet. But the orchestra was only one element. There was also a chorus of eight Siamese women and a third very important component, Rita Moreno, who narrated the ballet story while the dancers beside her portrayed it visually. A simultaneous performance of all these ingredients seemed impossible because, in the complicated medium of stereophonic sound, it is essential to keep all the elements separated. Otherwise, we would end up with a combined recorded hodgepodge of unpredictable balance, with no possibility of improvement through editing or mixing.

We solved the problem by the use of closed-circuit television, a first, I believe. My percussion orchestra was set up in the main recording stage; Ken's chorus was grouped in a second sound stage adjacent to mine; and Rita Moreno, Jerome Robbins, and his cast of dancers were in a third studio, across the street.

Each of us could see the other two on twin monitor TV screens, all of us were in audible contact by way of microphones and earphones, and each element was synchronously recorded on its own strip of 35mm magnetic tape, with complete isolation one from the other.

I can hear some of you thinking: "That's just like Hollywood, making a big deal out of a perfectly simple project!"

Let me explain that. Theoretically, motion picture recording techniques offer the will-o-the-wisp possibility of achieving perfection—perfection of orchestral playing and dynamics, of vocal interpretation, tone, and diction, perfection of inspired, one-of-a-kind total performance.

On the Broadway stage, tonight's performance drifts over the footlights and goes home in the ears of the audience. Tomorrow night's performance may be quite different, better or worse, but it is equally ephemeral. A film performance can be definitive. It becomes, in its optimum recorded form, a frozen entity, one that will be seen and heard again and again. The slightest flaw is magnified enormously through repetition. So we work very hard, sometimes making six or seven or more performance recordings, called "takes", of an entire ballet. Then, after hearing each take, we discover, if we're lucky, that three of our recorded efforts contain all the ingredients we were seeking. From take three we use the first forty-seven bars. Take five gives us bars forty-eight through ninety-nine, and take seven goes beautifully from bar one hundred to the end. Our music editor then intercuts the chosen takes, and we have our ballet, with infinite variables for obtaining a perfect balance of all the elements. I must tell you that the problems of *The King and I,* regardless of the laborious travail encountered along the way, led to a result of pure pleasure.

In *South Pacific,* Giorgio Tozzi, the great baritone of the Metropolitan Opera, became the voice double for Rosanno Brazzi. He was magnificent, but Rosanno insisted to the very end that he was going to replace Giorgio's voice with his own. Finally, after much rehearsal, Ken recorded Rosanno's singing on a tape machine in our office, then played the result back at full volume. Rosanno listened for a few minutes, reached for his hat and said, "You say it sounds like a nanny goat? Well, you're right. Brazzi, Tozzi, who will know the difference?"

South Pacific did not get good reviews. Perhaps the sudden leap from the confines of the stage to the immensity of all out doors was too tempting for the director to resist. Many scenes were added, and we used a number of antique Polynesian instruments, all of which looked better than they sounded, except one—the nose flute. It has a plaintive texture, but could never have been used on Broadway. Can you imagine sitting in the second row on opening night and seeing a solo flautist stand up and stick a bamboo instrument up his nose?

The Island of Bali Ha'i posed a musical challenge. Should we treat it as a place, or as a mystical, beckoning, illusive yet compelling female symbolization of Lieutenant Cable's desire? We decided upon the latter, using several harps, a curtain of Chinese glass, wind chimes and tree bells for the instrumental effect, and then superimposing the siren song of women's voices (all highly reverberated) over this glittering foundation. It was an electrifying experiment.

All the musical enlargements in *South Pacific* were dictated by the vast panoramic scenes photographed in the Hawaiian Islands. Shooting films on location has become a standard, though sometimes vexing, practice. The exteriors for *Carousel* were filmed in Maine, *Sound of Music* in Salzburg, *Camelot* in Spain, *Finian's Rainbow* all over the United States. By this method, directors and cameramen have created sequences demanding musical treatments never conceived by the composers of the original scores.

Here the work of the adaptor requires sensitive inventiveness and careful development of the melodies inherent in the score. To do otherwise would introduce foreign thematic material destructive to cohesive integrity, apart from insulting the composer.

Camelot was the most demanding in this respect, and in other respects as well. To begin with, a voice double had to be found for Franco Nero, and Ken found him, after much searching, in the person of Gene Merlino. It is strikingly coincidental that Gene's surname stems from Merlin, the magician in the Arthurian legend, and he became just that for Franco. Both were of Italian extraction, and Gene could speak the language. He explained the process of singing to Franco, then demonstrated the structure of each vowel and consonant until Franco acquired adequate ability to synchronize his lips, throat, and breathing with the finished prerecorded sound tracks, which we call playbacks, and, somehow, the illusion came off. Sheer magic!

Vanessa Redgrave would have been a vocal disaster were she not such a distinguished actress. Ken was heard to remark one day that she certainly could use a vocal transplant, but he was equally certain that *it* would reject *her*! However, her dramatic talents made her voice tolerable, although the effort she expended to produce useable sound tracks was beyond credibility.

Richard Harris discovered he could sing by listening to himself on Ken's tape recorder. Together they studied and explored the voice tirelessly, rehearsing the songs every day, including holidays and weekends. Richard's enthusiasm and vocal facility grew and

grew until he was confidently irrepressible. He delivered fine performances, and is now, as you know, one of the great hits on
record.

The final act of adaptation involves what is known on the
Broadway stage as incidental music. In the scoring of a film, this
musical connective tissue becomes anything but incidental. The
score for *Camelot*, for example, inclusive of the songs, added up
to two hours and forty minutes. Sonny Burke, head of Warner
Brothers' Seven Arts Music Department, lovingly called it "ankle-
deep, wall-to-wall music!" The kindest compliment of all was
from Frederick Loewe, who was enchanted that not once had we
violated, mangled, or raped his musical intent.

It has always been a firm premise of mine that the score for a
musical film should flow easily, as a stream flows, with the songs
appearing so naturally that they seem to float. There are, of
course, exceptions to this practice, as when a song rises out of a
quiet, unscored scene, softly stated by an unaccompanied voice, to
be joined at an appropriate moment by the subtle entrance of the
orchestral accompaniment.

Unless the conclusion of a song climaxes an act, or a scene
leading to a fade-out, or to an intermission, I have made it a point
never to attach the usual thundering coda. This device, used so
much in the Broadway show, calls for applause, and most usually
gets it on the stage. In the motion picture theater applause is rare
because it is meaningless to applaud someone who isn't there, so,
as the song comes to an end, the music moves on into the next
scene, leaving no awkward pause for the inevitable, intrusive
crunch of popcorn.

One further comment, which may reveal a subconscious hostili-
ty; call it a pet peeve. Sometimes a producer, director, composer,
or author will cut a great song out of the completed film and
replace it with an expository dialogue scene designed to illuminate
the plot. Too frequently this kind of surgery destroys continuity,
mood, and audience involvement, butchering the entire scene. The
film then falls victim to further panic editing; music goes out the
window; and you're left with a lot of redundant words. It's a bit
like Mark Twain's gift for sulfuric and all-embracing profanity.
His outbursts always embarrassed and irritated his wife, Olivia.
She objected, she cajoled, she remonstrated, all to no effect. One
day, after Mark Twain had let loose a torrent of purple language,

his sweet wife astonished him by repeating it word for word. For a moment Twain was speechless, but only for a moment. Then he said, "Livy, you have the words alright, but you ain't got the music!"

This brings us to the technique of film recording, something the stage musical doesn't have to worry about. In the early days of sound, Al Jolson or Bing Crosby would stand in front of the camera with a microphone overhead. The orchestra would be seated out of camera range, usually about a block away. When the director gave the cue, the camera, recorder, conductor, orchestra, and soloist would burst into activity, rooted to the spot, hoping desperately to stay together.

Before the advent of the synchronized acetate recorder, we had to wait for the film to come back from the lab to know the worst—and it usually was. We called this operation "direct" or "live" recording, and still do. Some of the generation beyond the gap think they've just now invented it. But, in reality, the performer had even less freedom of movement than on a theater stage, and there was no possibility of improving the balance of relationship between voice and accompaniment once the recording was locked in on the old optical film.

The invention of multiple-track recording and magnetic tape changed all that. The best musicals employ prerecorded tracks. Very briefly and simply it happens like this: All or most of the musical numbers to be used in the film are rehearsed, orchestrated in their new keys to fit the voices at hand, and recorded before the actors go in front of the camera. The orchestra is set up on a recording stage, the soloist steps into an isolated sound-proof booth, faces the conductor through a double wall of plate glass, and puts on an earphone. The orchestra may be recorded on four separate channels, as in Cinemascope or Panavision, or on six tracks for the 70-millimeter Cinerama or Todd-AO Wide-Screen process. The soloist is recorded on still another channel. It sounds complex, and is, but the recorded product is adaptable to unlimited adjustment and editing. Any one channel may be raised or lowered in volume, independent of the others, to produce any desired instrumental sonority. The soloist's performance may be raised, equalized, or softened to arrive at a perfect balance between all the factors involved. It is the only system I know where you can have your cake and eat it too!

If a chorus is to be added to the number, the singers come in on the following day, listen to the orchestra track on earphones, and record their voices on multiple microphones. Then all the elements are combined in the studio dubbing room to make a monaural tape or disc, which is sent to the set or location.

Here the actor has complete freedom. He hears his voice reproduced on a series of loudspeakers and sings along with it while being photographed riding a horse, or a train, or a boat or a carousel—in Spain, Hawaii, or Hongkong. No matter how the director wants to cut up his camera shots, the playback is the one fundamental anchor, the perfect measuring rod.

Some critics have stated flatly that spontaneity is lost by this method of recording. Let me go on record emphatically that this is absolutely not true. Consider the alternative.

An actor/singer makes a "live" recording in front of the camera with an offstage piano, frequently out of tune. The set is noisy; it may be an exterior with airplanes droning overhead. But the director gets his shot, and the actor looks fine, until the sound track is heard in the projection room and discovered to be worthless, because the piano is mixed with the voice inextricably and the planes have wiped out several words.

Now the actor must come into the studio, put on a headphone, listen to himself singing spontaneously, if slightly off key, watch his lips on a black and white screen, and try to recapture something which the director called "spontaneous" in the first place. One hundred and seventy tries later he is about as spontaneous as a soggy bath sponge. Maybe he finally gets a fair take. Now the conductor puts on his headphone, rehearses the orchestra, and chases the actor singer whom he cannot see, till the accompaniment fits the voice. I regard this as demented and irresponsible, a disastrous waste of talent and time and money, and a sure way to destroy the screen musical.

Yet is is being done, stubbornly and willfully, because someone believes that he has "discovered" a new thing, something the men of experience in the industry discarded as deadly and impractical more than thirty years ago.

Let me summarize briefly what is, by now, obvious to all of us. The stage is alive with three-dimensional actors. They respond to the laughter and applause of an involved audience. On the screen, the actors are photogenic and impersonal, preset, preserved, and unresponsive.

On the stage, the sets are prescribed by the limits of four walls. They are often extremely beautiful, effective, and even breathtaking. On the screen, the limit is not even the sky. Outer space is available, as well as the Grand Canyon, the Denver Mint, or the fantastic depths of the sea.

On the stage, an intimate love scene becomes a clutching blur of tangled arms and legs when viewed from the balcony. Facial expression is sometimes lost, and overt action must delineate ideas and emotions. On the screen, the camera is omnipresent, moving, turning, showing everything, allowing nothing to escape.

The flicker of an eyelid can be made to express a subtle hidden emotional decision, and you see it! A long shot can reach to infinity. A close-up can be overwhelming. There is a shot in *Camelot* where King Arthur's nostril is as enormous as the whole of Goliath—no pun intended.

In closing, I hope I have not left you as confused as I am. You see, I really am of two colors. William Buckley would call me dichromatic. I love the theater, especially the musical theatre. When it's good, it is tremendously exciting, entertaining, inspiring, even spellbinding. True, the stage has its peculiar limitations, but so has a novel, and so has the screen.

After all, a motion picture is actually a recorded illusion, an audible, visible, graphic imitation of what was once reality. That it sometimes succeeds in gripping and holding the emotions of people in movie houses all around the world is magic of the highest order.

Bernard Herrmann.

12
BERNARD HERRMANN

"I feel that music on the screen can seek out and intensify the inner thoughts of the characters. It can invest a scene with terror, grandeur, gaiety, or misery. It can propel narrative swiftly forward, or slow it down. It often lifts mere dialogue into the realm of poetry. Finally, it is the communicating link between the screen and the audience, reaching out and enveloping all into one single experience."

Bernard Herrmann's place in the history of film scoring is now quite easy to place: he was a master craftsman, and he was unique. A good case can be made for claiming him as the most important of all American film composers, and it is possible to support that claim with a generous amount of his work on recordings. Excerpts from half of Herrmann's fifty scores are available on disc, and they cover most of his best work, ranging from his first score to his last. Few composers are represented as well as Herrmann on records. The tragedy is not so much that he died at the relatively early age of 64, but that he died at a time when his services were more in demand than they had been for some years and at a time when he was engaged in making more recordings than ever. The recordings, made mostly in London with that city's finest musicians, presented optimum performances of not only his work but that of other composers. Herrmann's death was a most severe loss to the music world, especially to those who felt as did he that composition for the screen was an increasingly important outlet for serious musicians. Miklos Rozsa claims, "Herrmann was a Gulliver among the film music Lilliputians. He was a milestone in the history of films." However, it was not a milestone easily reached. Herrmann was never an easy man with whom to work, and he was extremely critical of much that was done in film scoring. He argued with producers and engineers over concepts and methods, and felt that few people seemed to fully understand the power of music as an adjunct to filmmaking. "The motion picture sound track is an exquisitely sensitive medium. With skillful engineering, a simple bass flute solo, the pulsing of a bass drum, or the sound of muted horns can often be far more effective than half a hundred musicians playing away."

Most of Herrmann's output as a composer was for the screen, but he bridled at being called a film composer because he was well aware of the pejorative ring that title has among the critics. He bitterly resented the suggestion that to write for films was somewhat of less value than writing for the concert hall or the opera house, and the quality of his scores makes it difficult for critics to prove their points. That much inferior music has been written for films over the years did nothing to dissuade Herrmann in his belief that it was possible to supply the medium with music of the highest order. No one was more critical than Herrmann himself; he despised those who wrote trash for films; and he despised even more the majority of people who produce films, almost all of whom were, in his opinion, generally tasteless and virtually moronic in their understanding of music. He was known on several occasions to berate producers who considered hiring him; after having been shown their product, he would wail, "Why do you show me this trash?" Such was his eloquent contempt and his ferocious manner that Herrmann begot a reputation for being irrascible that was almost as legendary as his composing skill.

Herrmann was a product of an era of American musical activity that is regretably long gone, the era of network radio broadcasting when the likes of NBC, CBS, and ABC employed orchestras and produced programs of symphonic, chamber, and operatic music, and by so doing did a great deal to further the cause of good music in America. Many musicians still recall how forceful and valuable Herrmann was in serving that cause. He, for example, championed the music of Charles Ives and gave first broadcast performances of many of Ives' works, at a time when no other conductors showed any interest in that composer. During his years in England, Herrmann, a decided Anglophile, conducted many American pieces for the BBC and for his concerts with the great London orchestras.

Herrmann was born in New York City in June of 1911. Neither parent was musical, but his own propensity for music was so strong that by the time he left high school, it was agreed by his family that he should study composition at New York University. This led to his becoming a fellowship student at the Juilliard School of Music, where he completed two years. While there he composed a ballet piece, which was included in the Broadway musical *Americana* (1932), and formed a chamber orchestra, which gave public performances under his baton. In producing these concerts, Herrmann often chose to include rare compositions; it was never said of Herrmann at any time in his life that he cared much about following conventional methods.

At the age of 22, Herrmann was hired by the Columbia Broadcasting System to write and conduct music for their serious and educational programs. A year later, in 1933, he was given the post of staff conductor of the CBS Orchestra, which included the production of most of their music programming. By 1936 Herrmann had worked up great enthusiasm for the art of dramatic scoring, which caused him to become associated with the brilliant young actor-producer Orson Welles, four years Herrmann's junior, but a kindred spirit in seeking new dimensions for the arts. They also shared a certain disdain for authority. Herrmann and Welles blazed a number of new trails together, the greatest of which was *Citizen Kane*. By 1940 Herrmann had written not only large amounts of dramatic music for radio, but a number of concert pieces as well. *Kane* was an ideal way for Herrmann to enter the film world because it gave him the luxury of working alongside Welles for three months and conceiving the score as the picture was made. Both the score and the film heralded a new day for the American screen. Herrmann followed it with *All That Money Can Buy*, which won him an Oscar, and Welles' second picture, *The Magnificent Ambersons*. From that point on, there was no doubt that Bernard Herrmann was a major contributor to the art of film scoring.

Herrmann did not choose to overplay his new-found profession and averaged less than one score a year in the decade following *Kane*. He maintained a home in New York and his standing in radio and concerts, but the arrival of television put an end to that particular way of life. The radio networks dropped their orchestras and most of the music staffs. Herrmann was fortunate in having broken the Hollywood barrier, something a great many prominent American composers and conductors were never able to do. For the most part he was careful in his choice of pictures and never signed a contract with any one studio. He seemed to find a fascination with stories of fantasy, both romantic and bizarre. Of *Jane Eyre* (1944) he said, "It's Gothic extravagances and poetic morbidities made it an ideal vehicle for music." A similar claim might be made about his next score, *Hangover Square* (1945), which required him to write a short and macabre piano concerto for a demented pianist (Laird Cregar) going to his death while performing his work as his home burns down around him. This ability to set weird and frightening scenes to music would serve Herrmann well some years later with Hitchcock. With *The Ghost and Mrs. Muir* (1947), Herrmann proved that lurking in his soul was a strain of pure romanticism. It is among the most delicate and romantic scores ever written and moves a touching story into an almost sublime atmosphere.

Four years passed before Herrmann returned to Hollywood, to do *The Day the Earth Stood Still* (1951). This showed another side of his nature, his empathy for the unreal and for science fiction. In 1955 came the meeting with Hitchcock, for *The Trouble With Harry*, and a marvelous association that was to produce *The Man Who Knew Too Much* (1956), *The Wrong Man* (1957), *Vertigo* (1958), *North By Northwest* (1959), *Psycho* (1960), and *Marnie* (1964). In 1966 their association sadly came to an end with *Torn Curtain* when Hitchcock decided, clearly with pressure from Universal, that he wanted a lighter score than the one Herrmann had written. They were never to work together again.

By the mid-sixties, Herrmann was increasingly disenchanted with Hollywood, as were many of the giants of film scoring, who found themselves being bypassed in favor of a more pop sound in scoring. He moved to London, where he spent the remainder of his life. He averaged one score a year, and as the interest in film music recordings grew, he found great satisfaction in making them, in addition to recording concert works, among which was his own symphony and several chamber works. In his last years, he found himself gaining in favor as a film composer, especially among the younger filmmakers. Brian De Palma used him to advantage in the horrific *Sisters* (1972) and again three years later with *Obsession*, a romantic mystery somewhat along the lines of *Vertigo* and containing a quintessential Herrmann score. The score for *Obession*, perhaps ironically, is almost a summation of his devices and style as a composer of this kind of picture. It was followed by the brutal and bloody *Taxi Driver*, for which Herrmann wrote a jazz-tinted, searing score. It was not only his final score, but the one which contributed to his death. In failing health for some years, he ignored the advice of his doctors and exhausted himself. The recording of the score for *Taxi Driver* was completed on the evening of December 23, 1975, at the Burbank Studios, with Herrmann preferring to finish the job, rather than do another session the following day. He died in his sleep that night at his hotel.

In his tribute to Herrmann in the March 1976 edition of *Films in Review*, film music commentator Page Cook wrote:

> The problems of setting music to film often lie in its coalescence of artistic as well as practical demands, a problem deepened by a complicated structure of imagery and symbolism and the cinematic forms, which no matter how many analogies have been drawn to musical forms (sonata, allegro, fugue, rondeaux) may or may not be enhanced by musical treatment. The miracle of Herrmann's solution is that while maintaining a highly individual style he attained a consistent subtlety and fluency in knowing when and where to apply lyricism and/or harrowing intensity. *And* a spiritual transcendence.

Bernard Herrmann was indeed an individual. He was among the few composers who insisted on doing his own orchestrations, believing that the subtleties he wished to convey in his instrumentation could not be left to someone else to fill in. Christopher Palmer, the English musicologist and orchestrator, who has provided the liner notes for many of the Herrmann records, describes the Herrmann sound in this manner:

> The steely singing spaciousness of his string lines, his evocative use of low woodwind sonorities, which often involve unusual combinations—it is quite common for a Herrmann score to call for two or more English horns, alto and bass flutes and as many as four bass clarinets. He has never seen any good reason to restrict himself to the standard symphonic specifications when the cinema offers such unlimited scope for unorthodox groupings. . . . But underlying everything is his belief in film music as an indispensable part of the emotional and dramatic argument for the film. As he once remarked, "A composer's first job is to get inside the drama. If he can't do that he shouldn't be writing the music at all."

Herrmann did not readily grant interviews. He disliked pon-
tificating and whenever he agreed to discuss the subject of film
music it was only after much persuasion. And the conversation
always encompassed more than film music. He was rather gruff
and often severe in his comments, particularly about people and
happenings in the film industry. Very little met with his approval.
That his standards were high is apparent in his work; he earned the
right to his opinions. The following interview was conducted by a
pair of film music enthusiasts, Leslie Zador and Greg Rose. It appeared in the *Los Angeles Free Press* in October 1970 and is here
used with their permission.

Bernard Herrmann on Film Music

ZADOR: American composers who write for films run a
tremendous risk of losing critical favor. The critic will cite a film
score that the composer's work resembles, or even say that the entire piece sounds like "movie music." Implicit in this castigation is
the view that anything that has been written for the screen must
necessarily be bad.

HERRMANN: This is purely snob appeal. One doesn't find this
situation on the Continent or in England, where music is taken
more seriously than it is in this country. There's no difference between being a composer for one thing and a composer for another.
You have a career as a composer whether you write for film, television, or symphony orchestra. Prokofiev's *War and Peace* sounds
very much in certain passages like his film music, but that has
nothing to do with *War and Peace* being a great opera. I don't
think that even as great a genius as Mozart thought that he wasn't
being a composer when he wrote ballroom music.

ROSE: But wouldn't you go along with the view that the requirements for a film score and a concert piece are not the same?
For example, your conducting of the suites from the Hitchcock
films is considerably different from what we heard in the films.

HERRMANN: Of course. One was the tempo for the concert,
the other for the film. The music in the film is conducted in relation to the visuals, whereas in the concert piece one has a different
set of relationships. And it is these relationships that the composer

should consider when adapting his score for the sound-track album, which unfortunately few of them do.

ROSE: In the love music from *Vertigo*, in the Hitchcock album, you have this marvelous crescendo built on a steady tempo. . . .

HERRMANN: Which you couldn't have in the picture, because the scene jumped too much and cut across the montaging. Writing for a picture is like accompanying a singer. When you go see an opera, you don't worry whether the orchestra's interpretation is different than what you heard on record, because the singer at that performance is doing it differently. Music is a living art; it is not a gelatined art. It is a fluid art, and that means that each time it is played, it is reborn, which is why it is probably the greatest of all the arts. I heard Toscanini do the Beethoven *Eroica* ten times, and each time it was a new experience. I mentioned it to him once. I told him that his interpretation of the piece was different from that which I had heard the previous year. And he said it was because last year he had been a fool. No one performance of a work can be definitive. A record is, therefore, a self defeating process, because once a piece is performed, no matter how brilliantly, after two or three times, you've had it. Each performance of a piece of music reveals something new about what's in it. There is no one interpretation that can reveal all of it.

ZADOR: At the time of Orson Welles' famous broadcast of *The War of the Worlds*, you were conducting the CBS orchestra and were working with Welles in preparing the musical portion of the program. Could you tell us how your association with Welles came about?

HERRMANN: I began working at CBS in 1934 when they made me staff conductor of the CBS Symphony Orchestra. Shortly afterwards, I don't remember when, Welles came to CBS as an actor. Long before he became the director of the Mercury Theater Players, he was acting in a number of shows, among them "The CBS Workshop," many episodes of which I scored.

ZADOR: But you didn't write any music for *The War of the Worlds*?

HERRMANN: No, I didn't. The purpose was to create the illusion of reality. We played some dance music at the beginning of the show until Welles "interrupted the program" to announce the discovery of the Martian spacecraft.

ZADOR: Did you find him easy to get along with?

HERRMANN: I always find difficult people easy. I only find glad Harrys difficult—the "nice guys"—they're difficult and vacuous. They pretend to be nice guys, but it's a disguise. They're vicious and vindictive people.

ROSE: And it's these people who are responsible for the deterioration of the quality of music written for films. Composers whose efforts for the screen could stand on their own as independent works have been replaced by hacks who can't even write Muzak. Instead of enhancing, they manage to detract from the film.

HERRMANN: But the problem ultimately rests with the audience. If you had audiences that cared more, you wouldn't have this. But they have been conditioned to accept the pop score as the dramatic common denominator and don't demand any more. In fact, they won't tolerate anything more cerebral these days.

ZADOR: And that is why you are no longer associated with Alfred Hitchcock?

HERRMANN: Yes. The last film we did together was *Marnie*. We had a disagreement over *Torn Curtain*. I had worked on the picture, and when I presented my ideas to him, he told me that the studio wanted a pop composer, but that if I could do it he would let me. If he wanted that kind of music, I told him, he ought to get that kind of composer. It wasn't Hitchcock's fault, mind you. He's a good man, but they were just putting too much pressure on him. Unfortunately he went along with them, which was a mistake, because a good score would have helped the picture. A pop score helped ruin it. The executives no doubt figured that a great pop score for *Torn Curtain* would sell ten million records. Of course, what *Torn Curtain* needed was a score that didn't help make the characters into ludicrous television characters, but into reality. So, instead, they got a TV score like the rest of their product. They've done a great job to strangle Hitchcock and other artists, all in the name of "doing their thing." "Doing their thing" means that they don't know what the hell they're doing and they hope it'll turn out all right.

ROSE: Of all the films you've done with Hitchcock, which one do you remember the most?

HERRMANN: I liked all of them, but I think that *Vertigo* manages to stand out a little from the rest. The yearning that was portrayed in the film, together with the theme of obsession—the film is truly a masterpiece.

ROSE: Before *Torn Curtain*, however, during those ten consecutive years in which you scored all of his pictures, did the studios interfere with your functions or attempt to in any way?

HERRMANN: No. There was greater respect for composers then. No executive told me that I had to employ a certain style here, or that he wanted something resembling what I had used in earlier film there. If they had, and if they had insisted, I would have walked away. I would look at each picture several times and decide which passages needed music and wrote as I saw fit. But, of course, the controls are a lot tighter today. You write music not for the film but to please some group. A romantic attitude toward music in films is no longer regarded as fashionable. Instead, what is fashionable today is to please a faction of common interests. "Doing your own thing" means that you're doing it in relationship to another group that's "doing their thing." The stagnation that has come about is depressing. They insist on repeating formulas that have already been proven and are unwilling to attempt anything that is a little different. I'll give you an example. In 1961 when I came back from England I brought back some of the early records that the Beatles had made for Deutsche Grammophon. I had met them when I was conducting in Liverpool. I was introduced to them and asked if I could do something here in Hollywood to help them. So I took their records to a few of the big powers here—CBS, Universal—but they all thought it was corny stuff. There's nothing in that crap, they told me. They could have had the Beatles for a small sum, maybe a thousand dollars. All they wanted was an appearance on television, maybe a chance at recording. If the formula is successful, the executives want an invitation, but they have no imagination of their own. They dress up in hippie clothes and grow their hair long, but underneath they're wearing gray flannel suits. If a fellow has a truck of gold dust, they will follow behind hoping that some will fall off. I told them at Universal that the Beatles were something new, but they didn't agree.

ZADOR: I think that this trend toward mediocrity in the film industry is paralleled in some respects by what has been going on in the concert hall as well.

HERRMANN: I would say so. The tastes of people who are in charge of what we hear when we go out to a concert are very safe tastes. They are the tastes of the new conservatives. They love any modern music as long as it is forty or fifty years old. Take Charles Ives. He finished writing in 1914. Why was he never played then?

But today he is played along with Schoenberg and the imitations of Schoenberg.

ZADOR: But yet we find that quite a few composers are being played who are different.

HERRMANN: Yes, but it isn't even music a lot of the time. It is merely problematical.

ZADOR: Problematical?

HERRMANN: Yes, problematical. I think you can see this best in the trend which opera has followed. From the eighteenth century until the third quarter of the nineteenth century people went to the opera to hear the singers. About 1880 it began to drift to who was conducting the opera. That lasted until the beginning of World War II. From that time until recently it was who was producing the opera. The conductors became nonentities. It was Webster's *Carmen*, Bing's *Tristan*. You would have thought that Wagner had never written the piece, but that it was the manager of the Met who was to be congratulated. And the new stage upon which it is entering is whether the opera is creating sufficient furor owing to its being problematical enough. How much publicity and notoriety has it received. The quality of the production, the music, the sets, singer, this is no longer or paramount consideration. Rather it is the outlandishness of the work that we should hold in highest regard. Yes, you do have new music. But if it's not of the percussion school, it's the synthesizer school, or else this rubbish where the orchestra makes up whatever it likes. But I'll tell you something. The audience is smarter than all of them. For the most part, they manage to stay away.

ROSE: Which composers do you admire?

HERRMANN: I admire any composer whom I believe to be genuine, whether I am sympathetic to his particular style or not. But you have a situation where the majority of your contemporaries are writing for these separate schools in the hope of pleasing their colleagues, all in order to be "in." I don't like opportunists and frauds.

ZADOR: But don't you think that at least some credit should be given for the fact that we bother to preserve music that is great. Beethoven we hear quite often. Bach, Mozart, others.

HERRMANN: The only reason you hear them is because they are free. Beethoven, Bach, Mozart, the composers you mentioned, are not popular composers. They are only free composers. Suppose the orchestra had to pay a hundred dollars every time they played a Beethoven symphony; you think you'd get it so often? I have acquaintances who won't play a piece by Ravel because they have to pay twenty-five dollars for the rental of the parts. A fellow called me the other day, and he was shocked because there was a fifty-two dollar rental to do *Carnival of the Animals.*

ROSE: Would you say this depressing state of affairs is something new?

HERRMANN: Of course. When I was working with CBS, ten commissions were offered a year, some of them up to ten thousand dollars. Not only CBS but the other stations as well. If you heard a piece of music on the air, then you heard it live.

ROSE: Why then and not now?

HERRMANN: Because the people who were at that time in charge of entertainment felt they owed something to the listening audience, that fourteen million people listening to a symphony concert were important to spend money on. But those were different days and long ago. . . .

13
ELMER BERNSTEIN

While it is true that the primary purpose of film scoring is to supplement and strengthen the visual and emotional components, it is also possible for a composer to speak with his own voice. Music for films does not have to be anonymous; there is nothing wrong with style. Elmer Bernstein is a foremost example of a composer who goes beyond the mere functions of scoring and supplies music that is recognizably his. When given an appropriate film, he has also supplied music that rises from the background and becomes a leading force, of which *The Magnificent Seven* (1960) is a good example. Its tuneful, rhythmic main theme has justifiably become one of the most popular pieces written for films, and being aware of it while watching the picture adds to the enjoyment. Being aware of the jaunty march that opens *The Great Escape* (1962) also adds to the pleasure of watching the picture being set up. In the cases of *The Man With the Golden Arm* (1957) and *To Kill A Mockingbird*, (1962) Bernstsin's music is far more than background. Both scores fully characterize and color the films. In a certain sense, they frame the pictures. It is Bernstein's good fortune to have been born with more than the ability to compose, but to have the gifts of melody and personal style. They have helped make him one of the most successful of all the composers who have worked in films.

Bernstein was born in New York City in April of 1922 and showed artistic leanings even as a child. He won a number of prizes for painting and also engaged in dancing, but by the time he was 12, it was clear that his major interest was in music. He studied piano and came to the attention of Henriette Michelson, a teacher at the

Elmer Bernstein.

Julliard School of Music, who took him as a student and guided his development. Although his interest at that time was in becoming a concert pianist, Bernstein also revealed a talent for improvising and was encouraged by his teacher, who took him to see Aaron Copland. The composer was sufficiently impressed to arrange for Bernstein to study composition with one of his own pupils, Israel Sitowitz. This led to scholarships which enabled Bernstein to study with Roger Sessions and Stefan Wolpe. He completed his education at New York University, majoring in music education, but still intent on a career as a pianist.

Bernstein began giving recitals in his late teens and steadily built a reputation, until the age of 21 when he was inducted into war service and joined the Army Air Corps. His ability as a pianist was of little value at this time, but he made known his considerable knowledge of American music and was assigned as an arranger with the Armed Forces Radio Service. One of his earliest jobs was making arrangements for Glenn Miller and his newly formed Ar-

my Air Corps Band. This led to assignments as a composer of incidental scores for radio productions, and by the time he left the
service three years later, Bernstein had written the music for some
eighty programs. Despite this impressive roster, he found there
were few opportunities for this kind of work when he left the service and he therefore returned to the life of a concert pianist.
However, in 1949 his ability as a composer for broadcasts was
remembered, and he was offered the job of writing a score for the
radio service of the United Nations for a program concerning the
armistice achieved by the UN in Israel. The program was carried
by NBC and was heard by the esteemed writer-producer Norman
Corwin, who engaged Bernstein to write a score for one of his
dramatic productions. This in turn was heard by a Columbia Picture executive, who invited Bernstein to Hollywood and offered
him the chance to write scores for two pictures, *Saturday's Hero*
and *Boots Malone*, both in 1951.

Bernstein attracted attention with his third scord, for Joan
Crawford's *Sudden Fear* (1952), in which he used a lighter and
more modernistic texture than was general in Hollywood at that
time. Despite the good notices, it did not result in many offers for
his services, and the following years were a struggle for Bernstein
as he attempted to establish a reputation as a film composer. His
assignments were mostly minor ones but *The View from Pompey's
Head* in 1955 caused Bernstein to be considered for Cecil B.
DeMille's *The Ten Commandments*. Victor Young, who had
scored the previous half-dozen DeMille epics had died, and the
great producer was doubtful about most of the composers whose
names were mentioned to him. Bernstein impressed him, and it
was arranged for the composer to score a single sequence as a test.
DeMille liked what he heard and retained Bernstein on a week-by-
week salary, but with no contract. Ultimately, over the course of
more than a year, he wrote the whole lengthy score. Before *The
Ten Commandments* was released, Bernstein had scored *The Man
with the Golden Arm*, (1955) which is generally considered to be
the first major score to utilize the jazz idiom dramatically. It
brought Bernstein an Oscar nomination and a firm place in the
Hollywood musical community.

By 1960, with *The Magnificent Seven*, Bernstein was among the
most popular of film composers and in line for major assignments.
He was also getting to be well represented on recordings, and more

than thirty of his scores have appeared in album form. In 1961, two of his scores, *Summer and Smoke* and *Walk on the Wild Side*, were nominated for Oscars, as was *To Kill a Mockingbird* the following year. *Mockingbird*, clearly a milestone among American film scores, did not bring its composer an Oscar, but he did receive one in 1967 for the music direction of the Julie Andrews musical *Thoroughly Modern Millie*. That he should be so rewarded for the one job, a fairly routine assignment, and not for a major effort is an irony all too characteristic of Hollywood.

Bernstein is an articulate and energetic man, who has found time for activities in addition to his busy career as a film composer. He was for a ten-year period the president of the Los Angeles Young Musicians Foundation, and since 1968 he has been the director and conductor of the San Fernando Valley Symphony Orchestra. In 1969 he also took on the job of president of the Composers and Lyricists Guild of America, for which he has been a vital force in establishing copyright credits and ownerships for its members.

In 1970 Bernstein expressed his concern for film composition in an article for *High Fidelity* magazine, calling it "Whatever Happened to Great Film Music?" The thousands of letters written in response confirmed that Bernstein was not alone in his concern. As a result of his efforts and those of other substantial composers, the standards of film scoring began to rise in the seventies. To further prove his belief in the value of first class composition for the screen, Bernstein opened his own record company in 1974 (Film Music Collection, P.O. Box 261, Calabasas, CA 91302) and recorded major scores by Max Steiner, Franz Waxman, Alfred Newman, Miklos Rozsa, and Bernard Herrmann, as well as his own score for *To Kill a Mockingbird*. It might well be said that no other composer has done more to advance the cause of good music in films.

Elmer Bernstein on
Film Music

In writing a film score, the thing that concerns me most is the philosophical attitude. The mechanical aspects of scoring, the actual technique of fitting music to a picture, are complicated, but

they can be mastered relatively easily. The philosophical requirement is something else. This involves factors like taste, intelligence, and imagination, and those are things that cannot be
taught. The philosophical aspect involves the composer's attitude
toward what the function of music in the film is going to be. And
that function is particular with each and every picture.

Let's take two examples, *The Magnificent Seven* and *Birdman
of Alcatraz*. They both have certain ambient factors, but they are
very different films, and the music in them functions in quite different ways. The purpose of the music in *The Magnificent Seven*
was largely to accent excitement, but it also served in a quite
specific way to provide pacing to a film which would have been
much slower without the score. When next you see the film,
observe that the music is often faster in tempo than anything that
is actually happening on the screen. The film needed music to help
give it drive. In that sense, it is a quite physical score, as much
foreground as background. It was a film that also needed music to
suit its locale, and in this case I felt it should have a definite
Chicano sound, a blending of many elements of American and
Mexican music. In other words, this was a picture which required
an obvious kind of music.

The Birdman of Alcatraz is an example of the opposite end of
philosophical scale. Here the music could not be obvious. It had to
be subtle in order to state many things that were implicit rather
than explicit. The music had a lot to do with the fact that beauty is
something that lives inside people much more than outside people.
It's an internal life, and even within the bleakness of a prison, a
person could live a life of beauty. The beauty was internal. It was
my function to supply music that would enlarge that attitude and
do it in a subliminal way.

The first hurdle the composer has to leap is the business of spotting the film, that is, finding out the points at which to bring in
and bring out the music. This is a very difficult set of decisions to
arrive at—not simply because the choice of spotting is vital to the
effectiveness of the score, but because it involves opinions other
than the composer's. The producer and the director have a right to
say where music should appear in their picture. This touches on
ego because all creative people have egos. If you are a composer,
you want to express in your score those points which will make it
more effective. If you are a director, you perhaps feel that the film

stands on its own and doesn't need anything. All the composer can do at this stage is to ask for a chance to demonstrate what he thinks his music will do to help. Most directors agree to this, provided they feel they are not being nailed down. Sometimes we have the situation in reverse, where the director may want music in a scene which suggests absolutely nothing to the composer. Oftentimes, this is to "wallpaper" the film, which means covering up what the director considers to be deficiencies in his work. There is a strange notion in this business that if scenes don't work out as well as directors hope, then music can be brought in to fill in the holes and the cracks—that music will take the curse off it. As a composer I don't believe this should, or can, be the function of scoring.

I remember quite vividly an incident of this kind when I was working with Cecil B. DeMille. I had done *The Ten Commandments* for him, and because of that I was assigned to score *The Buccaneer*. DeMille had a reputation for tongue-lashing his people, and one day he called director Anthony Quinn and producer Henry Wilcoxon into a conference with me and proceeded to lay into them about a particular scene he hated. Then he turned to me and said, "Well, Elmer, you'll have to save it with the music." I was embarrassed to have even witnessed this scene, but even more embarrassed to have him suggest I could save the scene. All I could say was, "You know, Mr. DeMille, I would rather work on a film where the picture helps the music." Fortunately he laughed.

I think that music badly spotted in a film can injure the film quite severely—much more so than good music being able to help a bad scene. It may be better than nothing to provide the wallpaper, provided the composer can find a way to write something that does not call attention to itself or the weakness of the scene. The music should have a balance throughout the film, unless the film is terribly specialized. By this I mean it is possible for the dramatic structure of a film to need a lot of music at the beginning and not much at the end. This is why a composer must view the film in its entirety and work out a program for it. Ideally, the composer should be in on the filming from the start of production and be able to develop his concepts along with the director and the others, but this seldom happens. It did happen early in my film career with *The Ten Commandments* because DeMille liked to have his composers with him through the production. He had a solid sense of music and regarded it as a story-telling device, and he would discuss scenes in detail, seeking my advice on whether music was needed or not.

I was also fortunate with Otto Preminger in doing *The Man with the Golden Arm*. Preminger has a reputation for being difficult with composers and for being dictatorial in general. He was not that way with me. He wanted to have me at the first cast reading of the script and then expected me to turn up for every day of shooting. He did not, however, require me to play anything for him, although he gradually became curious when he sensed I was coming up with something very different from the norm. The beauty of this method was that it enabled me to write a score that was intrinsically a part of the film. In other words, the music grew with the picture. The same luxury was available in working with Alan Pakula on *To Kill a Mockingbird* and his other pictures. He didn't ask me to be on the set every day, but we did discuss the projects before they went before the cameras. This is the ideal way to work because otherwise the composer is put in a terrible position. The director may live with his film for years before he actually gets to shoot it. Then, in most cases, a composer is brought in and expected to make his contribution in a matter of weeks.

We tend to think of film music as a fairly new art form. In a sense it is, and in another sense it isn't. The concept of using music as an adjunct to what is basically a mixed medium is ancient. Greek drama was basically mixture of media. Opera and ballet are both forms combining media. Music in its inception was really adjunctive. It was used for religious purposes and to encourage work. Its emergence as pure entertainment was relatively late in history. Music really is an art whose life begins where pictures and words leave off. It's a totally nonplastic art, and it is, in my opinion, a nonintellectual art on the appreciation level. You receive it through an emotional medium. Music is rarely something to which you listen and wonder what it means. Music is basically a fantasy, an emotional fantasy. It is for this reason that I think music functions so ideally in the motion picture, because you have in music a tremendous, seductive, manipulative tool. You can manipulate your audience, provided the music doesn't become intellectualized This happens when the music is so obvious and familiar in its devices that the audience is told nothing it doesn't already know. It allows for no emotional response.

On the other hand, even this business of not allowing for emotional response can sometimes be used to advantage. A good example of this is the score of *Young Frankenstein* by John Morris. He used all the old clichés of horror-movie scoring and used them so obviously the audience had to laugh. They were so familiar they had no emotional response, except in an absurd and amusing way. So the idea that we react to music because of a certain conditioning and learning is essentially correct. But it sets up a great problem for the film composer if he is looking for a really fresh response. This applies to all film production. The photographic and the editing devices can be stimulating when first used, but they become weary after a few years. We all have that problem.

However, the composer has a problem that differs from those of his fellow film workers. The problem of communication with his director or producer over the language of music. More often than not I am asked to demonstrate my ideas on the piano, which is a far from satisfactory method because many of my ideas are purely orchestral and the effects I have in mind cannot be demonstrated on the piano. Sound is very important today, and our sophisticated recording techniques and electronic devices give us a limitless range of possibilities. Yet we always seem to come back to the piano, although there is no denying its practical and constant nature. I can even think of times when the mere presence of a piano solved immediate problems. One of the directors with whom I have most enjoyed working is George Roy Hill, and the reason for this is that he is a good amateur musician. I found this out when we were doing our first film together, *The World of Henry Orient*. We had discussed the music on many occasions, and all went well until one point during the recording session when we got to a sequence that didn't jell with what he had in mind. He stopped the session, went over to the piano, and started to play, saying "No, I wanted something more like this." Since he hadn't told me about his ability in music, it left me with my mouth hanging open. But after that I knew we were on a different footing, the kind of footing that makes a composer's job much more practical and comfortable.

The film composer is an employee, and his relationship with his employer is a difficult one at best. It is rare even in this enlightened age to find a producer or director with a long and disciplined career in any field of the arts. And it is too much to expect. Producers need be businessmen, and as such they come from a completely different world. Directors tend to graduate from film editing or cinematography or allied crafts. The getting together of a well-trained composer and the average producer or director is often akin to having a heart specialist try to convince an Amazonian tribesman to submit to open-heart surgery. While the analogy may at first glance seem a bit bizarre, it is a very good analogy. In both cases we are talking about highly trained experts attempting to improve the quality of life in one way or another. In both cases the people are fearfully ignorant, and if they refuse the treatment, they endanger their lives and frustrate the practitioner in the process.

There is of course no question that the overall concept of a film is the province of a director. In a very general way, this also includes the music. In recent times, the field has been invaded by some younger men whose egos far exceed their talent, and there is then a tendency to treat the composer as some sort of mechanic who produces some sort of product by the yard and can, on demand, produce three yards of this and three yards of that. Once again, I must go back to the operating room with the patient on the table for open-heart surgery: the question is where, when, and how to treat him and what type of anesthesia to use, if any. As a matter of fact, it has often been on my mind to let the producer or director do my music if they would allow me to do their surgery. It will never come to that, of course, but perhaps it is not too much to expect producers and directors to give more thought to the contribution of music, and perhaps read books such as this one.

It is not, to state the obvious, easy to compose for the screen because it's a matter of imposing one art form on another. It's easy, if you are a trained composer, to write a piece of music that has good internal structure of its own, but it may not work in a film because the structure of the film may be quite different. The composer is at the mercy of that structure. When it is good, when the picture has a solid design, with developments that peak and resolve logically, then the programming of the score becomes that much easier. All arts, of course, have certain self-imposed restrictions. If you set out to write a short story, your problems are very different than if you set out to write a novel. Music has many forms—sonata, fugues, canons, and so on—all forms that are in themselves structures. The one thing, the one circumscription, that is different in films is that the composer must learn to write and live within a time medium. This is unique in the world of composition. You have to learn to adapt music techniques to composing a piece which lives, for example, within one minute, thirty-four and two-thirds seconds. If the composer cannot learn to do that, he finds himself doing artifical things. It is a technique peculiar to films. It is extremely difficult, and it cannot be learned in classrooms. No matter how good a composer may be, he cannot survice in films without this highly acute sense of timing.

The most important thing for the aspiring film composer is simply to see as many films as he can and study them with both his eyes and his ears. It is vital to understand that film is a combination of sight and sound. Those composers who are simply looking for an outlet to write music had best forget films.

14
HENRY MANCINI

The composer who made the most valuable contribution to the major stylistic changes in scoring techniques that began taking place in Hollywood in the late fifties was Henry Mancini. The power of the recording industry had already made producers aware of the advertising value of issuing movie music on discs, so much so that it had an adverse affect on scoring standards. Producers began to think of film music in terms of records rather than as functional tracks. In Mancini this dangerous situation found an ideal resolution. Here was a composer who could serve both directions, pleasing producers with scoring that was adept and fully serviceable and yet later able to adapt much of his scoring into interesting and often profitable record albums. With the success of *Breakfast at Tiffany's* (1961) and its Oscar-winning theme song "Moon River," Mancini was able to work both sides of the street. Unfortunately his success moved producers to assume that other musicians could do likewise—an assumption that became more lamentable with every year of the sixties and that occasionally resulted in the hiring of pop music groups for scoring sessions. It took a man of Mancini's caliber to know that a score was one thing and a record album something else. The popularity of his scores in album form was a result of his rearranging and rerecording them for the record market.

More than any other composer in Hollywood, Mancini opened up the craft of scoring by insisting on better recording methods and on newer concepts in orchestration. It may seem strange to anyone not familiar with the Hollywood studios, but the quality of their sound technically was in fact behind the times by the late fif-

Henry Mancini.

ties. The thinking on the administrative level was conservative—with the recession in production it almost became spastic—and the actual equipment was on the verge of becoming outdated. The technical standards were certainly behind those then employed in television and in the commercial recording studios. Mancini was in the foreground of those who forced the studios to restructure both their thinking and their systems. He was also successful in introducing new and younger musicians to the studio scoring sessions, bringing in men with experience in jazz and contemporary music, thereby helping to break the barrier set up by executives who considered only musicians of classical background capable of film scoring. What Mancini was after were men in both camps.

Mancini's success was not without a certain price tag, in this instance the same tag that had plagued so many film actors—type casting. His skill with light, amusing scores, with the accent on adroit instrumentation, caused producers to think of him as a composer for light and amusing pictures. It was a case of nothing succeeding like success, and in Mancini's case, it was happily aggravated by the fact that he was in demand as a performing pianist-conductor.

It has been Henry Mancini's great good fortune to be blessed with the gift of melody, in addition to the ability to understand the mechanics and the sonics of film scoring. The gift is traceable to some extent in his family background. Both parents came from the Abruzzi region of Italy, and both had a love of traditional music. When they settled in the steel-producing region of Pennsylvania the father, Quinto Mancini, enrolled in one of the many brass bands that flourished in Italian communities in those days. He was a steelworker by trade, but a strong enough music lover to crave success for his son as a musician. Mancini junior confesses that he had little interest in music as a youngster and might never have taken it up had it not been for the push of his father, who started him on the piccolo at the age of 8 and a few years later had the boy performing with the Sons of Italy band in their town, West Aliquippa. A feeling for music gradually grew upon young Mancini, who came to appreciate the sacrifices made by his father in order to send him to music teachers. It was not, however, until he learned the craft of arranging music, rather than merely performing it, that he realized he wanted to make a living as a musician. A new world opened up to him when he began studying with Max Adkins, the conductor and arranger at the Stanley Theater in Pittsburgh. In 1942 Mancini graduated from the Aliquippa High School and went directly to the Juilliard School of Music in New York.

Mancini was able to spend only one year at Juilliard before he was called for military service. He returned to civilian life three years later, in 1946, and landed a job as a pianist and arranger with Tex Beneke's newly formed Glenn Miller-styled band. It was while working for Beneke that Mancini met the woman who would become his wife, Ginny O'Connor, who was then under contract to Mel Torme as a member of his singing group, The Meltones. And it was through his wife that Mancini was first exposed to film scoring. After leaving the Meltones, Ginny joined the Mello-Larks. They were hired to make a short subject at Universal, and Mancini was offered the job of arranging the music for them. The job brought him into contact with Joseph Gershenson, the head of music for that studio, who took a liking to Mancini's capabilities and asked him if he would like to do some work on an Abbott and

Costello film called *Lost in Alaska* (1952). It called for two weeks of work, but another project followed immediately, and Mancini was soon under contract. It developed into a six-year period of doing every kind of work involved in the scoring of movies and became the kind of apprenticeship that can only be the envy of aspiring film composers today since such positions are pitifully rare.

Mancini's prior experience with dance bands made him an obvious choice as the arranger of *The Glenn Miller Story* (1953) and *The Benny Goodman Story* (1955), but he became ever more interested in the art of dramatic scoring. His first major opportunity came in 1958 with the Orson Welles classic *A Touch of Evil*, although it was a film that called more for the subtle use of jazz than symphonic music. As such it served as an unusual counterpoint to the sleazy sting of the subject matter. The film was not a box office success, although with time it has acquired esteem as a superb *film noir*. And despite his exhibition of skill, Mancini's services were shortly thereafter terminated by Universal. It was not a happy time for making feature films in Hollywood. Television had taken a severe toll of cinema receipts, but ironically it was television that opened up Mancini's career and helped to bring a new concept to feature film scoring.

Among the people who had been impressed by Mancini's score for *A Touch of Evil* was Blake Edwards, who had already directed and produced a number of features, but was just about to start a television series about a sophisticated private detective called *Peter Gunn*. Edwards reasoned that part of the approach should be a new kind of scoring—light in texture and modern in style, using the jazz idiom and also taking advantage of the new recording techniques. The results exceeded even Edwards' high hopes. The Mancini scores for *Peter Gunn* won him great public approval, plus a contract with RCA Records and eventual reentry into feature film scoring on his own terms. In 1960 Blake Edwards directed the Bing Crosby comedy *High Time* and hired Mancini to do the score, touching off a string of successful Edwards-Mancini cooperations over the next decade, among them *Breakfast at Tiffany's*, (1961) *Experiment in Terror*, (1962) *Days of Wine and Roses*, (1962) *The Pink Panther* (1964) (and all its sequels), *The Great Race*, (1965) and *Darling Lili*. (1970).

His concerts did well, as did the continual stream of recordings.

The only problem was in getting producers to hire him for the more serious pictures. Fortunately Blake Edwards knew the value of his composer and assigned him to several projects that were intended to do more than amuse, such as the genuinely scary *Experiment in Terror* and the poignant *Days of Wine and Roses*. In time other producers recognized Mancini's other side. In 1967 he scored the eerie *Wait until Dark*, and three years later he wrote a majestic score, one considered by many as his magnum opus, *The Molly Maguires*, a sad and dramatic account of life in the Pennsylvania coal fields in the late nineteenth century. *The Night Visitor* (1971) is yet another study with an eerie atmosphere achieved using a small orchestra in a chilling, unsettling manner. With *The White Dawn* (1975) Mancini wrote a superb aural accompaniment to a picture of stark splendor and tragicomic adventure. No reasonable critic, on hearing this particular score, could accuse Mancini of being a lightweight composer.

Henry Mancini has now plied his craft long enough to be considered a veteran. He is long past being a new boy in the business, although his youthful manner and his penchant for writing bright and pleasing melodies tend to make people think of him in terms of the younger set. But he is now in the position of having young musicians, some a whole generation younger, seeking his advice. A generous slice of Mancini advice follows.

Henry Mancini on Film Music

I had the good fortune to spend a six-year period, from 1952 to 1958, at Universal, and it was like an apprenticeship. It was six years of training in which I was required to do just about everything a film composer comes across in the course of his craft—arranging, adapting, orchestrating, using stock material, working fast, working against time and slim budgets, and generally functioning. It prepared me to face just about any assignment that would come up in the years ahead. Sad to say, that kind of training is almost impossible to get in the industry today.

Those years at Universal were like taking a doctorate in film scoring. Joe Gershenson was head of the music department, and he taught me a great deal. He was a great one in dealing with the diverse kinds of directors you come across when you're in such a position at a major studio. We had everyone from Orson Welles on down. Down included cheapie westerns, the Ma and Pa Kettle series, *Francis the Mule, Bonzo the Ape, Kelly the Dog,* and *The Creature from the Black Lagoon.* Sometimes there was hardly any budget at all, and it was necessary to "stock" the picture. They had a tremendous music library, dating back many years, and I would take a scene and work from my timing notes exactly as if I was going to compose the score. The only difference was that I would have to take the music from the library. The music, of course, was recopied and rerecorded in its new form. It was a challenge but very interesting because it gave me the opportunity to study other people's work. Many fine composers had written for Universal, including Miklos Rozsa and Frank Skinner. It was a fascinating experience, and it helped me to understand the technique of film scoring. So many composers, when they do their first film, become so involved with technique they forget about the quality of the music. Mastering technique is comparable to a director mastering his devices—the director's job is to tell a story, not to show how it got there.

One thing Joe Gershenson taught me was the value of cooperation. He had an expression "Take partners," which means let people know what you're doing. This is very important in dealing with directors, few of whom can articulate what they want musically. They indicate, and you have to draw it out of them—you have to drag it out sometimes. One of the most common problems lies in talking directors out of using music for scenes that don't require it.

By the time most filmmakers get to the stage of working with the composer, they have been with the picture so much and are so close to it that sometimes they lose their perspective. When the composer arrives on the scene, he can easily be made to feel like a man going in the ninth inning with bases loaded and two men out. He's got to get the other guy out, and the director may lean over backwards depending on him to do it. There are many times when I have had to put up a strong argument to convince a director that a scene is fine, that it is strong and doesn't need scoring. But by the same token, I have often written music for a scene where the director or producer didn't ask for it or in fact, had told me it wasn't wanted, but I felt the scene needed it. I'm happy to say that in the majority of cases the directors have gone along with my unsolicited contribution and utilized it.

One instance comes to mind. Howard Hawks, as you know, isn't a musician, but his pictures have always been memorable for their scores. He's always been conscious of music's role. *Hatari* was a series of incidents without a rigid storyline. They were very colorful incidents, and every little piece was a story in itself. Several could have been taken out of the movie and no one would have ever known. Two of them, in particular, Howard had doubts about. "Let me see what I can do," I said. One was the baby elephant sequence and the other was the ostrich barnyard sequence. I wrote a piece for both, and the music proved to be very effective, the most successful pieces in the picture.

I've been very lucky with many of the people I've worked with: Blake Edwards, Howard Hawks, Stanley Donen, and Orson Welles, among others. One thing we had in common was an agreement on the common goal of what was needed for the film—what it was about and what the music could be expected to add to the film.

I found out a long time ago that if a person isn't musical, you have to present your work in terms he can understand and recognize. You can't expect a nonmusician to understand what you're talking about—although some composers do! Communication is the most important thing between composer and director. I try to write my scores so there are no surprises for the director.

Then, too, a composer's relationship with each producer or producer-director is different. For example, when I was involved with Blake Edwards on the *Peter Gunn* series, he challenged me weekly with long scenes without any dialogue, already hearing the musical score in his mind's ear. Blake regarded the music as a vital voice in the total picture. He has always been astute musically. Normally, we would look at the picture a number of times. We rarely got into many deep conversations because we didn't have to. He trusted me, so we didn't have many big discussions about what the end result was going to be. Our ideas seemed to coincide nearly always.

On the other side of the coin is Orson Welles. The only contact I had with him was exactly one meeting having to do with *Touch of Evil*. He is an extremely knowledgeable filmmaker who knew precisely what he wanted musically. Welles once sent a letter to Joe

Gershenson while I was off staff. He set down in about four or five typed pages his ideas about what the music for his film should be. I read the letter after I had already screened the film and had my own thoughts about what it needed. Fortunately, my own thinking was largely confirmed by Welles' notes.

Touch of Evil was one of the first pictures to take advantage of what we call "source" music, which simply means music coming from a visible source, such as a radio. In this film, we used horn speakers outside all the bars in a Mexican border town. I heard later that Welles was very pleased with the score.

Among the first of the title songs in a dramatic picture that made sense and proved a commercial success was *High Noon* by Dimitri Tiomkin and Ned Washington. It pulled out the plug on everything. Now a composer is preconditioned to start work on a picture and to expect the director or producer to ask for a title song. I have to tell them that sometimes it works, sometimes it doesn't. On some films we've written complete songs, then did not use the lyrics because we felt they would serve no dramatic purpose. The minute you put a song over the titles or in any part of the picture, you're unconsciously trying to play on the viewer's pocketbook—you're trying to get him to listen, to go out and buy. Often these songs don't really make the action progress or make any kind of comment. We had a title song in *Charade*, which played under a boat scene and worked fairly well. It didn't go over the titles because the titles were not designed to take it.

In *Two for the Road*, we had a song that had no place in the picture, so we agreed not to use it. *Sunflower* also had a title theme with words. It was originally planned to be used at the beginning, but it proved distracting so it was used in an instrumental form only. In *Days of Wine and Roses*, a title song worked just fine, as in *Dear Heart*. A couple of others I have written have also worked. It's simply a matter of whether the song fits with the story and mood, or whether you're doing it for pure exploitation.

I have special feelings about the role music should play in a film. I think that when it's obtrusive or the audience is unduly aware of it, it isn't serving its best purpose. The audience is in the theater to see a story told. When they are very much aware of arty camera angles, or tricky directional touches, or music that belts them—and all of this happens in some pictures—you're distracting from the story. I was once asked by a director to write very dramatic music for a high point in a film. I pointed out to him that it was unnecessary, that the drama of the scene would work best against a quiet theme, that the music should provide a canvas against which the scene could play and not embellish action that didn't need embellishment. He agreed and it worked.

I don't think there is any advantage in seeing the film being made. I would rather wait until everybody else is finished, then look at it and start my contribution, unless, of course, special research is required beforehand. Doing the many other things that I do, I have to have a discipline. I find that there is no reason for me to think about a picture until I'm doing it. I prefer not to do two or three things at once; when I start scoring a film, everything else is out. And it does take a lot of mental discipline to shut off your other involvements.

Although I write on deadlines always, it's again a point of self-discipline with me that if I have not finished my score at least several days before recording, I worry. Ideally I like to have it done a week in advance. I don't believe in putting things off for some reason or another, then finding yourself writing right up to the recording time. Many other people are involved, such as copyists, and it all takes time.

One of the advantages of having arrived at the position I am in now is that I do have considerable choice of what assignments I'm going to take. I try to take them with directors or producers with whom I can communicate. However—and this is a very big however—no matter how good you think you are at your job, or how famous you think you may be, you can still fail at the assignment if the chemistry isn't right. Many of the best composers in this business have had scores rejected and tossed out. It happened with me when I worked for Alfred Hitchcock on *Frenzy*.

We scored *Frenzy* in London, and Hitchcock was there throughout the recording session, which I found disconcerting. Not his being there, but the fact that he didn't say much when we were doing it. He sat through every piece and nodded approval, and finally, when he was alone in the dubbing room, he decided that it didn't work. His reason, I was told, was that the score was macabre, which puzzled me because it was a film with many macabre things in it. It wasn't an easy decision to accept, and it was very crushing when it happened, but I thereupon joined a very exclusive club, the composers-with-scores-dumped club. If I were doing the score again, I really don't know what I would do differently. It turned out that Hitchcock wanted a lighter score, which also confused me because he and I had discussed the musical requirements beforehand, and we seemed to be in agreement. He afterwards hired Ron Goodwin, who is a friend of mine and with whom I later discussed the situation. Ron read me a detailed analysis of what Hitchcock had in mind after he decided he wanted another score. It was interesting because I wish I had had something like that to go by. It might have been a different story. But it was quite an experience. Apart from the film, I found Mr. Hitchcock to be a gracious and generous man. During lunch one day, we got into a discussion about a mutual interest we had—wine. The next day, a case of Chateau Haut Brion (magnums) was delivered to me. Come to think of it, I guess the whole adventure was not a total loss after all. I still think what I did on *Frenzy* was good—a score completely without themes, because it seemed to me the film didn't require any.

On the other hand there are films which definitely require themes, or at least one powerful theme. If you go to see a Broadway musical, it's good to know what you will hear. The same thing applies to some films. It can help if it has a song or theme that is greatly popular because it puts it on everybody's level. But what has happened recently is that there have been a lot of talented people who write both words and music, and with a few exceptions the message of the lyrics has taken over and become more important than the melody. It has to do with writers wanting to communicate more fully, but this is something apart from the functions of film scoring.

One thing I have learned is that good music can improve a fine film, but it can never make a bad film good. We composers are not magicians. We write music. We are one of the elements that go to make up a final piece of work. When it works and when we feel we've made a contribution, it's a great source of satisfaction.

Is it easy for a young composer to get into films? It's not easy for anyone to get in anywhere, whether you're a doctor, a lawyer, or whatever. It's all very personal. It's a matter of wanting very badly to do your chosen thing, and if you want to do it badly enough, you'll find ways.

Fred Steiner.

15
FRED STEINER

The only problem involved with becoming successful as a film composer in Hollywood with a name like Steiner lies in identification with the man who made such a mark in the golden years of the movie industry. Fred Steiner has explained many times, and will doubtless continue to explain, that he is not a relative of Max Steiner but that he is an admirer. Indeed, as a teenager in New York he once visited the famed composer to express his admiration. Max was staying in an apartment, and the nervous young man called from the lobby, and upon giving his name, he was asked by Steiner if he was a relative. Learning that he was not, the composer replied, "In that case you can come up."

Fred Steiner has remained an admirer of his celebrated namesake, although there is almost nothing in his own work that stylistically resembles the Viennese-born master of movie music. Fred Steiner is a product of another generation and a completely different musical background. He was born in New York in 1923, the son of George Steiner, who was a violinist and composer, and who derived much of his employment from working for film and broadcasting companies. His son early acquired an inclination for the same outlet but considered success in the major league of Hollywood almost too much to hope for. Steiner began his study of the piano at the age of 6, and by the time he was 13 he had progressed to include the cello and music theory. He graduated from Townsend Harris High School and won a scholarship to the Oberlin Conservatory of Music in Ohio, where he studied with Normand Lockwood. Steiner received his Bachelor of Music degree in 1943, terminating the requirements with a recital of his own compositions, performing as both a cellist and a pianist.

Faced with making a living, Steiner felt his possible future was that of a musician, but with the aid of his father, he obtained an introduction to radio conductor-composer Van Cleave, in whose orchestra Steiner senior was then playing. The 20-year-old Steiner was engaged as an orchestrator, although his knowledge of that craft was limited, and he admits that his quickly developed skill came from a close study of Van Cleave. Employment from that point onward was continuous, and two years later Steiner was appointed the music director of ABC's weekly radio series *This Is Your FBI*. With the decline in radio production caused by the arrival of television, Steiner turned his attentions to the new medium and moved to Los Angeles, soon to become the main center of U.S. television activities.

Steiner was fully occupied with arranging, composing, and conducting scores for television programs until 1956. He scored many of the prestigious *Playhouse 90* dramas and UPA's television cartoon series, as well as supplying music for comedy series such as those of Ed Wynn, Red Skelton, Joan Davis, and Danny Thomas, plus the more dramatic programs like *Gunsmoke* and *Perry Mason*. His output was so plentiful that he had no time to think of scoring feature films. His transfer to the big screen came about almost accidentally as a result of an argument he had with the then head of music for CBS. Not wishing to continue his association with the gentleman, Steiner put out for work in feature film scoring and was soon engaged, thanks partly to the high opinion of him voiced by Bernard Herrmann, who had admired Steiner's work broadcast in New York. As a graduate of that school himself, Herrmann valued anyone who had met its high demands. After a number of assignments as an orchestrator, Steiner was given a film to score, the 1956 release *Run for the Sun*, a mystery drama set in Mexico and starring Richard Widmark. His colleagues still consider it a major effort, particularly since it was his first feature score. It contains one episode, involving a stricken airplane making a crash landing in the jungle, that remains a textbook example of dramatic scoring. The suspense and fearful anxiety in this episode is made almost unbearable by the searing but restrained underscoring.

Steiner was well represented in 1957 by five scores, the most memorable of which is *Time Limit*. While not a box office winner, the film is highly regarded for its adult and touching examination of psychological warfare in Korea. Richard Widmark starred in the film and coproduced it, with Karl Malden as director. Steiner's score eloquently underlines the anguish of the principal character, an army major (Richard Basehart) on trial for collaborating with the enemy in order to alleviate conditions in a POW camp. The music also communicates the chill and the bleakness of the winter Korean setting, as well as the sad circumstances of the prisoners. As with all his scores, Steiner achieved these effects without musical exaggeration.

In 1958 Fred Steiner accepted a position as the manager of a recording company in Mexico City, and for a two year period lived there with his wife and two daughters. It was a period of security, which enabled him to devote time to the writing of absolute music, including a cello sonata, a string trio, and a woodwind quintet, all of which were performed in recitals. He returned to Los Angeles in response to continual offers for television scoring and to his feeling that to stay away longer would not be wise. Steiner was again almost trapped by the abundance of television work, which involved large amounts of composition of the kind required instantly. It included the series *Have Gun, Will Travel, The Twilight Zone, The Untouchables, Rawhide*, and perhaps most conspicuously, many of the scores for the greatly popular *Star Trek*. The demands of television kept Steiner away from feature films until 1967, when he wrote the music for *First to Fight* and *The St. Valentine's Day Massacre*.

Steiner is among the most knowledgeable men in films on the art of scoring, not only as a practitioner but as a student. He is an authority on the work of his colleagues. In 1979, he was completing his doctorate in musicology at the University of Southern California and writing a thesis on the career of Alfred Newman. Steiner was associated with Newman as a collaborator on *The Greatest Story Ever Told* and *Airport*, and he believes that Newman's contribution to the development of film scoring was both profound and powerful.

Fred Steiner has also found time to serve on the executive board of the Composers' and Lyricists' Guild of America. In a profession often marked with personality conflicts and frayed nerves, Steiner is notable for his even temper and affable nature. It is no exaggeration to claim him as one of the best-liked men in the film music community. A busy and productive man, Steiner is generous in his praise for the outstanding composers in the history of film scoring, especially of Newman and Bernard Herrmann. In London in late 1976, he conducted the National Philharmonic Orchestra in a fresh recording of Max Steiner's ground-breaking (in every sense) score for *King Kong*. He believes that this 1933 work has much to say to would-be composers for the screen and that it sets a standard of effectiveness that is rarely surpassed even today. What Fred Steiner himself has to say about film music follows.

Fred Steiner on Film Music

Like most people in the movie business or in other areas of the world of entertainment, I have kept press clippings, reviews, letters, photos, and other mementos of what is now more than a thirty-year career as a composer and conductor. No less of a ham than most, I confess that every now and then I do enjoy sitting down and leafing through this very personal assortment of memorabilia. Although it is far from complete, my collection of odd bits of paper, old letters, and yellowing snatches of newsprint evoke vivid memories of certain times, people, places, projects, and pieces of music I have almost completely forgotten.

Most of the memories are pleasant, but some are admittedly painful and perhaps would better be forgotten, except that I have luckily been blessed with a sense of humor. That, plus the merciful intervention of time, makes it possible for me to look back on some of those misadventures with a smile.

Now, since I am no less susceptible to flattery than the next person, I must admit that some of the items I treasure most are those which have revealed to an otherwise unsuspecting world how good I really am at what I do. Among these are letters from directors and producers telling me how much they like my work and a few press reviews which speak approvingly of the contributions my scores made to certain motion pictures.

Here, for instance, is a letter I received from the producer of *Gunsmoke* in 1963. It says, in part, that my music for the episode entitled "My Sister's Keeper" made a fine picture out of what could have been something maudlin and slow.

When *Time Limit* was reviewed by *The Hollywood Reporter* in 1957, I was understandably gratified when the reviewer stated that my music, "unobtrusive and gentle, is just right for the picture." In 1967, the *Daily Variety* critique of *First to Fight* said in part, that my score was "appropriate to the action and moods."

As I reread these gratifying words, I remember other flattering remarks on my work,—some which were not made in writing, but were said in my presence, and which I really should not allow myself to forget. When the director of *Hec Ramsey*, a film for television which spawned the series of the same name, heard my score on the dubbing stage, I overheard him telling one of his staff members that my music had transformed a B picture into an "epic Western." Although there were several gifted composers who contributed scores to the popular TV series *Star Trek*, the associate producer told me I was the only one who wrote music "with balls."

There are other pleasantly comforting things of this sort in my memorabilia. But my purpose here is not to impress upon the reader what a fine composer I am or how skillful I may have been in apparently capturing in my music the correct or essential mood of a film. My reason for citing these encomiums is that I want to make a confession. Having thought about these expessions of approval many times, I occasionally find myself troubled by one nagging question: What did I do that apparently worked so right? Or to put it more precisely, what were the ingredients in my music that made it do the things they said it did?

How does music turn a maudlin film into a fine picture? Or a Grade B story into an epic Western? What makes a score "just right" for a film? How can music have "balls?" In other words, what is it that makes music for the movies or TV work the way it does—or not work, as the case may be? How many times I have thought how useful it would be to know the answers so that I could be assured of always doing things the right way!

According to Tony Thomas, describing the values and functions of the art of combining moving pictures with musical tones is rather like describing a beautiful woman—there's no way of doing it adequately. "But," he adds in his 1973 publication *Music for the Movies*, "no one should be condemned for trying." Although modesty would probably impel me and my colleagues to disregard Tony's flattering comparison of our music to female pulchritude, most of us would certainly agree with his basic premise.

Like many creative people, we find it difficult to talk about our work, but we do make the attempt sometimes, especially when queried by students or others who express interest in our composing problems. However, music is the most abstract of the arts, and because its creation and appreciation are so largely governed by emotional factors, it is extremely hard to verbalize. For this and other reasons, most film composers have discovered that it is much easier to discuss the technical or mechanical aspects of their scores than the creative or aesthetic.

Speaking for myself, in classroom and lecture situations, I can demonstrate what kind of music I wrote for this scene or that, which theme or melodic motive stands for which character or idea, how I developed the motives, my principles of orchestration, how the mood of the music is varied according to the changing visual image or its dramatic content, and so on. But can I explain, in any meaningful or systematic fashion, just why I wrote the music I did? Can I give reasons for rejecting certain melodic ideas which occur to me and utilizing others? Can I make it clear to anyone, or even to myself, why one musical effect or device seemed right to me for a particular scene, and another wrong? Can any composer who has written for the screen really declare, in terms which would have significance for a music scholar or analyst, just what film music is all about, what it is supposed to do for a picture, and how one should go about doing it?

Far from being condemned for trying, film composers and music directors have frequently been urged to state their views regarding the functions and artistic principles of music for the screen, especially since the advent of sound. Consequently, many notions regarding this new, strictly twentieth-century form of musical composition have been set forth in articles, lectures, symposia, interviews, and whatnot. But it seems to me that few of the ideas expressed thus far have shed any light on the sort of thing I have been wondering about: What is the fundamental nature of film music? How does it function in relation to the cinematic entity? How does it influence the emotions and reactions of the spectators?

For example, some of the most interesting and highly treasured contributions to the slim body of film music literature are certain articles written by composers for that now-defunct and much-missed little periodical, *Film Music Notes* (1941-1957). However, most of them are very brief, and they usually deal with specific films. Important as these writings are for the researcher in film music history, they are mostly of the here's-what-I-wrote-for-this-scene and there's-what-I-wrote-for-that-scene sort. The writers often explain the development of motifs, provide harmonic analyses, discuss orchestration, and so forth, but none of them really come to grips with certain basic and admittedly perplexing questions: What should music contribute to a film? What are its duties and obligations toward the total filmic entity? And just how does a composer go about writing music which fulfills those obligations?

Questions regarding the aesthetic functions of film music are often put to composers in interviews and symposia, but, as a rule, their answers consist of vague and enigmatic phrases such as "music must support the image," "create an emotional ambience," "underline the basic emotions," "bring a counterline," express "the inner workings," add an "emotional third dimension," make "dramatic implications," give a "smoothness of continuity," and so on. All of which is undeniably valid, but unfortunately of little help to the composer seeking to know what he or she is doing that is right or wrong. Nor is much help to be found in the writings of the few film historians and theoreticians who have attempted to explore this relatively un-trodden ground. For instance, Manvell and Huntley, in their com-prehensive book, *The Techniques of Film Music* (1957; 1975) state that music "points, underlines, links, emphasizes, or interprets the action, becoming part of the dramatic pattern of the film's struc-ture." But what they do not reveal is how it does these things.

Siegfried Kracauer, in his *Theory of Film* (1960), directs our at-tention to the fact that films are practically never shown without music, and then proceeds to give some well thought out and rather convincing hypotheses on why this is so. His chapter on music also includes a valuable and provocative discussion of what he calls "parallel" and "contrapuntal" accompaniments, and their rela-tions to the narrative. But, as able and eloquent as Kracauer and some other film theoreticians are, in none of their writings have I been able to find a clear, systematic explanation of the means by which movie music does all the marvelous things ascribed to it thus far.

So, here is something to think about: If it is true that music for the films can do all the things that composers have said it does or should do, if it has all the qualities which writers like Manvell and Huntley attribute to it, and if it is indeed capable of expressing such artistic and aesthetic subtleties as Kracauer's parallelism and counterpoint, why has no one held up to scrutiny any of the musical means used by screen composers to accomplish such things?

What I am talking about, obviously, is the formulation of a theory or philosophy of music for motion pictures. What I am suggesting is the possibility that someday the literature of film music may yield the equivalent of an Eisenstein, a Bazin, Kracauer, or Sarris—those men who, with varying degrees of success, have attempted to discover and analyze the essential nature and language of the cinema.

If there are any among my readers who may be repelled by the sight of that often misunderstood word "theory," let me assure them that I am not using it to signify merely a dry, lifeless set of academic rules and regulations governing procedures for composing music. Neither, to my mind, does it always indicate nothing more than speculative or abstract reasoning—something cerebral which is distinguished from or opposed to actual practice and experiment.

Nor should it ever, as is often the case, consist of a mere set of general assertions made to justify an individual's own point of view and to vindicate his or her own prejudices, likes, and dislikes. To me a theory denotes a system of knowledge based on principles and assumptions which have evolved from accepted practices and procedures of the past and present. This knowledge can be employed to clarify, analyze, and explain the special nature of a musical phenomenon, and to illuminate, point out, and possibly predict the subtle and complex relationships among its musical events.

When that rather heady statement is stripped of ornaments, passing tones, and chromatic embellishments, it simply expresses my belief that (1) theory is based on practice, and (2) theory can be used to explain practice. But is a theory of film music a real possibility? Are there, so to speak, some general principles and assumptions floating around, perhaps out there in the ozone, waiting for a future historian-theoretician to come along, gather them in, and convert them into a systematic body of knowledge?

To this date, the only person to try and deal with film music theory qua theory has been the German composer Hanns Eisler, whose small book, *Composing for the Films* (1947), was written as the result of a Rockefeller Foundation grant for research in this field. Although still required reading for any serious student of movie music, Eisler's otherwise worthy effort is too badly marred by his musical and sociological prejudices to qualify it as a genuine theory. He too obviously dislikes and too quickly repudiates such things as structural tonality, leitmotivic technique, melodic music in general, and Hollywood music in particular.(It has been noted that, in his own film scores, Eisler did not always practice what he preached.)

The admirable article on film music in the fifth edition of *Grove's Dictionary of Music and Musicians* (1954) is the combined work of British musicologists Ernest Irving, Hans Keller, and Wilfrid Mellers. But, of the three, only the last delves into specific theoretical matters, and, even at that, his discussion is mainly a restatement of Eisler's precepts, and he duly echoes some of Eisler's prejudices.

Accordingly, despite its deficiencies as a purely theoretical work, *Composing for the Films* remains the only treatise which talks of specific aesthetic problems in a theoretical manner. However, it is possible to glean some further indications as to the feasibility of formulating a systematic exposition of film music philosophy if one examines certain comments by other authorities, persons who do not themselves deal explicitly with this topic, but who acknowledge, if only by implication, that such a possibility exists.

For instance, in 1924 French composer Eric Satie characterized his film score for the Surrealist ballet *Relâche* as "musique D'ameublement" (furniture music). Satie's seemingly odd concept found its origin in something that Matisse had once said when he envisioned a new art without any distracting subject matter—in his words, "something analogous to an easy chair."

Whether one agrees with the premise or not, Satie's notion of cinema music as a kind of furnishing surely ranks as one of the earliest assertions made by a composer as to the functions of music for the screen. He apparently envisioned its purpose as somewhat analogous to that which a frame serves for the picture it encloses.

Interestingly enough, this idea was to be echoed in later years when Bernard Herrmann remarked that his music for *Anna and the King of Siam* (1946) "was intended to serve as musical scenery."

During the first decade of the sound era, there was quite a flurry of writings by composers, conductors, and music critics on various musical problems connected with the new medium of talking pictures. The writers rarely used the word theory or alluded to any definite theoretical concepts; nevertheless, those articles which discuss specific compositional or stylistic matters offer some intriguing glimpses of what the skeletal framework of a film music theory might look like and the material some of its chapters might cover.

For example, the polemics against illustrative music (otherwise known as "mickey-mousing") which started in the mid-thirties—and continue to this day—can be said to constitute some of the first discernible gropings toward a general theoretical principle. And the same claim could be made for certain assertions made in those days regarding the general unsuitability of standard or traditional musical forms (sonata, rondo, and so on) for use in film scores.

Subtle indications of the concept of a viable film music theory occasionally show up in the most unexpected places, and not necessarily in the thoughts of the musicians. There is a particularly apt example in a 1933 interview with Alfred Hitchcock, one of the first directors to experiment with the dramatic possibilities of sound. Expounding on the use of music in films, Hitchcock asserts his belief that almost any scene has, somewhere, the "correct musical accompaniment." It could be argued that a scene can have more than one "correct" musical accompaniment, but even that contention would imply that some general principles of aptness are to be found somewhere.

In the chapter devoted to music in his book, *Filmmaking: The Collaborative Art* (1975), film historian Donald Chase uses the following interesting phrases: "influences on *traditional* sound film scoring," "radical shifts in the *theory* and *practice* of film music in recent years," and "the *traditional form* of motion picture scoring," (Emphases added.)

The reference to a theory of film music is striking but puzzling: as noted earlier, no one except Eisler has thus far attempted to formulate any kind of theory, and his precepts have been largely ignored by practicing screen composers. All the same, as Chase suggests, if there is or was such a thing as a traditional form for scoring, it seems to me that it should be possible to define it. And such a definition would clearly constitute a major element of a film music philosophy.

Overt or hidden allusions to a potential theory can be found in other sources, but one more example will suffice for now. It is an intriguing remark once made by my good friend and esteemed colleague, David Raksin, one of the finest composers in Hollywood.

Notwithstanding his stature a recognized authority on movie music matters, David has sometimes voiced strong opposition to the concept of theorizing about the aesthetic problems of our profession. Here is what he said in an interview with Allan Ulrich, in *The Art of Film Music* (Oakland, 1976):

> I am very reluctant to speak of an aesthetic of film music; the world is so full of estheticians who do so much harm that I don't wish to abet their little scene. I have seen writings about film music that are so ill-informed and so *wide of the mark* that they have aroused a revulsion in me. [Emphasis added.]

Once more, it seems to me that the implication is clear; for if, as David avers, certain extant writings are so wide of the mark, it must be inferred that there is a mark to be aimed at. And therefore, can one not presume that someday a writer may come along who will come closer to that mark, or maybe even hit it?

One thing is certain: Whoever decides to tackle such a project—the formulation of a theory of music for motion pictures—will find it a fascinating and richly rewarding field of investigation. Among the fascinations to be encountered will be the business (and this is an absolute must) of trying to construct a logical, step-by-step order from the helter-skelter growth process of an artistic phenomenon whose evolution consisted mainly of learning by doing, experimentation, trial and error, emotional or intuitive reasoning, and just plain hunches.

And if our future historian-theoretician is successful, the richest reward of the work will be a deeper and better understanding of this unique new art form which has contributed so much to our twentieth-century existence, which has reached into the homes and enriched the lives of countless millions of people all over the world, and which in so doing, has been so instrumental in shaping their musical tastes.

Speaking for myself, my only purpose in writing these words is to open the minds of film music lovers and to start them thinking, talking, and writing about certain things which are usually taken for granted and which have been rarely, if ever, closely examined. Obviously, in these few pages I have offered only an inkling of what can or should be done. The rest must be left to the imaginations and zeal of our future historian-theoretician, who will help us all—composer and devotee alike—better understand where the art of film music is, what it went through to get there, what should be done to make it better, and possibly find some answers to the question, "Where did we go right?"

16
WILLIAM ALWYN

If British film music ever had a golden age, it would have to be the period beginning in the late forties and lasting through most of the following decade. The British film industry, ever constant since the coming of sound, enjoyed a period of expanded creativity and production with World War II and something of a box office boom thereafter. Although never geared to the output of Hollywood, studios such as Ealing and the J. Arthur Rank Organization produced a steady stream of good films and employed most of the top composers of Britain. The British composers, unlike their counterparts in Hollywood who were contracted to studios and left with little time to pursue other musical paths, were in the fortunate position of working both sides of the street. They scored films while they continued to write for the concert hall and the various forms of theater. Among the most active British composers for film were Sir Arnold Bax, Anthony Collins, Benjamin Frankel, Malcolm Arnold, Richard Addinsell, Constant Lambert, and, most conspicuously, William Alwyn.

The British school of film composition was founded in 1935 when Sir Arthur Bliss wrote his superb score to *Things to Come*. It was the same year that Sir William Walton began his scoring career, somewhat modestly, with *Escape Me Never*, but advancing to great craftsmanship a few years later with his scores for Olivier's Shakespearean films. It was also in 1935 that composer-conductor-author Constant Lambert stated the case for his fellow composers:

The sound film opens up fascinating new possibilities of

William Alwyn.

aesthetic and is bound to have strong influence on the trend of music in this century. It offers the serious composer what has been lacking since the eighteenth century—a reasonable commercial outlet for his activities, comparable to the "occasional" music which the greatest classical composers did not disdain to write. And in addition to its intrinsic interest as a new craft, writing for films will have the salutary effect of keeping composers in touch with a large audience and its human reactions.

Lambert's views were certainly made valid by the British film industry in the fifties. The force and vitality dwindled with the sixties, with the decline in the number of films made in England and with the steady invasion of pop music. Sadly, what happened in California also happened in London—the foremost, serious composers of film music were gradually shunted to the sidelines. Conspicuous among them was William Alwyn, who has not scored a film since 1960.

Alwyn, who was born in Northampton in 1905, recalls that he became intrigued with the cinema and its music while still a schoolboy. He was taught flute by a man who worked in a factory during the daytime and played piano at a movie theater in the evenings. Eventually, as the theater expanded the accompaniment to a small orchestra, young Alwyn was hired to play the flute and rapidly came to know a vast repertory of standard concert pieces, such as the overtures *Zampa* and *Poet and Peasant*, plus the catalogue items written especially for the screen. As Alwyn describes it, the catalogue was designed to meet any known human situation. Each session was frantic, as the musicians strove to keep up with the large number of pieces required, in addition to the immediacy with which they were required. Pieces of sheet music were whipped on and off music stands with lightning speed, often with ensuing confusion. It was the pianist-leader who bound the enterprise together with ad-libbed modulations and improvised chords. For young Alwyn it was a most basic education in the craft of supplying films with music. It was some years later that, as a musician in London, he had further experience in performing in film theaters, and by that time the craft was much more sophisticated, with prepared scores and efficient timing devices.

Alwyn, who is a professor of music and who was awarded a Fellowship at the Royal Academy of Music in London in 1936, received his education in Northampton and studied music at the Royal Academy. He taught composition at the Royal Academy from 1926 to 1955, while also pursuing his career as a composer. Alwyn has always been among the most prominent forces in British music, serving as the chairman of the Composers' Guild of Great Britain in 1949, 1950, and 1954, writing on musical topics for magazines, lecturing on music, serving on sundry committees, and eventually becoming a working member of the British Film Academy.

The list of Alwyn compositions, aside from his film work, is a long one and includes five symphonies, several concerts for various solo instruments and orchestra, many concert pieces and a great deal of chamber music. He began his film career in 1936 by scoring a modest picture entitled *The Future's in the Air*, following it over the next few years with a number of documentaries and films for the British government. He did not really hit his stride as a major film composer until the war years, particularly with *Desert Victory* (1943), *The Way Ahead* (1944), and *The True Glory* (1945), each one being a distinguished item about the war and a mixture of documentary and drama. His scoring of each was free of the bombast which characterized most war pictures of the era.

Alwyn became one of the most employed of British film composers following the war. *The Rake's Progress* (1946), which did much to propel Rex Harrison's popularity, contained some witty music, including calypso melodies for a South American sequence. It was the same year that he wrote a masterful score for Carol Reed's stark drama *Odd Man Out*, set in Northern Ireland and starring James Mason as an IRA agitator who is wounded during a raid and spends the remaining hours of his life trying to elude the police and shuttling between those who help him and those who would turn him in. The score perfectly matches the bleak settings, the anxiety, and yet the tenderness of the dying fugitive and the girl who loves him and dies with him. It is interesting that Alwyn has written effective music for two other films about the Irish—*Captain Boycott* (1947), an historical adventure, and *Shake Hands With the Devil* (1959). The latter is a darkly realistic account of the IRA in Dublin during the troubles with England, and it stars James Cagney as a dedicated revolutionary. Alwyn's fine score was issued as a recording, unfortunately one of the very few of his many distinguished compositions for the British screen to be made available in such form.

Alwyn also scored *The Rocking Horse Winner* (1949), an

unusual drama about a boy who fantasizes while riding his rocking horse and actually predicts winners at a local race track and thereby helps his family's need for money, but with tragic results. The score is highly important as an undercurrent of tension. Other interesting scores by Alwyn include *The Card* (1952, titled *The Promoter* for U.S. release), one of the most charming of the Alec Guinness comedies; *The Million Pound Note* (1953), with Gregory Peck as the man with the million pound note in the Mark Twain satire; *The Seekers*, a costumed adventure set in New Zealand and incorporating Maori music; and *A Night to Remember* (1958), an excellent account of the sinking of the Titanic. Alwyn also wrote the music for two classic swashbuckler items—*The Crimson Pirate* (1952), with Burt Lancaster, and *The Master of Ballantrae* (1953), one of the last and best of Errol Flynn's costume adventures.

William Alwyn has long been known as one of the erudite and articulate British composers. The following article appeared in the March 1959 issue of the magazine *Films and Filming* and is a transcription of a lecture given by him at the National Film Theatre in London. It is used here with the permission of the composer.

William Alwyn on Film Music

The art of film music is a specialized branch of the wider art of the film. Because it is a specialized art, the purpose for which it exists and the separate functions it fulfills are sometimes misunderstood. The musician himself is inclined to confuse it with descriptive music, which is called program music in the concert hall. Oddly enough, direct description plays a relatively small part in film music.

Composing for the film demands from the composer a purely dramatic approach to music and provides a welcome additional outlet for his theatrical instincts, other than opera, ballet, or incidental music for the stage. Perhaps that is why it has attracted composers of the caliber of Walton, Bliss, the late Dr. Vaughan Williams (who composed his first film score at the age of 69 and, as with everything he did, brought to film music his ever youthful spirit), Aaron Copland, Georges Auric, Shostakovitch (who learned his technique in the cinema and, by 1937, had already composed a number of important Russian feature films), Honneger (again a pioneer of film music), and Prokofiev, to mention only a few.

It also requires from the composer a considerable degree of versatility. His technique must be such that it is adequate to any situation—comic or tragic—and any style, Shakespearean or Wild Western. Versatility is sometimes regarded as a debatable asset in a composer. Contemporary criticism is inclined to question the ability of a creative artist to be versatile. The composer must be channeled and docketed. But versatility does not mean an abandonment of individuality. An individual style can remain inviolate although it rings all the changes on comedy, tragedy, period, colour, and form.

It should be established at once that the functions of the symphonist, the opera composer, and the writer of ballet music or of the score for a cinematic film are distinct, specialized, and various; and each demands a different critical approach from the intelligent listener.

The conscientious composer brings to absolute music, or serious music if you like, an utterly different approach from that which he adopts for the film. In absolute music he is concerned with the technical problems of formal design and construction. Even an essentially atmospheric work such as Debussy's *La Mer* is more dependent on its exquisite sense of line, phrase, and climax rather than on the sea, which is its inspiration, and more concerned with evocation rather than description.

One of the first lessons a composer learns is that music can do most things; but it cannot describe, except by verbal or visual implication. It is a constant association of visual ideas with music which unhesitatingly makes us think of the sea when Mendelssohn's *Fingal's Cave* is played. This piece could quite as easily have been associated with forest murmurs. Again, Debussy's piano piece, *Jardins Sous la Pluie*, would still function as music if he had called it less poetically, but equally appropriately, *Hail on a Hot Tin Roof*.

I myself had the amusing experience of hearing some music of mine, aptly I thought, composed to accompany a film about butterflies; just as aptly, some years after, fitted to a film about elephants (without my permission, of course)!

The points I hope I have made, then, are that film music forms an entirely specialised function, distinct from any other musical function; and that far from being descriptive music, this is the one thing it is worst fitted for, and for which it is most rarely used in film (I am, of course, speaking of good films, films that are intelligently made).

As a film composer, I come to the film as a specialist, one of a team of specialists, of technicians concerned with this complex conglomeration of visuals, sound effects, music, and dialogue which go to make the completed contemporary sound film. I, myself, have a very clear idea of what I can achieve and what I should be asked to achieve.

"Film Music: Sound or Silence?" could well be my theme. It seems both provocative and paradoxical, but to me, at least, it makes good sense. Sound can only make its effect by contrast with silence. As a hill to a valley, fortissimo can only be relative to pianissimo. Music depends for its maximum effect on the absence of music.

Mozart, I think it was, once made the profound remark that the most important thing in music was no music at all. This most important paradox seems to be in danger of being forgotten in the very medium where it is all-important. The continuous stream of background music which mars so many present-day films negatives the intelligent approach of the composer to the sound track. He cannot make his effect if music is laid on with a trowel. The continuous flow of musical sound begins by merely irritating, and then the ear tends to ignore it. If you go to a factory, to make yourself heard above the din of machinery you must first of all shout, but after a time the incessant noise becomes a mere background to normal conversation.

After his visit to America about two years ago, I asked Sir William Walton what was his main impression. "Oh," he said, "music never stops. In the hotel, at the drugstore, even at the dentist's music is always being churned out, relentlessly and unceasingly." Unfortunately, this is becoming true of other countries as well as America.

The public has become conditioned to a continual background of musical sound in everyday life, but will still expect it as a background to its entertainment. It is with regret and foreboding one sees this encroaching upon the film score. This attitude cuts at the very roots of film music as an art. Without silence the composer loses his most effective weapon. It is a point to which the director must be increasingly alive and in which the composer is only too willing to cooperate. I do feel that far too much of my ingenuity is spent nowadays in persuading the filmmaker to keep music out of the film rather than to put it in.

"Silence is golden;" without it film music can make little impact. The circus and variety hall turns exist on such contrasts. Who can fail to be shocked into awed admiration when the performer reaches his most impressive act? The band abruptly stops. As the artist totters precariously on the top of his trapeze, he performs the incredible with the aid of silence—followed by a gunfire "roll" on the side drum. You top this with a triumphant fanfare and musical drama is enacted before your very eyes.

This is film music in all its pristine simplicity—the dramatic function of music as understood by playwrights from Shakespeare to Shaw, the theatrical use of music, which is the very origin and foundation of music in film. Indeed, film music stems from the theater and not, as often imagined, from the background of piano music which accompanied the silent film. Although some of the methods involved in silent film accompaniment were carried on when the changeover began, particularly in the accompaniments to some documentary films and travel films. I am not referring to the imaginative treatment of sound in documentary films such as *Night Mail* or Rotha's *World of Plenty*, but to those routine films which are used to fill up a feature program.

Film music is essentially dramatic music, not descriptive music. Music functions to point the dramatic atmosphere of the film and add one more emotional plane to an attack which is already being made on the visual sense.

Music in films has the remarkable faculty for portraying something which is happening in the actor's mind, and not what you see in his face or in his actions. In the old silent film the actor had to rely on exaggerated gestures, the art of mime to express his emotions. In the sound film he can behave naturally with the aid of words; the "method" can come into its own; but he can also remain silent and poker-faced while music expresses for him the emotion which is to be shared by his audience.

This is an entirely new weapon in the film director's armory. With imagination he can shoot on two planes. I remember using a different version of this technique in *October Man*. The central character (John Mills) is suspected of murder. In all the bustle of C.I.D. questioning and investigation, he is utterly detached and thinking only of the girl he has just left. You, as an audience, realize this, not because of anything he says, but because you can hear remotely and intensely, high up on a solo violin, the persistent sound of a tune that you have already learned earlier on in the picture to associate with the girl.

Music can operate on a plane completely contrary to the visuals. There is still a wide field for experiment in this. One of the fascinations of composing for the cinema is that it is a young art, and to pioneer in any aspect of it is rewarding and stimulating to the creative artist.

Another function of film music more obvious because of familiarity is its use to secure dramatic tension. This has now become the commonplace of the television thriller, but usually you are only too conscious of it because little attempt is made to use it with subtlety. Generally it is the blatant use of the circus performer's drumroll. But to me it loses its effect when it becomes a cliché, and I know that I am being cheated emotionally by an extraneous device.

The whole art of the cinema is in its planning. It is coordination of a team, director, producer, designer, cameraman, musician, and actor, all working together and interlocking to obtain a dramatic whole in which no single aspect is predominant. This applies particularly to the music. It should be sensed and not predominant; predominant but only sensed.

I am always a little worried if somebody says to me, "I liked your score for such-and-such a picture." It makes me wonder whether I have stepped outside my brief, which is to provide music which is as indigenous to the film as the camera angles and the film sets.

John Addison.

17
JOHN ADDISON

John Addison is possibly the most productive of all the British composers associated with films. Since his first major score in 1950 (*Seven Days to Noon*) he has written music for more than sixty pictures, in addition to a large body of music for the theater and a dozen pieces of concert and chamber music. Gifted with melody and a firm sense of drama, Addison has a style that is a happy compromise between traditional and contemporary methods, and as a film composer, he has sought devices that differ from the norm. The best example of this is the score for which he won an Oscar, *Tom Jones* (1963). The obvious approach to this costume romp would be the use of a full orchestra; it occured to Addison that it would be more humorous and piquant if the titles were accompanied by harpsichord and piano. He credits this economical approach to film scoring to his years working in the British studios, where budgets were more often than not on the meager side and required composers to be resourceful. He also strongly believes that light instrumental forces are sometimes more effective than the symphonic. Another case in point is *The Maggie* (1954), a comedy set in Scotland and dealing with the adventures of a battered old fishing boat and its skipper. For this Addison singled out the harmonica to carry the burden of the score. On the other hand, he has also made use of large-scaled orchestras,, as with *The Amorous Adventures of Moll Flanders* (1965), *The Charge of the Light Brigade* (1968), *Start the Revolution Without Me* (1969), and *Swashbuckler* (1976).

Addison was born in Surrey in 1920, the son of a British army colonel who desired his offspring to follow his own choice of career. He finished his formal education at Wellington College, a respected school for sons of the military, but then explained to his father that his primary interest was in music and not in the service. Addison senior accepted this and the 17-year old proceeded to enroll in the Royal College of Music in London. He excelled in composition and won the coveted Sullivan Prize. However, he was there for only one year and left to join the army for wartime service. Addison was commissioned in the twenty-third Hussar Tank Regiment in 1940 and took part in the invasion of Europe. He was wounded at Caen and later stationed in Germany.

Returning to London in 1946, Addison decided to resume his study of music and took advantage of the government's willingness to give grants to ex-servicemen seeking to establish themselves in business. He resumed study at the Royal College of Music and, after winning his A.R.C.M. degree, stayed to become a member of the teaching staff. Up to this time Addison had had no interest in film scoring, but a chance meeting with director-producer Roy Boulting changed his mind. He had met Boulting while both were in the service; the filmmaker said then that he would be willing to help Addison if the need arose. Boulting was as good as his word. He came to the college to hear a performance of a piece by Addison, liked what he heard, and invited the composer to write a section of a film on which he was then working. Several such opportunities came his way thereafter, and in 1950 Boulting decided to hire Addison for a full score for an important film, *Seven Days to Noon*, a suspense thriller about a scientist threatening to explode an atomic bomb unless his demands were met. Addison's score helped supply the strained, exciting mood of the picture and firmly established him as a strong, new voice in film scoring. His assignments from that time have been plentiful and varied.

A signal year for Addison was 1950. It not only saw the start of his career in film scoring, but it was the year in which he had a chamber work, his Sextet for Woodwinds, performed at the prestigious Festival of the International Society for Contemporary Music at Frankfurt, Germany. Its success triggered off a steady stream of concert pieces over the years. Among them are a Concerto for Trumpet, Strings, and Percussion (recorded by the Louisville Orchestra on the Louisville label, S-695) and his Divertimento for Brass (recorded on the Argo label, ARG-813, by the

Philip Jones Brass Ensemble). His other works include the *Wellington* Suite, commissioned for the centenary of his alma mater, Wellington College, in 1959; a Partita for Strings; and various works for chamber groups. His most widely performed orchestral work is the suite from the ballet *Carte Blanche*, which was commissioned by the Sadler Wells Ballet and first performed at the Edinburgh Festival in 1959. The suite has been conducted by the likes of Sir Thomas Beecham and Leopold Stokowski and recorded by the composer with the Pro Arte Orchestra (PYE GGC-4048).

Addison has also been one of the most productive composers for the British theatre. In 1955 he wrote the score for the London musical revue *Cranks*, which played on Broadway a year later and which Addison recorded with the original cast, headed by Anthony Newley (HMV CLP-1082). His association with director Tony Richardson began in 1957 with Addison's incidental music to John Osborne's *The Entertainer,* starring Laurence Olivier. He subsequently scored several Richardson and Olivier stage productions, including *Luther* (1961), *Hamlet* (1963) and *I, Claudius* (1972). Over the past twenty years, Addison has scored more than twenty stage productions.

Concurrent with his work in films and the theater, Addison has made occasional forays into television, beginning in 1955 with a BBC childrens' programme called *Steps into Ballet*. Six years later he scored the BBC-TV film *Sambo and the Snow Mountains*, and in 1964 provided the music for two BBC series, *The Orchestra* and *The Detective*. His first assignment for American television was the score of CBS' *The Search for Ulysses*, and since then there have been various dramatic and documentary scores on both sides of the Atlantic.

Addison's track record for the cinema has been both distinguished and profitable right from the time of *Seven Days to Noon*, more so than most composers working for the screen either in Europe or America. It can be argued that luck plays a part in the career of any composer, but in terms of writing for the screen, the luck that wins the most points is that which comes from a combination of a solid musical education and what can best be described as a knack—an innate flair for inventing music that supports and enhances the visual. Addison has this knack in large measure. *Tom Jones* is the best known example, but there are other instances, such as the opening sequence in *Pool of London* (1951), in which the scenes of busy wharves and shipping movements on the Thames is underscored with a sustained rhythm in the lower strings. In *The Man Between* (1953), a dark account of espionage in divided Berlin, Addison states the sadness of the main character, a doomed spy (James Mason) with a quiet theme for the saxophone, which becomes poignant when pointed against the empty ruins of the bombed city. The saxophone served Addison well much later when he scored Hitchcock's *Torn Curtain* (1966), also a story of spies in East Berlin, but this time the saxophone theme was used more humorously, albeit with a muted sense of danger, to characterize a bus carrying the two leading characters, as they try to escape to the West.

Addison's military background has proven useful in films such as *The Red Beret* (1953), dealing with the wartime adventures of parachutists; *Cockleshell Heroes* (1955), about Royal Marine commandoes; and *I Was Monty's Double* (1958). The ease with which Addison has been able to write marches with a marked British flavor is evident in *Reach for the Sky* (1956), concerning the exploits of RAF fighter ace Douglas Bader, and *Guns at Batasi* (1964), a film about the British army in modern Africa. The Bader assignment was of particular interest for Addison because the celebrated ace is his brother-in-law. However, lest anyone accuse Addison of writing overheroically for films about the services, he can justly point to his sly music for the Boulting Brothers' satire on the British Army, *Private's Progress* (1956).

With the decline in the volume of film product in England and with most of his assignments coming from Hollywood producers, Addison moved to Los Angeles with his wife and two children in 1975. In 1976 he was well represented with his good-humored scores for *Swashbuckler* and *The Seven-Per-cent Solution*, and there is every reason to believe he will continue to be one of the film world's foremost contributors to the art of scoring.

John Addison on Film Music

I wrote my first film score, *Seven Days to Noon*, soon after finishing my studies at the Royal College of Music in London, and

I was very fortunate to be associated at the outset with Roy Boulting, who directed it and who was not only knowledgeable in all departments of filmmaking, but genuinely musical as well. He guided me through that first score, and he was always available for advice. From the beginning, therefore, it seemed natural to me to work closely with the director or producer of a film. At that time I was writing concert music as well as film scores and had the opportunity of writing purely for myself when I wanted to. In writing for films I regarded myself as one of a team, in which the director was the all-important guiding light. As I gained experience in film writing and worked with other directors and producers, I found that getting into their minds, finding out what they wanted, and then interpreting what they said into musical terms was just as important as writing the music itself. There are often many ways of treating a film sequence musically, but it is no good going against the director's overall conception for his film.

In 1960, when I had already written about thirty film scores, I met Tony Richardson, who asked me to write the music for John Osborne's play *The Entertainer* at the Royal Court Theatre. This was my introduction to the English Stage Society, who, under George Devine's direction, was dedicated to finding new playwrights and new actors, reflecting the changing social attitudes of the times. Working at the Royal Court Theatre, I was one of a team which had shared goals. Later, when Tony Richardson and John Osborne formed Woodfall Films, to make such films as *A Taste of Honey, The Loneliness of the Long Distance Runner*, and *Tom Jones*, there was a similar spirit. In these films I was involved early and would visit the unit on location. It was unthinkable that the composer would be brought in at the last moment on any of the Woodfall productions. And having worked closely with the director throughout, I would stay with the picture after the recordings, attending the dubbing, where the music finally joins all the other sounds on the track.

Another factor when I started writing film music in England was the prevailing attitudes towards Hollywood, with its factory style of film production and the kind of music scores associated with that style. There was a reaction against large orchestras, nineteenth century harmonic language, the automatic use of strings under every love scene, celestial choirs, and so forth.

The reason technical devices become cliches is that they have proved successful over and over again. For instance, strings are effective under dialogue because they don't fight the voices. It was not easy to find new ways of solving old problems, ways which would work as well as the proven methods. In some of these films, instead of mixing music and effects, the effects would be dropped altogether, leaving the music in the clear. On the other hand, sequences such as chases, which usually have music, would be carried by the effects alone in the interests of realism. The combination of sound effects, movement, and clever editing can often create its own music. I have, for example, been complimented on my music for the stag hunt in *Tom Jones*. Actually, there was no music until the hunt was over!

We found that small instrumental combinations could make more effect, with more presence, than an orchestra of sixty or seventy players. On *The Loneliness of the Long Distance Runner* I used a traditional jazz group of four players, combined with a string octet and a few legitimate woodwinds and brass instruments.

Film music is full of opposites—there's an exception to every rule. So, although one tries to avoid writing music which underlines what is going on on the screen, it is sometimes necessary to do so. It is more satisfying, however, when music can say something that isn't happening on the screen. I often find, too, that certain musical forms, such as a dance or a march or a fugue, can be extremely effective even though they do not exactly match the action. The result can sometimes be more strange and more satisfying than "mickey mouse" fitting or the use of mere mood music. There are examples of this in my score for *The Seven Percent Solution*. I suspect, however, that more important than technique is a sort of instinct, a hunch that a certain thing will work—a dramatic feeling for the medium, which would not necessarily apply to other forms, such as opera.

This is not to say that one sits down and waits hopefully for an idea to come. I usually begin by thinking about the film as a whole, analyzing the action and what the characters are feeling, before I think in specifically musical terms. By way of illustration, I will discuss some random examples from some of my scores, both distant and more recent.

I found it very interesting writing music for the comedies of the Boulting brothers, whose attitudes to whatever it was they were satirizing was quite detached, as if from a pedestal, taking no sides. *Carlton Brown of the Foreign Office* is a good example. This was about an emerging black state, an island almost forgotten by the Foreign Office, which suddenly becomes a pawn on the board of international power politics. There was a sequence in which the Big Powers decided to divide the island, and this was done in a montage by a little man with one of those machines that mark tennis courts, pushing it across the entire island. For that I wrote a tune played on solo piano, with an oom-pah accompaniment on brass instruments. This is an example of having an instinct for a sound, which works well when married with the visual, although one can't quite explain why. There are several reasons why one shouldn't use a piano in a scene like this. In the first place, a piano is associated with interior, rather than exterior sounds, and secondly it is liable to sound like source music, as if someone is playing it off-screen. Orchestral instruments or a chamber group does not give this impression. But in this sequence, it worked because the piano became a sort of character, as if it were the voice of that little machine being pushed across the island, over the hills, and through the jungle.

In doing *The Entertainer*, I was dealing with a film that had been a play, although completely rewritten for the screen. The main point about the score is that it was based on songs written for the play, with lyrics by John Osborne, and those songs characterized Archie Rice and his seedy act at the seaside resorts where he performed. On one level the songs were meant to seem authentic, but on another level they were far from the real thing because the lyrics were related to the whole play as well as to Archie's act. Since Osborne was not a lyricist in the technical sense, the shape of his lyrics forced me into correspondingly unusual musical constructions, creating an atmosphere that combined reality with another dimension. The actual background score was kept to a minimum and as simple as possible. For instance, in several spots I used only an echoed solo piano version of Archie's theme song "Why Should I Care?" to create a certain hollow emotional effect. In this case, the use of the piano was justified because its character related to Archie's life.

A Taste of Honey was a romantic film about a lonely girl (Rita Tushingham), who starts up a relationship with a homosexual boy. There is an extraordinary dignity about him, which is one of the most touching things in the film. The girl has an affair with a black sailor and eventually bears his child. What kind of music do you write for that? I remember quite clearly Tony Richardson saying to me that the music should be formal, which struck me at first as an odd approach to this material. But he was right. To have done a conventional romantic score would have taken away from the realism of the picture and made it corny. So the music actually consisted of two elements. One was the use of the children's game song "Alley, Alley O." I had been up to Manchester, going around the schools in the poor areas, recording some of the songs the children had grown up with, and this was the main one, and I combined it with various contrapuntal structures. The other element was the use of rather formal music for certain characters, as for instance, the theme for the homosexual boy and girl, played on the mandolin and based on a dance form in 2/4 time. The score's formal organization, not often found in film music, worked in this romantic but realistic picture in a way that ordinary, less cerebral scoring might not have done.

When Richardson came to make *Tom Jones*, he made a little speech at a party before the unit went on location and said that he intended to see that they all had a jolly good time. Which is what they did, because they returned fourteen weeks later exhausted but happy, and that joyful quality is apparent in the film. When Richardson started to talk about the score he said, "It's going to be a pop score, isn't it?" which was his way of telling me I shouldn't make it complicated and symphonic. My interpretation of his admonition was to give the score eighteenth century mannerisms without necessarily using eighteenth century instrumentation (except in the source music). This was the basic approach. The film opened with a sequence in silent film style, for which I used the very simple device of a harpsichord to represent the eighteenth century and a slightly out-of-tune upright piano to denote the silent movie element. Later in the film I did what many other composers have done, namely, use different groups of instruments for the main characters. What may have given the music a special flavor in this instance was the fact that although the orchestra consisted of sixty players, I often used quite small groups for many sequences. For example: Tom Jones himself was characterized by a concertina; the "profane" love theme was marked by an alto saxophone and bassoon duo; the "pure" love theme was characterized by solo violin, harp, and piano; Squire Weston's theme was played mainly on horns; and the highwayman was accompanied by a banjo tune.

Another feature of *Tom Jones* was the treatment of the commentary spoken by Michael MacLiammoir. We had decided that whoever spoke the narration should be someone whose voice would have the same kind of stature as one of the leading actors in the film. Naturally, the music accompanying it would be equally important. I decided therefore to set all the commentaries to music as if they were recitatives in an opera, and record them with the full orchestra. This involved rehearsing MacLiammoir with a repetiteur for three weeks before the sessions. It was worth it, for MacLiammoir was able to react to the music and I was able to punctuate his timings and pauses. There is no doubt that this treatment of the commentary made an important contribution to the film.

The Seven Per-Cent Solution was an especially intriguing film to score. I started out, as I always do, by seeking out the director, Herbert Ross, and we spent several days running the picture together and discussing it. The film is a fantasy, in which the imaginary (although almost real) character, Sherlock Holmes, is involved with the historical character, Sigmund Freud. In directing the film, Ross had striven not to allow the humor to become camp, but to try to retain as much as possible of the literary value of the novel on which it was based, without taking itself too seriously. It was a thin line of balance, and Ross was anxious that I should not do anything in the score that would push the film in the wrong direction.

One of the first ideas I had was to use, in the early part of the picture, short musical statements in the form of chapter headings, and I was intrigued to learn that Ross had himself thought, at one time, of having visual chapter headings. Obviously we were thinking along the same lines. I next engaged myself with the problem of Holmes' addiction to cocaine, with which the music would have an important part to play. It was made up of a plaintive phrase for the oboe and a rushing sound on the violins, combined with a string synthesizer effect. The string sound was associated both with the compulsion to take cocaine and the overexcited state induced by the drug. Throughout the film the oboe phrase preceded or followed a high trill, which accompanied the periodic, very brief flashbacks (only two or three seconds at a time) of a boy mounting a staircase. These had an eerie effect, and their full significance only became clear at the end of the picture, during Freud's analysis of Holmes. We learn that Holmes was very fond of his mother and that during his childhood a traumatic event connected with her had given him an emotional block in his relations with women. The oboe phrase suggests his pent-up emotional feelings and his capacity for tenderness, so that every time we see the boy in these flashbacks, the phrase was used, and at the end it turns into a lyrical melody when Holmes has been cured by Freud and meets again the singer he has previously rescued. Now at last he will be able to develop a loving relationship with her. At that point the mother theme is able to express itself in a fully resolved statement.

Another feature of *The Seven Per-Cent Solution* is my use once again of dance forms. When Holmes and Watson first entered Austria it was a natural thing to do to go into a waltz—Straussian in flavor though not an exact pastiche. At the beginning, the theme is fairly exuberant, but as they approach Freud's house in Vienna, Watson has misgivings, and at this point the waltz theme begins to sound less sure of itself. Later in the picture there is a scene where Holmes and Watson rush out of a hospital in pursuit of the wicked baron, and this is marked by hurried music but also in waltz tempo. Then, towards the end of the film, there is a chase sequence, which included a spectacular sword fight between Holmes and the baron. Having greatly admired Richard Rodney Bennett's inspired waltz theme for the train in *Murder on the Orient Express*, I was concerned about doing something that would be different from what Richard had done so well. Since the characters were bound for the Balkans, it occured to me that I might use a theme in czardas form. The rhythm of the czardas actually has something in common with that of a train travelling fast and is susceptible to changes of tempo, including accelerandi. It was an interesting technical exercise to synchronize the music to the varying movements and maintain the tension over an extended period of time.

Just how one arrives at these decisions is hard to describe, but as I have said, it is largely a matter of instinct. As a vital member of the team, the composer has the added advantage of coming in with a fresh eye. Moreover, by discussing the shape of the film and the director's intentions, the composer discovers important clues that will lead him to the right style and show him what his score ought to achieve. It cannot "save" a bad picture, but it can make a thrilling contribution to a good or even fair one.

To sum up: I get the impression that in Hollywood film composers are expected to take every job as it comes along. Fortunately, the pressures were not quite as great in England, and after a spell of doing several film scores one after the other, I was able to take a break and work in the theater or write a concert piece. Looking back, I would say that I have been lucky in the period and the places I worked in. That is to say, there were ten years when some of the most interesting work in films was being done in London, and I was right there and given opportunities I might otherwise not have had. At the same time, having come to know Hollywood better, I now appreciate the advantages of the system as it works today, which is less rigid than in the past. The composer is provided with every kind of assistance regarding the administrative side of scoring—copying, music editing, all the devices of the trade, even what I would not have believed possible in my English days, having one's score proofread by a librarian before it goes to the copyists. It was in Hollywood that I first made use of an orchestrator, on *Torn Curtain*; I had orchestrated forty-seven films before this myself. Such things take a lot of the angst out of the job. But of course, there are always those first moments of horror when you sit down in front of that empty piece of white manuscript paper, wondering if the right ideas will come. Later, if all goes well, there is the excitement and the satisfaction of knowing that your score, recorded and dubbed so soon after it was written, has really helped a film to work in a way it never could have without the music.

Jerry Fielding.

18

JERRY FIELDING

Jerry Fielding established himself as a major film composer in 1962 with his score for Otto Preminger's *Advise and Consent*, a film dealing with subtle and occasionally evil political connivance in Washington. It required, and received, a score which would simmer in the background and bind together a group of characters ranging from sympathetic to vicious. Largely filmed in Washington, the film had a near-documentary feeling, and Fielding's music provided an uneasy, rather ethereal emotive undercurrent. The success of the score raised the question of why such a talented musician, then 40 years of age, had taken so long to gain a foothold in Hollywood. The answers involve some of the political chicanery touched on in *Advise and Consent*. Fielding, an admitted maverick by nature and a man deeply concerned about the ways of the world, was blacklisted because of leftist leanings and for being an unfriendly witness in the hearings on un-American activities. As with so many victims of that sad era, it is not difficult to understand why he, and others, were so damned. One of the issues for which Fielding was criticized in the early 1950s was his pointing up of racial prejudice in music assignments and the almost complete refusal to hire blacks, an issue that now seems far removed from reality.

Fielding was born in Pittsburgh in June of 1922, the son of Russian imigrants. He describes his father as a man not successful in business, a dreamer and an intellectual, with a great love of music. Fielding senior collected recordings and encouraged his son to enjoy them, in addition to taking him to concerts. This leaning was strengthened by the then common practice in Pittsburgh public schools of including radio programs on music appreciation as part of the arts and humanities. Fielding considers himself fortunate to have been a schoolboy in those years and regrets that such exposure is not available to young people today. On the other hand, the Pittsburgh of his youth was an unhealthy environment; fumes from the coal industry polluted the air. At the age of 14 his health broke down, and he was confined to his home for a two-year period, much of which he spent listening to the radio and supplementing his growing interest in music. He recalls the dramatic broadcasts of Orson Welles with their music scores by Bernard Herrmann, the great variety of concert programs; and the increasing sophistication of the arrangement then being done for the leading dance bands. It occurred to Fielding that the arrangements of the famed swing musicians utilized elements of classical music and that it was an area in which he would like to become involved.

In his late teens, Fielding joined the studio of Max Atkins, a legendary figure in American music. Atkins was the music director and conductor of the Stanley Theater in Pittsburgh, long one of the top presentation houses in America, with a large pit orchestra providing accompaniment to stage and films. Atkins' best students, who included Henry Mancini and Billy May, were gradually taken into the orchestra as players and also given assignments as arrangers. It was, recalls Fielding, an ideal place to learn, since the theater had a different show every week and required enormous amounts of music material. Atkins was a man with the ability not only to spot talent, but also to encourage it. He was constantly called on by band leaders who needed young players and arrangers. After a year with Atkins, Fielding was hired by Alvino Rey to make arrangements for his band and vocal group, the King Sisters. He toured with Rey and eventually arrived in Los Angeles, where he decided to stay. Fielding found that the biggest market for arrangers was in radio and mostly for the shows that featured the name bands. An important opening came his way when Kay Kyser's arranger, George Duning, was called into the armed services and Fielding, turned down by the services on grounds of health, took over the job. By this time Fielding had made many arrangements for the likes of Tommy Dorsey, Charlie Barnet, and Claude Thornhill, but he now found himself writing daily arrangements for Kyser and learning a great deal about sound and recording techniques.

Fielding secured his first job as a conductor in 1947 with Jack

Paar's radio program. Other assignments followed, leading to an association with Groucho Marx as the music director of his radio and television program. In 1953 Fielding ran afoul of the political blacklist—he describes himself as a loud-mouthed crusader—and was suddenly unemployable in Hollywood. Fortunately, the blacklisting was almost entirely confined to the film and television industries in Los Angeles, and Fielding, like many others, went elsewhere. The early fifties were the burgeoning years of Las Vegas, and Fielding found a profitable outlet for his abilities as a director and arranger for stage presentations. Among the people for whom Fielding worked were Abbott and Costello, Debbie Reynolds, Eddie Fisher, and Mitzi Gaynor. Fielding was away from Los Angeles for almost ten years, and he credits Betty Hutton with making it possible for him to resume his career there. He had directed and arranged her act in Las Vegas, and when she was contracted to do a television series, she asked for Fielding. When told he was still considered somewhat *persona non grata*, she demanded that he be hired. Several famous names had implied that they would back him in such circumstances, but Betty Hutton was the only one who actually did so. Once resettled in Los Angeles, and with a more sane political atmosphere, Fielding's career entered wider and more interesting channels. He was hired to write music for various dramatic and comedic TV series, and when Otto Preminger was looking for a composer to score *Advise and Consent*, Dalton Trumbo suggested his good friend Fielding. Preminger, himself a maverick by nature and the most independent of independent producers, was impressed with the composer's track record and gave him the assignment. In coming up with an interesting solution to the job of scoring a difficult subject, Fielding put himself on the film music map.

Ever interested in exploring new musical avenues, Fielding was fascinated with the concepts of serious, dramatic scoring, and to widen his knowledge of theory and counterpoint, he studied with esteemed composers Ernst Toch and Maria Castelnuovo-Tedesco. In 1967, he met a man with whom he would become a close friend and associate—director Sam Peckinpah. The two were both hired to work on the television drama *Noon Wine*, in ABC's *Stage 67* series. Peckinpah had won a name for himself in 1961 with his fine western *Ride the High Country*, but he had run aground three years later with his ambitious production of *Major Dundee*, which was considered by Columbia Pictures to be not only too long but too cerebral a western. It was drastically cut without Peckinpah's cooperation, and his loudly voiced and bitter condemnation of Hollywood caused him to suffer a period of unemployment. However, Fielding and Peckinpah, kindred spirits in many of their nonestablishment views, found a working partnership, and when the director managed to get *The Wild Bunch*, which he had written with Walon Green, into production, he assigned Fielding as his composer. Peckinpah took his time about making the picture and employed the composer for almost a year, resulting in a near-perfect situation for such a job. It allowed for considerable study of Mexican music and much time on location with the film in Mexico. Since then Fielding has also scored Peckinpah's *Garcia, Straw Dogs, Junior Bonner, The Killer Elite,* and *Bring Me the Head of Alfredo.* He also formed a profitable association with English director-producer Michael Winner and scored his remarkable gothic exercise *The Nightcomers,* using a full orchestra in the romantic fashion and following it with much grittier scores for the Winner westerns *The Lawman* and *Chato's Land.* Fielding has also written music for Winner's more modern and harsh subjects *The Mechanic* and *Scorpio.* Fielding is a musician who forms deep associations with certain directors. More recently, he has written scores for actor-director Clint Eastwood, whom he describes as an easy man for whom to work, since he accepts the composer's concept of what a film requires and allows him to function without interference. It has resulted in Fielding's work on *The Outlaw Josey Wales* and *The Enforcer.*

Jerry Fielding continues to find new methods of scoring films. He keeps an open mind about all means of composition, including electronic, and believes the public is far more sympathetic to progress in music than most film producers imagine. Fielding has not followed an easy path in his career, and he is not given to repeating musical situations no matter how successful they may have been. His talents and his views have produced a body of work which makes for rewarding study.

Jerry Fielding on Film Music

I think that anyone comtemplating becoming a serious composer today would be best advised to gear himself toward the films—unless he happens to have a rich parent who can buy him a symphony orchestra. Films need serious composers, and they are going to need them even more in the future. Film music is the main forum for composers of serious intent to possibly create something of value, something that has a real function and can reach a mass audience. I love films; to me it is a fantastic medium. What better way is there to reach people? You can touch them quickly and compactly, and assuming that they are watching the film in a theater, you have their full attention.

Film composers often say they would like to be in on a picture from the beginning, in order to get to know it and develop their music along with the production. This approach does not appeal to me, mostly because of the great length of time producers and directors take to make a film. They write the script over and over; they shoot scenes in a variety of ways; and then they edit this way and that. They listen to all kinds of opinions on their product, and they often get confused and end up not really knowing what they have. It's a case of being too close to the forest to see the trees, and that's a dangerous situation because each film must have a unique architecture, a certain balance.

I like to avoid all those confusions and come in with what I think is a valuable contribution to the producers, which is the matter of coming in with a fresh eye. The job of the composer has to be done very carefully. You can't lead a picture by the nose: you can support it, you can help to give it its proper color and feeling, you can cause certain situations to be weighed one against the other, you can heighten scenes, and you can help reduce visual excesses. There are many things you can do. You can simply fill up silences. Or you can leave silences, which are very important to films, which is something many directors don't realize. There's nothing more eloquent than a proper pause, a pregnant silence.

In order to do all these things, I want to see the picture when it's completed. I don't want to be told that a scene was taken out, because I then might start to miss it. I study every film I am about to score several times before going in to discuss it. In most cases the producers and directors don't really know where music should be used. Sometimes they admit that there are parts of the film they don't like and that they want me to bale them out by laying in music. They lament that the picture "needs" something. What it mostly needs is reshooting. If it is badly shot, then it simply isn't there and music won't put it there.

I don't like people who come to me and say, "I don't like this cue; take it out." He may not like the cue, but it is there for a purpose. There are certain syndromes and certain things I do in the course of scoring that relate to moments in other parts of the score. What happens musically in reel nine may make little sense if the device I've planted in reel three has to be deleted. It isn't a matter of the director not having a musical education, but he should have a sense of architecture to appreciate what a composer is trying to do. This is true of everyone who contributes to film-making; they must have a sense of architecture. For me there is nothing more important than form. I take great exception to those people who let everything spill out on the floor and then try to piece something together.

I try not to limit myself stylistically. I feel, for example, that rock has its place and can be interesting to work with. I did a picture called *Supercops* and scored it with rock because it was pure exploitation subject, a very black comedy, commenting on certain aspects of the contemporary scene. Although there are many places where it won't fit, sometimes a rock score is the only kind you can do. This was such a picture. We did it with a Brazilian rhythm section, seven drummers, because there is a rhythmic quality in Brazilian music that is tremendously exciting. That was one of the few swinging things I've been able to do in scoring. I still dearly love to do things that swing.

One of the most intriguing things about film scoring is the opportunity it gives to explore all kinds of music. In scoring Michael Winner's unjustly ignored picture *The Nightcomers*, for example, I indulged my love of the baroque school. It was a labor of love, and I think it is Winner's best picture to date. It was beautifully filmed in winter landscapes in England, largely in and around a magnificent country manor, and it is a forward projection of the characters in Henry James' *The Turn of the Screw*. The task as I saw it was to deal with the period, the real estate, and that peculiar scent which must brush the ear ever so gently to remind us that all is not quite right and that we are dealing with two sweet children, who have become depraved killers in all their honest, naive sweetness. For the most part the score is tonal, classical, pastoral, and drawing-room-proper, but with intimations of tragedy. Of all my output through the years, it is among the film scores of which I am most proud.

It often happens in this business that some of a composer's most interesting efforts are spent on films which fail to make much impression on the public. I enjoyed scoring the short-lived television series *The Chicago Teddy Bears* because it was a chance to work with ragtime. Peckinpah's *Junior Bonner* was a modern western and needed country music. I love those kinds of innovations. If you can bring off reality in films to where people totally accept what you've done, because it is so real, then the score fits and belongs. That's where it's at.

If I had to settle for the use of just one word to describe the function of scoring, I think I would choose "portend." Film is full of portents—things which are suggested or implied by the mood of the script, the acting, the direction, and the photography. I feel music can serve that purpose probably better than the other elements. Sometimes you want to tell the audience what the picture is all about, to help set it up. Sometimes you don't. On those occasions when you don't, you can supply music which grabs attention in some ambiguous way. Often this is done to set a mysterious or tragic tone. "Unexpected" is the word. Once you have seized on a workable device, you develop it and try to intimate something which is otherwise not visible. For myself I try to make it something that is not necessarily melodic. Opinions vary on this but I don't advocate the leitmotiv method in film scoring because I don't think audiences, other than those who are musically disposed, can retain melodies on short acquaintance. What I try to create by way of getting attention is a certain sound; most people can recognize a sound, even though subconsciously. Think for example, of what Rozsa did with the theme in *Spellbound*. It was at that time a new and unique sound, and it immediately summarized the psychotic condition of the hero. That sound not only told the audience something potent about what they were watching, but signaled that something strange and exciting was likely to happen. This is what I mean by portend. If you can set up a mood with the score, people will react to it, even though they may not be aware of it. This is the function of the composer—to serve the picture.

The composer who works in films must subordinate his ego. This is not to say that he can't take pride in what he does, but the fact of the matter is that what he does is often unrecognized. Music has a crucial and critical function as part of a conglomerate, but it is not always a necessary increment in picture making.

Sometimes it is not. It depends on the kind of picture you have on hand. A picture is, after all, a composite of many different kinds of crafts. It's the result of the work of many; it cannot be done by one man, not even by the likes of D.W. Griffith or Charlie Chaplin; and this is even more true now than it was in their times. The various functions in filmmaking have become ever more specialized, demanding more and more expertise, although not always getting it. However, there are some films which simply do not require music, and there are sequences in almost all films which cannot stand music. There was a time in Hollywood when the music started with the titles and kept going to the end, but that style is long gone. You must write music for a reason. You put it in a picture for a purpose. I am a firm believer in the philosophy that if the film is working and doing its dramatic job successfully, then leave it alone. The problem for the composer is in looking at those first prints that are shown to him and having to decide immediately what kind of sound is needed. You must have the ability to project in your mind what that film will sound like with music and without it and after the proper sound effects have been added and the dialogue properly dubbed. This is all a matter of judgment, and it is the composer's toughest job. Any director who edits a film—and this applies to nine out of ten of them—doesn't seem to know what is needed musically. They become confused. They look at a rough cut, the first assemblings, and they begin to reedit the picture to where it feels comfortable to them. If they get to the point where they are satisfied and happy with what they have, then to call in a composer is almost a redundancy because to cut a film to the point where it is perfectly balanced and where there is no room for repose or further statement, leaves no leeway for music. Here is my point: music alters the tone of a scene, and directors should bear this in mind when they are editing. They should not make a final editing until they have heard the picture with music. What most directors don't realize is that they cut material unnecessarily. Material that doesn't work well without music might work well when scored. It might. I find that my biggest battle is seeing a film in the long cut, going home to map out a musical plan, and then coming back and finding that much of what I had planned no longer makes sense because the director has kicked out sequences he felt were not essential. This leaves me with few places in which to function. I have to constantly point this out to them.

Sometimes they agree to put back some of the deleted material, which usually causes them to become even more confused.

What I am getting at is this: filmmaking is a conglomerate art, a composite of the input of a lot of people. You cannot exclude any element of this business from the importance of its impact on the other elements. This has been my complaint about the whole *auteur* period, when we went into that ridiculous few years of utter worship of directors, endowing them with the knowledge of God and giving them the right to overrule everybody, including the Supreme Court and the Catholic Church. No one is that wise. You must allow for discussion and for the input of all the factors. However, common sense is no more common in filmmaking than in any other business. For example, I find that it is difficult to get the studio executives to take seriously my request that the sound department be included in whatever I am doing. I feel that the sound technicians should be privy to what I have in mind and that I should be privy to what they are planning. Otherwise we might obviate each other.

I have always felt that the duty of serious artists is not primarily to please the public; the primary obligation is to speak the truth. That is the function of the artist, and although the public may not at first like what they hear or see, they may eventually change their minds. Unfortunately, we have to make a living in the meantime. We should be able to be honest without having to worry about whether something is going to pay off, but such a nirvana does not exist and probably never will. For a composer, the business of scoring films offers something as least half way there. It allows us to exercise our craft and at the same time earn a living, and, on certain wonderful occasions, to write honestly.

I do not know if any of the work I have done in films is of any real value. I try, and there is value in that. As I grow older, I keep finding that the more I do, the more I want to do. And there are new areas within the framework of music, even as we know it now, that offer opportunities. I do not want to go into electronic music, nor do I have any desire to hit pianos with axes to discover new sounds. There is much left in conventional forms that has not been tapped yet. We are only just beginning to break away from the shackles of tonality, which Schoenberg realized decades ago and which Charles Ives also realized without ever having heard of

Schoenberg. My interest is in finding new means of musical expression within concepts that make sense to listeners and that can affect their emotions and sensibilities, which is the basic job of film scoring.

I am fascinated by those composers who have developed this craft. Men like the late Bernard Herrmann, who was one of the most capable composers of this century. So too is Alex North. In France we have George Delerue, and in England we have Richard Rodney Bennett. However, the sad truth about this business is that the best composers are not necessarily those who get first crack at the best pictures. Some of our most highly regarded men are unemployed much of the time. There can be no other industry in which the finest craftsmen are pushed aside in favor of lesser craftsmen. It is difficult to explain this to anyone not engaged in the film business, but it is the result of limited musical intelligence on the part of producers and directors. It is also a result of the influence of the record industry, with its consuming need for commercial material. What film producers fail to understand is that not every movie can stand a blatantly commercial score. Wrong music can lessen the impact of a film. There are even films that simply don't require music at all. Ingmar Bergman's *Cries and Whispers* is a case in point. There is no written music in it, but the way dialogue and sound are used in that picture is in itself a form of music. That film is a work of art.

Writing music for films is a fascinating business. It is probably the most challenging outlet for composers today. It offers enormous opportunities, but because of the nature of the film industry, it is also a line of work more than full of frustrations. Any composer who doesn't realize that or who hasn't the strength to cope with it, had best keep away. Mervyn LeRoy once said about movie acting, "Talent is not enough." That goes double for the film composer.

19
JERRY GOLDSMITH

There was little surprise in the Hollywood music community when the 1976 Oscar for the best score went to Jerry Goldsmith for *The Omen*. The general feeling was that it was long overdue. Goldsmith had been nominated eight times, and it was a matter of concern among knowledgeable film music students that it had taken so long for Goldsmith to be so honored by his colleagues. A good argument can be made in claiming Goldsmith as the foremost film composer of the seventies. His track record over the previous twenty years has been almost astonishing for its consistency of quality, and for his ability to continually devise new ways of making musical comment in films. Goldsmith was more productive than any other composer during those same years, and he seems to thrive on being busy. In the same year as *The Omen*, he also scored *Logan's Run, The Cassandra Crossing, Twilight's Last Gleaming* and *Islands in the Stream*. These are films ranging from horror to science fiction to action-adventure to political intrigue to romanticism. Each contains a substantial score that is quite distinct from the others.

Goldsmith is one of the few film composers actually born in Los Angeles. He was born in February of 1929 in an average but comfortable nonmusical family. His father was, and is, a structural engineer. His late mother had a normal interest in music and encouraged her son to take piano lessons. Goldsmith displayed no unusual musical aptitudes until the age of 12, when his skill with the piano led his parents to believe he might have a future as a musician. He was placed with the distinguished teacher and concert pianist Jacob Gimpel, with whom he remained during his

Jerry Goldsmith.

teens and through whom he was able to meet a great many of the
European musicians and composers who had left Europe because
of the Nazi era. Among them was composer Maria Castelnuovo-
Tedesco, who took young Goldsmith on as a pupil in composition,
theory, and counterpoint. The interest in becoming a composer
replaced his earlier interest in being a concert pianist, especially
with the realization that performing required more technique and
stamina than he felt he had. After completing his years of normal
schooling he enrolled in Los Angeles City College to study music
further, and at the same time he attended classes on film composition given by Miklos Rozsa at the University of Southern California.

In 1950, at 21 and a newly married man, Goldsmith sought work
in anything that would give him access to music. He was able to
land a position as a clerk-typist in the music department of CBS in
Hollywood and gradually made known his interest in composition.
The head of the department, Lud Gluskin, took an interest in
Goldsmith and invited him to join the studio musical workshop.
After a couple of years he was given minor assignments in radio,
and in time he was put in charge of providing music for radio series
such as *Romance, Suspense, Escape,* and *CBS Radio Workshop.*
Goldsmith recalls the assignments as being modest because of the
small budgets. In 1955 he graduated to television and started to
work on *Climax*, which was the first live dramatic program to
come from the CBS Los Angeles studios. They were also modestly
scored because of funds. Goldsmith was required to write a score
each week and to perform it as live accompaniment, which called
for a certain amount of ad-libbing in order to meet the timings and
to cover errors in performance by the actors and the technicians.
He himself played in the small orchestra, performing on piano,
organ, and novachord and occasionally improvising while on the
air. It was far from easy, but it was an education in scoring such as
no aspiring composer today can possibly have, since all scoring
now employed in television is prerecorded.

Goldsmith stayed with CBS until 1960, having by that time acquired a reputation as a dramatic composer with his scores for the
acclaimed series *The Twilight Zone.* He did his first feature film
score in 1957, *Black Patch*, and two similarly modest features in
1959, *City of Fear* and *Face of a Fugitive*, with the more impressive *Studs Lonigan* the following year. Goldsmith was hired by

Revue Studios in 1960 to score their *Thriller* television series, which furthered his reputation and made him known to the more important musical figures in Hollywood, such as Alfred Newman, who one day phoned Goldsmith to tell him that he was impressed with his work and would see to it that opportunities came his way. It was Newman who persuaded Universal to hire Goldsmith for what would be his first important film, *Lonely Are the Brave* (1963). Later the same year he went to Rome to record his score for John Huston's *Freud*, a score which registered him as a distinct new force in the scoring fraternity. It is still a remarkable composition, stark in character, contemplative in its shifting moods, gentle, sad, eerie, and somehow entirely suitable to this account of the early years of psychiatry. Alfred Newman brought Goldsmith to Twentieth Century-Fox in 1963 to score *The Stripper*, the first of the composer's pictures with Franklin Schaffner, which started his long association with that studio. When not working for Fox, Goldsmith has been hired by other studios, such as Paramount for *Seven Days in May* (1964) and MGM for *A Patch of Blue* (1965), both of which were aided by his music but in very different ways. The first required a dry and searing kind of music to back up an almost emotionless story of political chicanery, while the other needed a gentle and delicately toned score to underline the love between a black man and a blind white girl.

In 1966 Goldsmith scored two epic adventure films: *The Blue Max*, a grandly heroic picture of first World War aviation, and *The Sand Pebbles*, a tragic story of U.S. Naval affairs in Chinese waters in the twenties. In 1968 he scored the first of the popular films about like in the future, *The Planet of the Apes*, with a pulsating symphonic score that was somewhat Bartokian in color and a major element in the success of that bizarre fantasy. He received wide acclaim with his score for Schaffner's outstanding account of the warrior *Patton*. The main theme, a jaunty march, captured the bravura of the American general, but it was a particular device that made its mark in this score. It was a new dynamic—a solo trumpet fanfare in triplets which echoed across the screen, fading out, and used to pinpoint Patton's thoughts on the history of warfare and his belief that he had lived in previous times. It is both heroic and slightly eerie, and skillfully underlines an important aspect of the famous soldier's character.

Like all composers, Goldsmith has written interesting scores for films which did not find favor with the public, pictures like *The Illustrated Man* (1969) and *The Ballad of Cable Hogue* (1970), both of which he considers among his best efforts. He also wrote the music for such diverse films as *Tora! Tora! Tora!* (1970), *The Mephisto Waltz* (1971), *Klute* (1971), *Papillon* (1973), the rollicking western *The Wild Rovers*, the television film of *The Red Pony* (1973), the swashbuckling adventure film *The Wind and the Lion* (1975), and the greatly successful horror yarn *The Omen* (1976), a film which would be not nearly so frightening if it were not for Goldsmith's score. It does for the film what John Williams' music did for *Jaws*—it gave the film an atmosphere of tension that was quite missing in the film prior to scoring. The contribution of composers like Goldsmith and Williams can truly be gauged only by those who have had the opportunity to see the films with and without the scores.

Franklin Schaffner makes this comment: "Jerry Goldsmith is an artist who meets all the demands upon the composer in film. He communicates, integrates, subordinates, supports, and designs with discipline." His contribution in other words, is precisely what film scoring is all about.

Jerry Goldsmith on
Film Music

I compose music for films, which makes me a film composer. Which is fine except that the tag "film composer" in this country has come to have a kind of second-class ring to it. This is ridiculous. People have never tagged Paul Hindemith or Arnold Schönberg as "professor composers," with the implication that it was a lesser rank. Some men who write music earn a living by teaching. Others pay their bills by winning grants and commissions. Still others, like me, make our way by working in films. We are all composers. I tackle every assignment just as seriously as if I were aiming it at a concert hall. The fact that a great many of the films themselves are second rate is beside the point. Hundreds of films are made; the odds are against every one of them becoming a masterpiece or even a minor classic. But I would be cheating the audience and myself if I tried to judge a film's place in history before I decided whether to give it my best effort, or only half an effort.

If a film story is less than inspiring,I find something in it to challenge me. I create a musical problem and then try to solve it. If my work is successful it adds a special dimension to the movie, even though I know right from the beginning my contribution is certainly not the single most important element, the glue that binds it all together. I don't want to sound falsely modest. I like to think that I have a hard-eyed recognition of my role. If ego is the fuel that keeps the engine running, I have plenty of it. Without ego I would be depressingly unproductive. But ego has to be controlled in any field, and most particularly in the performing arts, where there is a constant risk of getting drunk on the strong brandy of applause. Too many compositions in the concert hall suffer from lack of control by the composer. Some pieces sound like a child throwing tantrums. At times the same lack of discipline shows up in painting and literature. A close rein would work wonders. Perhaps that is the one advantage that film composition has over the other forms of music—it cannot be anything else but disciplined. The composer has to abide by strict rules, he has to work fast, and he must write music that is direct and effective.

I believe discipline is vital for creative people. If left to their own devices, they sometimes flail around, not knowing what it is they really want or how to get there. They speak vaguely about inspiration. Writing for films doesn't allow for any such doubtful luxury. Waiting for inspiration to strike is like waiting for one's ship to come in—it rarely does. I am not comparing myself to Stravinsky, but his style of work set a good example for me. He was highly disciplined. Every morning at eight he was in his study writing music, or at least putting notes on paper. He would stop for lunch and a brief nap, then go back to writing for a long afternoon. Whether he produced a little or a great deal was beside the point. What counted was the disciplined act of sitting there, day in and day out, trying to be creative. It takes on special importance for the composer because music is, I believe, the most difficult of the creative arts. A painter begins with identifiable colors, a palette, a brush, perhaps a model. A writer begins with a large vocabulary and some real-life characters, perhaps disguised but nonetheless real. A composer has almost nothing to start with. There are twelve different tones and that is all he brings to the game. So each assignment for me begins with an agonizing experience. Where shall I begin? What notes shall I play? What combination of sounds will be at once so melodic and original and attention-grabbing that the audience will be hooked? To me, ninety-five per cent of the agony is finding a point of departure, a place to begin.

I have heard some of my colleagues say that the music writes itself, but I'm skeptical. My guess is that creative people are reluctant to admit they suffer in the process of creation. But I see suffering as an inescapable part of the experience. I agonized for a month looking for an approach to scoring *Logan's Run*. Once I found it, the music took off like a racehorse. I may stumble through a lot of false starts, but that is part of the discipline of sitting there at the piano and working. Everything I do takes a tremendous amount of feeling my way around dark corners, like a blind man in a curved tunnel. When I was a student, I had to fight discouragement because I was unbelievably slow. Over the years I have developed technique, but I still haven't found an easy way to be a composer. And when some snide critic refers to film music as if it were a breeze, I am as angered by their ignorance as their impertinence.

I consider myself a serious composer. I know that much of the driving force in the studios over the years has been for popular music and that in recent times a good many serious film composers have been passed over in favor of the pop sound. But this does nothing to change my own views on film scoring. This is not to say that there isn't a place for popular music in films. It clearly has a very real place in what is largely a popular medium, and particularly in those films which deal with comtemporary issues and scenes. I agree that *Easy Rider* had the right kind of music. The score for *Midnight Cowboy* was excellent; I can't imagine a better way to do it. What I object to is the forcing of pop music in scores for blatantly commercial reasons. It ignores the real function of scoring, which is to support the film's impact on the mind and the emotions of the audience.

I have no tolerance for the critics who put down film music. The film composer today functions in much the same way as did Mozart, Haydn, and Bach with their weekly commitments to the church or their patrons, except that we haven't yet produced a Mozart, a Haydn, or a Bach. But it can happen. Just because one is composing for films doesn't mean that one has to write inferior or unimportant music. The possibility exists for excellent work, which is something our lofty music critics apparently don't even want to admit. But I consider my own efforts in film composition to be serious, and I encourage other composers to take the medium seriously.

I look upon film scoring in terms of fabric. It's a composition tailored for a film, and all its elements must relate to one another. Thematically there must be something that ties the score together; you can't just write a string of unrelated pieces. This is where I think the seriously trained composer is of more value, simply because part of the study of composition is the concept of musical relativity and development. I also think the serious composer is likely to be able to make statements more precisely and economically than the musician from the pop field.

Economy is a strong factor in my own theories about scoring. I feel less is better than more. Music should be used only when it is really necessary. However, that was not the guiding force in the pioneering days in Hollywood scoring, partly because the old films lacked reality and were steeped in fantasy—and as Jack Warner said, "fantasy needs music"—and partly because studio heads like Jack Warner loved to have their pictures afloat in music. The reason so many of Max Steiner's scores are long is that Warner demanded they be that way. Steiner often argued that the pictures would be better with less music but he was overruled. Today we don't have any Jack Warners, which is good in one way, but far worse in another. A man like Warner knew how to run a film factory. Today we have studio heads and producers who barely have any understanding, or interest, in music at all.

But to get back to economy. My main interest in scoring is in examining the characters in a film and making comment on them, and I think you can only do that if you use music sparingly. *Patton*, for example, is a three-hour film, but it has only about thirty minutes of music. The longest score I have done is *The Sand Pebbles*, which has about an hour, or one-third of the running time. One of my most talked about scores is *Seven Days in May*, and that has only about ten minutes, and *A Patch of Blue* has less than half an hour. So I can't help but feel that most of my best scores are those that use the least amount of music. I strongly feel that music is a problem in our time. The ear has become numb to it. We hardly exist without it—in elevators, in restaurants, in super-markets, in doctor's waiting rooms. It's going on all the time, and the whole value of music in films is being vitiated by this surfeit of music in which we all live. So if music is to be used in a film it must be used not only sparingly but with calculated effect.

A good film score requires two elements: it must have com-patibility, and it must have musical quality. It's hard to come to terms about the latter, but in the former I would say the composer must realize his job is not to dominate. The job is to supply addi-tional understanding to what is being said or what is being done. If, for example, you were writing an opera, you would need a sub-ject so profound that no other form of expression was possible. The same should be true of a film and its score. The composer must wait for those moments in the picture where there is a scene so special, where there is something to be said that only music can say. Then the presence of music will bring that extra element you need, and, if it's done right, it will elevate the scene.

As an example of this: in *Patton* there is a scene in which the general demands that his chaplain write a prayer for victory. The prayer is then read against a background of battle. It seemed to me to be a really vital scene and one in which I could make a com-ment that was counter to the almost overpowering visual. I saw it as an antiwar scene—in fact I think the whole film is a statement against war—and I wanted to play up the sadness and the sorrow and the irony of it all. Visually, you see the brutality of war, and yet you hear this prayer to God while men are being blown to bits. I decided to make my statement for solo violin. This brings up another important point: I was working for a man who was totally understanding of the function of music in film, Franklin Schaff-ner. We had the kind of rapport that encourages good work. As long as there are men like that and films like that, there will be op-portunities for serious composers in the picture business.

All that I can say about my method in writing music for films is that it is intensely personal. I work completely emotionally. I can-not intellectualize about the role of music in film. I decide if it should be there purely by my emotions. My reaction to what I see and hear in other people's films is also entirely emotional—and sometimes painful. I remember seeing Stanley Kubrick's *2001: A Space Odyssey* and cringing at what I consider to be an abominable misuse of music. I had heard the music Alex North had written for the film, and which had been dropped by Kubrick, and I thought what Kubrick used in its place was idiotic. I am aware of the success of the film but what North had written would have given the picture a far greater quality. The use of the *Blue Danube* waltz was amusing for a moment but quickly became distracting because it is so familiar and unrelated to the visual. North's waltz would have provided a marvelous effect. He treated it in an original and provocative way. It is a mistake to force music into a film, and for me *2001* was ruined by Kubrick's choice of music. His selections had no relationship, and the pieces could not comment on the film because they were not a part of it. So I come back to my theory that a score is a fabric which must be tailored to the film.

There is a danger in writing music for films year after year in becoming repetitive and not developing one's skills and technique. We all worry about that. In my own case I think I could have grown more, but I also think I have become more skillful over the years and broadened my reach in terms of style. At least, I'm conscious of trying. There are lots of areas left to grow in. The main drawback of writing for films is that is it restrictive. You have to hold yourself back. Most concert composers, like Stravinsky and Schoenberg, could not write for films because their ego would always get in the way. They would not condescend to stop the flow, the natural flow of creativity to accommodate the needs of the picture. You must recognize that limitation when you write for the screen. On the other hand, film does teach you to say something quickly and concisely, which is a lesson all composers should learn.

My hope is that audiences will improve. If they do, then directors and writers and composers will have to improve. I see signs of it. The whole range of musical literature is available to the public today, and their ears are attuned to everything. It's possible to use almost any style in film scoring and not shock audiences. A generation ago *Le Sacre du Printemps* was considered way-out. Now it isn't. Avant-garde music is readily available and so is electronic music, and all these forms can be used in scoring. However, I would caution would-be composers to be careful about becoming tricky with devices. The message is what counts. I've noticed that despite all the sophistication of our times, the greatest device of all remains the simple, straightforward melody. Using it in a sparse and simple way is still the best way. I'm also wary of the overuse of electronics in scoring, because it tends to have a depersonalized sound. People seem to think I used a lot of electronic instruments in *The Planet of the Apes.* Actually there wasn't a note of it in the whole score. I still feel that the standard orchestra has many untapped resources. I took conventional instrumentation in that score, but did unconventional things with it. For example, I used the French horn and had the player take off the mouthpiece and just blow air through it. There was a bass clarinetist who at one point didn't play notes, but just clicked the keys. I also used a ram's horn. In other words I achieved a wide range of effects outside of orthodox music, but within the range of a normal orchestra, which has almost no limits.

It's nice to think about the Golden Age of Hollywood, with the big studios and their fabulous music departments and the hundreds of films coming out every year. But it's gone. In some ways the composer today is more fortunate, provided he can find a good film, because he can attempt more than he could two decades ago. Twelve-tone music was unheard of during Max Steiner's heyday, as were any other avant-garde techniques. Finally, the future of film music rests with the composers themselves. If they take their work seriously and turn out the best that is within them, then perhaps we can persuade not only the public, but the filmmakers that good music is valuable in films. The public is not stupid. If our music survives, which I have no doubt it will, then it will be because it is good.

20
LEONARD ROSENMAN

There are seemingly few instances of actors taking a vital interest in film scoring and hardly any of actors coming to the aid of composers. The most shining example of an actor actually being responsible for a composer being hired for a film is that of James Dean, who advised Elia Kazan that Leonard Rosenman should be brought in to write the music for *East of Eden* (1955). Rosenman had had no prior experience in films, but Dean was insistent and Kazan decided to take a chance, albeit a calculated one, since Rosenman did have a reputation in serious music and had written scores for several plays in New York. The success of *East of Eden* made the composer an obvious choice for Dean's next picture, *Rebel without a Cause* and he would doubtless have been involved in other Dean projects but for the death of the actor. However, the two films were sufficient to launch Rosenman on what has proven to be an interesting and productive career in film music. What makes Rosenman's case even more interesting is that his work in films has been concurrent with his career as an avant-garde composer for concert halls and that there is little comparison between what he writes for one medium and for the other. The gentle, lyrical Americana of *East of Eden* is not to be found in his much more abstract and more involved chamber pieces. No other composer in California has divided his output more clearly than Rosenman.

Rosenman was born in New York City in 1924 and reached the age of 15 before showing any real interest in music. He describes his family background as being ordinary, with a father who ran a grocery store. None of his relatives or immediate antecedents were

Leonard Rosenman.

musicians. He discovered a liking for the piano when an aunt acquired one, which soon led to his deciding to study the instrument. With music as a hobby, Rosenman decided to make a living as a painter and took art courses to that end. His studies were interrupted in 1943 when he joined the Air Corps and spent the next three years in its informational and educational branch. After leaving the service Rosenman went to Berkeley, California, to study art at the Pratt Institute, but gradually found his interest in music overtaking the desire to follow a career as a painter. At Berkeley he became acquainted with the eminent Swiss composer Ernst Bloch, from whom he took theory and composition. He was also able to spend some time studying with Arnold Schoenberg in Los Angeles. Rosenman concentrated on his ability as a pianist and eventually, after returning to New York, received bookings as a performer, although supplementing his income as a teacher. One of his students was fledgling actor James Dean, who became a close friend.

Composition fascinated Rosenman more and more, and he broadened his knowledge by studying with Luigi Dallapiccola and Roger Sessions. He considers Sessions an ideal teacher because he encouraged the tendencies and tastes of his pupils rather than imposing his own. Rosenman's winning of a fellowship in composition took him to Tanglewood, Massachusetts, for further study, followed by the offer of a post as a resident composer. Serge Koussevitsky, then the guiding force at Tanglewood, as well as being the veteran conductor of the Boston Symphony Orchestra, was impressed with Rosenman and commissioned him to write a one-act opera, the success of which led to performances of other compositions. Then in 1954 came the completely unexpected offer from Kazan and entry into a totally different musical environment.

Rosenman admits to little prior interest in film scoring and to coming to his first job with almost no idea of how he would accomplish it. He was fortunate in working with Kazan, who was not only sympathetic and helpful, but who took his own, good time about making *East of Eden* and ignored studio pressure. Rosenman learned by doing and admits to being so limited in his knowledge of scoring devices that he had to ask someone at Warners what a click track was. He smiles in remembering that the man he unwittingly happened to ask was Max Steiner, who had pioneered the click track system. Rosenman was also fortunate in his next assignment, *The Cobweb* at MGM, because producer John Houseman agreed to let him write a score in an avant-garde style, using the twelve-tone scale for the first time in a commercial Hollywood film. The film was set in a mid-West psychiatric clinic, staffed by people almost as neurotic as their patients. Rosenman was delighted to find his score well received at the studio and praised in the industry. It led him to think that perhaps the tales he had heard about musical ignorance and limitations in Hollywood were false. However, once he settled into a career as a film composer, he found the general views to be largely true and that very few unrestricted opportunities came his way.

Despite the limitations of working for producers and directors with little interest in serious music, Rosenman was able to infuse his scores with ideas and devices removed from the norm. *The*

Young Stranger (1957), John Frankenheimer's first film and a touching account of the generation gap, has a romantic score, but a tone more in keeping with German lieder rather than the usual mock-Tchaikowsky. For *Pork Chop Hill* (1959), Rosenman discovered an ancient Chinese melody and used it as part of his dry comment on this Lewis Milestone picture about the bitter Korean war. He next scored *The Savage Eye* (1960) a bleak look at life in Los Angeles, for which he employed a small orchestra in a nonromantic score. Rosenman afterwards adapted the score into one of his chamber music pieces, the only time so far in which he has taken film music and used it in another form. He feels that scoring does not lend itself to concert adaptation, a view that is not shared by most composers in the industry.

Despite his views about the lot of composers working in Hollywood, Rosenman has applied himself to what he considers conventional, commercial music, and, as he explains, he has done it without shame, since it is a matter of knowing what is needed for certain products. His music for television is largely of this kind, such as his scores for *Combat, The Defenders*, and *Marcus Welby, M.D.* Rosenman admits that apart from the high income, there is also some pleasure in writing straightforward melodic music because it gives a sense of rationality to what is a largely irrational business. Nonetheless, he derives much greater pleasure in writing absolute music for chamber and concert groups. He describes film music as a craft having most of the attributes of music, with the exception that its primary motive is literary and not musical. He feels it is essential for any composer working in films to come to this understanding. Rosenman believes that despite its basically secondary nature, musical expression can or should have a virtually unlimited scope in film scoring. More often than not, the outcome is the imagination of the director rather than the composer. In scoring *Fantastic Voyage* (1966) Rosenman was able to persuade the director and the producer that jazz, which is what they had in mind, was not what this clever science fiction story needed, but that the music should come close to being avant-garde and that the sound track should contain no music until the moment the scientists begin their fantastic voyage. Up to that point all the sounds heard in the picture should be electronic. They agreed, and the result was an added dimension to an exceptional film of its kind.

Rosenman wrote two of his most unusual scores in 1970, for

Beneath the Planet of the Apes and *A Man Called Horse*. For the first, he helped enlarge the nightmarish quality of the story by giving the cruel ape warriors an accompaniment of piercing brass chords over shrill string passages, and he parodied the mutated humans with distortions of the hymm "All Things Bright and Beautiful." In *A Man Called Horse*, starring Richard Harris as a white man devoting his life to becoming an Indian, Rosenman employed genuine American Indian melodies and instruments, and even hired a choir from the Rosebud Sioux Reservation of South Dakota. It remains one of the most striking examples of combining avant-garde techniques and primitive musical material.

It is ironic, and also strangely typical of Hollywood, that Leonard Rosenman's winning of an Oscar came not from his own composition but from arranging the score of *Barry Lyndon* (1975) from the works of Handel, Mozart, Schubert, Vivaldi, and others. His next assignment was of a similar nature, but with vastly different material. For *Bound for Glory*, an account of folk balladeer Woody Guthrie, Rosenman arranged a large number of Guthrie songs and built his incidental score along similar lines. These two films, so very different in their musical needs, illustrate the range of knowledge required of any composer who would excel in the craft of film scoring. Such a man is Leonard Rosenman, who also happens to be one of the most erudite and articulate musicians in the film industry. The following is a slightly shortened version of an article the composer wrote for the Fall-Winter 1968 issue of *Perspectives in New Music*, published by the Princeton University Press, Princeton, New Jersey, and used with his consent.

Leonard Rosenman on Film Music

Several years ago I was invited by a university to teach a course in musical composition for films. I declined the offer saying that composition is composition and that I felt such a course would be better taught under the aegis of the Business Administration Department. My reply to this invitation was only half-facetious, for in functional music media, there are in fact no special compositional techniques to be learned. Nevertheless, such composition depends on a unique combination of aesthetic, musical, and dramaturgical considerations, which may be of interest to discuss here.

By "functional music" I mean music written not primarily for performance alone, but specifically for literary-image media over which the composer has no control, unlike opera for example. Since this field is so vast and complex that a full treatment is impossible within a comparatively short space, I shall limit myself to a discussion of music for films, as it is practiced, and as it possibly should be practiced, in the United States.

Music in the silent film era had several functions, all of which can be said to be literal in character. The first and most obvious was the transliteration of sound effects into the musical realm. At first, all this was done by way of either a live pianist or, in more lavish cases, a live orchestra. Eventually recordings were used. The second function, not only literal, but pragmatic, was that of covering up the noise of the projector. The third function, and perhaps the most interesting, involves a fear of silence, still ever present in our time. There is, in addition to the plain truth that the early filmmakers simply did not trust their products (and often with good reason), an aesthetic basis for this fear.

Dramatically, the concepts of a film and a live stage play are larger than life. Physically, however, while one medium depicts people up to ten times life-size, the other, using living performers, is framed in a smaller-than-life reference by both the audience's vantage point and the proscenium arch. However, through the characters in a play seem physically smaller than life (by the optics of perspective), they are indeed alive and fill the silences with a living aura: breathing, footsteps, the rustle of clothing, and so on.

In the silent film, the only sounds emanating from the product were mechanical and not alive. Therefore, in a medium in which audience empathy is mandatory for success, it was felt that during the silences the audience would subtly begin to fixate not upon the film, but upon the only source of life in the theater, namely, the sounds of the audience itself. Psychologically it is interesting, even today, to find an audience rapt with attention during noisy parts of the film, but beginning to cough and fidget during the silent moments. I think that this kind of restlessness embodies a need for the reassurance of a live environment.

The early filmmakers had an even more difficult problem than the filmmakers of today. Their product was totally silent. They lacked even a fair-sized arsenal of attention-getting weapons. It was therefore much easier for the audience to lose its empathy. Thus, music served to mask the silence. The results of this panic over silence were often grotesque.

Stylistically, film music of the silent era was another manifestation of American concert music of the time. The influence of the major European composers of the late nineteenth and early twentieth centuries was primary in concert music, and in film music too—but in a literal manner. Film scores consisted of the actual works of these Eurpoean composers. Those of us who remember seeing *The Son of the Sheik*, with Rudolph Valentino, recall to this day the score, which consisted of repetition ad nauseam of the slow movement of Tchaikovsky's Fifth Symphony. And for some strange reason lost to time the filmmakers picked the B section.

After the emergence of sound, and a subsequent transitional period of literalism, a new development began to take place. Quite unconsciously the filmmakers discovered that music had the power to embellish and change an audience's perception of the dramatic context of images and words, that music, though in itself not possessing universally codified applicable emotions, could, in a catalytic way, cause affective reactions in various contexts. The force of this idea emerged more out of the general trial-and-error methods of film work than from a knowledge of drama, film, music, or aesthetics. Moreover, as a more sophisticated extension of some of the aspects of the literal period, it was discovered that where the filmmakers had not fulfilled the dramatic requisites of the film, music in many cases served to give the illusion of completeness and of dramatic clarity.

Also, since music was (and still is) the only abstract element in a medium which has always depended on an audience's empathy with literary images and words, it followed that music's misunderstood essence imbued it with an aura of magic and mystery. Composers were, and still are, regarded as witch doctors who dispense their musical salves and ointments to be applied liberally over parts of the film felt to be ailing. Thus, out of the discovery of the catalytic nature of music in its relationship to images and words there developed the tradition of the huge scores found in films of the thirties through the fifties.

It was common at that time to find, in a film of approximately ninety minutes duration, almost every frame of film scored. Of course, this practice was, on the face of it, self-defeating. Music, by its constant and overbearing presence, canceled itself out. Its potential affective catalytic power was emasculated through a failure to provide constrast, to delineate ideas, and to use discrimination in dramaturgic placement.

Stylistically, the musical lag from the culture to the subculture could now be clearly perceived. While concert music in the United States had begun to come into its own, film music continued to follow the path of music in silent films. Progress had been made, however. No longer were the actual works of the old European concert composers played as film scores. Instead, there arose a crop of film composers who were steeped in and wrote in the nineteenth-and early twentieth-century styles of Tchaikovsky, Rachmaninoff, Wagner, Strauss, and Mahler. Many of these film composers were Europeans and came from the opera houses and theater pits of Vienna, Berlin, Paris, and Odessa. There were, for the most part, well-trained musicians whose close association with the music of the composers mentioned above manifested itself in the well-known "schmaltzy" style of almost all movie music of that period.

With the demise of the original Mesozoic film giants, a new class of filmmakers and composers gradually emerged. The influence of naturalistic European films began to be felt at the box office. The successes and popularity of such younger and more imaginative filmmakers as Fellini, Kurosawa, Bergman, and Clouzot con- tributed materially to the dawning necessity for a more imaginative and truthful use of the now vast and complex mid-twentieth- century film technology.

In previous periods of the short history of films, behavior on the screen had been taken at face value. Scenarios were, with few ex- ceptions, soap operas where two-dimensional characters flickered down their predictable paths towards the fade-out. This aspect of the portrayal of human behavior was probably consistent with the way the filmmakers of the time saw all human behavior (including their own) in "real" life. It was an era of a kind of nineteenth- century operatic lack of insight into what motivates real people to do real things.

Viewed in the context of mid-twentieth-century American society, one can see that the dawning interest in the "inner man," influenced by Freud and his investigations, soon began to penetrate the subculture of the entertainment media. This pursuit of truth in the subculture had and still has complex ramifications of both a felicitous and sinister nature. What are these ramifications and how do they apply to functional music?

The answer is found by noting how the subculture makes use of all elements of the culture—artistic, social, and scientific. Behavioral studies, especially, and their findings on how people live began to play a crucial role in the determination of techniques of salesmanship. Advertising agencies, radio and television heads, and filmmakers developed techniques for the use of "hidden persuaders," "subliminal" public messages, and psychologically oriented guidance to buy, to pay attention, to be sold along avenues which were psychologically constructed, paved, and walled in for the purpose of making the audience buy the sometimes unbuyable.

In film music it was found that the catalytic element could be psychologically more effective when capsulized in the form of a theme, ballad, or motif. This element worked best when "plugged"—repeated over and over, in no matter what the context, thus making any given context understandable by conditioning and association.

A good example of the felicitous use of this technique is probably one of the first of its kind. The film *Laura* was a slightly better-than-average suspense melodrama, based on a contrived and absurd premise. Its musical theme, a haunting ballad by David Raksin, was totally responsible for the film's becoming something of a "classic." In this example the hidden persuader, having almost the character of an early Alban Berg song, transcended the product which it was written to sell and catalytically imbued that product with the illusion of deep meaning.

An example of another sort is the score to the recent film success, *Dr. Zhivago*, by Maurice Jarre. "Lara's Theme," which is the central selling point of the score, is plugged and replugged by an orchestra seemingly in the last stages of elephantiasis. Even the most superficial scrutiny of "Lara's Theme" disclosed its imperfections (a charitable term). Its amateurishly twisted progressions aiming at modulation (and missing the mark), its actual wrong notes and unlettered harmonic choices simply make a bad tune. But all these elements, repeated incessantly by a huge and bloated instrumentation, succeeded in successfully selling the product and itself to a brainwashed consumer public.

But, as Lionel Newman, head of the music department of Twentieth-Century-Fox Studios pointed out, both composers in these examples have given the filmmakers more than their money's worth in the discharge of their duties as film composers. This is true, and serves to underline the fact that the film composer plays the role of catalyst in the subculture. His function is to help "sell" the film.

As can be expected, there followed from the premise of psychological salesmanship the conclusion that, if songs and songlike themes can sell a film, then song writers would make better film composers than composers of a symphonic background. Thus there arose the condition in which pop tune writers, pop music personalities, pop singers, and the like were called upon to compose music for films. At the moment of this writing most of the new "talents" in film music composition are refugees from the overworked and dying novelty-fad of cool jazz. It is at once comical and tragic to see their discomfort in attempting to write counterpoint, to essay a symphonic style, or to write dramaturgically in any fashion outside the limited ken of their musical experience.

To summarize, music in films began as literal sound effects and as a palliative to the fear of silence. It grew into a generalized and self-defeating "open" persuader. It now assumes the role of hidden persuader and acts to humanize mechanical images. It acts specifically to endow those images and words with meanings not immediately perceived by the eye and ear.

In this short history, I have not meant to give the impression of stratified historic periods; nor do I wish to imply that, while the previously discussed musical mainstream developed, there was not another dimension of functional music worth discussing. On the contrary, this latter topic is perhaps the crux of the entire discussion, which I propose to treat at this time.

Reality is, in films, an interpretation of naturalism. The image of the film, vastly larger than life, is by itself not real. For its reality it depends on its cohesive intellectual and affective statement. It is often the musical statement in the film that gives it its reality. This is somewhat paradoxical because music is, within the filmic frame of reference, its most unnaturalistic element.

Considering the catalytic and psychological aspects of film music previously discussed, it becomes increasingly clear that film music has the power to change naturalism into reality. Actually, the musical contribution to the film should be ideally to create a suprareality, a condition wherein the elements of literary naturalism are perceptually altered. In this way, the audience can have the insight into different aspects of behavior and motivation not possible under the aegis of naturalism.

Film music must thus enter directly into the plot of the film, adding a third dimension to the images and words. It is an attempt to establish the suprareality of a many-faceted portrayal of behavior that should motivate the composer in the selection of sequences to be scored and, just as important, the sequences to be left silent. I cite a simple example of a specific use of music to illustrate this precept.

The image is that of a long shot of a large city, perhaps New York or San Francisco. The camera comes in for a closer shot of the city. Now we can see, in some detail, the crowds, moving vehicles, and the general hustle and bustle indigenous to this environment.

The composer has several choices in interpreting this scene: First, he can elect to write one of those "big city" tunes most often heard as scoring to such scenes. The usual accompaniment to the Gershwin-like tune consists of an energetic ostinato, with a great deal of percussion, especially the xylophone. This kind of approach, often mingled with the naturalistic sound effects of the scene, does nothing to emphasize, improve upon, or say anything else about what the eye and ear already perceive, naturalistically. Second, he can elect not to score the scene, allowing sound effects to give the scene an aura of naturalism. Third, he can substitute composed and orchestrated "big city" noises for the sound effects, thus reverting to the old practice of literalism.

On the other hand, let us suppose that he elects to say something with music that will change the audience's perception of the image. Suppose he wants to make the statement that, "The city, for all its movement and activity, is actually a lonely place." Perhaps he would then score this sequence with solo instruments playing long lines, using disjunct intervals and phrases. In "playing against the scene" in this way, he will have intruded into the plot of the film.

He will have created that suprareality in altering the naturalism of the image, so that, as a work of art, the image can be perceived interpretively and not merely actually.

Throughout the mainstream of film music, there has been a parallel minority stream which, in my opinion, points toward a more creative and imaginative use of music in functional media. It is not coincidental that music of this minority was written by composers who wrote not only functional music, but concert music as well. Concert composers who are awake to and interested in functional music are, by their training and interests, the potential possessors of that kind of original musical vocabulary and musicodramaturgic syntax which constitute the culture, from which the subculture borrows and derives its driving forces. I use the word "original" not necessarily in terms of literal originality of compositional style, but rather in a larger sense—that of the very basis of descriptive comparison between the culture (original) and the subculture (derived).

It is the immediate and firsthand impact of a cultural force upon the subculture that imbues the subcultural industry with a deeper and more communicative spirit almost approaching "art." As it exists today, the big-studio film concept can only approach "art" but not achieve it. The closer to a concept of "art" we get, the more we observe that "art" is something of a one-man show. The achievement of a cooperative art, as the film is sometimes called, is, as yet, a thing of the future. (By "cooperative," I mean film media using all the arts, including music.) Certainly an examination of the works of today's film "artists" will bear this out. The works of Fellini, Bergman, and Kurosawa are almost completely one-man shows. They exemplify that branch of the arts into which film aesthetically belongs, that of literature, of pictures, and verbal ideas. It is no coincidence that, in the works of the filmmakers mentioned above, very little music is used. And if and when music is used, it is of a decidedly literal and/or naturalistic character. This does not mean that the concept of a "cooperative art" as applied to films is either false or impossible to realize. It does mean, however, that, by implication, in order to fashion a cooperative art one needs artists in all fields to do the fashioning.

In the musical realm the contemporary composer with a dramaturgical awareness can contribute greatly to this realization. He has a compositional technique superior to most, if not all, of the home-grown Hollywood film music producers. He has a greater sense of musical history and style, which would enable him to adjust his articulation more imaginatively to the basic intent of the film, both in terms of variety and, if necessary, style. He has, besides, a more imaginative and articulate sense of musical interpretation of the potential reality of the image than a bandleader or jazz musician engaged in scoring a film demanding a more sophisticated symphonic treatment. Furthermore, in an age of economy, in which studios want to get the most out of the least, the contemporary composer has that knowledge of the practice of chamber-music composition vital to the production of new scores involving small combinations of instruments.

Surely the great composers in musical history who dealt with opera and theater had these abilities. One can imagine (and composers in Hollywood often do!) what kinds of film scores that Mozart, Schumann, Hugo Wolf, Mahler, Strauss, Berg, Schoenberg, and Stravinsky (and the list merely begins here) would have written.

Previously I have discussed the catalytic ability of music to change the audience's perception of images and words. I now turn to the corollary: that of the effect of the image and words upon the music. There is a symbiotic catalytic-exchange relationship between the film and the music that accompanies it. I have personally had the experience of hearing musically unenlightened people comment positively and glowingly on a "dissonant" score after seeing the film. I have played these same people records of the score without telling them that it came from the film they had previously seen. Their reactions ranged from lukewarm confusion to positive rejection—no doubt their potential reactions on hearing a contemporary work of similar style in the concert hall.

It is therefore more than ever possible, in today's film of contemporary and even experimental images and words, for the composer to write stylistically the kind of music he would write for the concert hall. The important qualification to this statement is that the whole problem of musical style must be viewed strictly within the context of the functional field. Thus, the problems of form and style which arise in any serious approach to functional music must be discussed within a basically more complex definition of functional music than has been hitherto discussed in this article.

Within the strictest sense of musical definition, most functional music is not music at all. This is not a critique of the practice of functional music, but rather a musico-aesthetic statement about the circumscription of the field itself. For, while most of the elements of music as we know them appear to be present in the functional field, there is one element that is conspicuously absent. It is the propulsion of the score by means of musical ideas. As stated at the beginning of this article and implied throughout it, functional music is impelled by literary ideas. In an opera, the composer can manipulate the image or the text to satisfy the demands of the music. In films, he must manipulate his music to express literary ideas. Thus any truly musical aspect of a film score comes as a by-product and not as a direct result of the marriage with the literary form. By this I mean that any potential concert music which may ultimately arise from the body of the functional score must be reconceived and rewritten after the fact of its original intent and creation in order that its Gestalt be that of a musical nature.

The functional field is a potential laboratory for the composer in which he can try out almost anything he wishes, provided it fits into the schema of the literary form. In today's film media, there are always opportunities for sequences in which experimentation and "serious" composition can be carried out.

In the film *Fantastic Voyage*, I experimented with *Klangfarben* and varied counterpoints of these kinds of sounds. At that time, I was also writing a symphonic work in which this kind of texture played an important part. The opportunity of utilizing this particular technique in the film score enabled me to write certain sections of my concert piece with less speculation than if it had been otherwise.

Since the composer is usually given from four to ten weeks to write more music than is found in Beethoven's Ninth Symphony (I naturally speak quantitatively), several barriers exist to the composer's deriving any musical benefit from the assignment. But these can be overcome by a combination of attitude and experience.

Obviously, unless the composer is a Mozart, it is not possible for him to approach this kind of assignment with the same attitudes manifested toward the creation of a concert work of that length. It is mandatory, for practical reasons as well as reasons of sanity, to approach the assignment with both limited and realistic compositional goals in mind. Usually, in a film which requires, say, forty-five minutes of music, the sequences in which the composer can treat somewhat experimentally are comparatively few in number. Besides, most film music consists of rather simple elements: long chords, repeated impacts, single long lines, ostinati, and so on. These elements need not be complex to say whatever is needed.

Since, as I have pointed out, there is a two-way catalytic interaction between music and film, the serious musical intent of the composer in the context of the laboratory is of mutual benefit to both film and composer. If, throughout the pursuit of these realistic musical goals, the composer understands that his music serves a literary context, then he is giving both his audience and his employer their money's worth. The intensity and seriousness of the composer's musical intent will thus cause the image to be more vitally communicative.

In conclusion, I feel that functional music has the potentialities of providing at least some of the answers to the composer's questions of survival as a spiritual and economic being. As the functional field can use the services of the contemporary concept composer so can this composer use the field. As influx of knowledgeable and serious composers into functional fields is needed by both parties. Since music appears to be a permanent part of the film expression, the music of the concert composer who is dramaturgically aware will contribute to the possible creation of the yet unfulfilled idea of a cooperative art.

Film Music Discography
Since 1970
Compiled by Page Cook*

John Addison
 Smashing Time.   ABC Records ABCS-OC-6
 Sleuth (with Dialogue Highlights). Columbia S-32154
 Swashbuckler.   MCA 2096
 A Bridge Too Far.   United Artists LA762-H

Jeff Alexander
 Dirty Dingus Magee.   MGM ISE-24ST

Daniele Amfitheatrof
 Salome; Dance of the Seven Veils. RCA ARL-42005
  Conducted by Charles Gerhardt.

David Amram
 The Arrangement.   Warner Bros. WS-1824

Malcolm Arnold
 David Copperfield (TV Score).   GRT Records 10008

John Barry
 Mary, Queen of Scots.   Decca DL 79186
 Diamonds are Forever.   United Artists UAS 5220
 The Last Valley.   Dunhill DSX-50102
 Alice's Adventures in Wonderland. Warner Bros. BS-2671
 The Day of the Locust.   London PS 912
 The Dove.   ABC ABDP-852
 King Kong (1976).   Reprise MS 2260
 The Deep.   Casablanca NBLP 7060

Sir Arnold Bax
 Oliver Twist (Two Lyrical Pieces). London SPC 21149
  Conducted by Bernard Herr-
 mann.

Arthur Benjamin
 An Ideal Husband (Two Scenes). London SPC 21149
  Conducted by Bernard Herr-
 mann.

*Mr. Cook has, since 1963, been the film music commentator for *Films in Review.*

Richard Rodney Bennett
   Nicholas and Alexandra.   Bell 1103
      Conducted by Marcus Dods.
   Lady Caroline Lamb.   Angel S-36946
      Conducted by Marcus Dods.
   Murder on the Orient Express.   Capitol ST-11361
      Conducted by Marcus Dods.
   Equus (with Dialogue Highlights).   United Artists LA839-H
      Conducted by Angela Morley.

Elmer Bernstein
   The Buccaneer (Reissue).   Columbia ACS 8096
   The Miracle and *Toccata for Toy*
      Trains.   Filmmusic Collection FMC-2
   To Kill a Mockingbird.   Filmmusic Collection FMC-7
   The Midas Run.   Citadel CT-6016
   The Trial of Billy Jack.   ABC ABCD-853
   Gold.   ABC ABCD-855

Sir Arthur Bliss
   Things to Come Suite.   London SPC 21149
      Conducted by Bernard Herrmann.

Roy Budd
   Flight of the Doves.   London XPS 591
   Kidnapped (1971).   American International A-1042
   Paper Tiger.   Capitol SW-11475

John Cacavas
   Airport '75.   MCA 2082
   Horror Express.   Citadel CT-6026

John Cameron
   A Touch of Class.   Brut 6004
   The Ruling Class.   Avco Embassy 11008

Bill Conti
   Rocky.   United Artists LA693-G
   An Unmarried Woman.   20th Century Fox T-557

Frank Cordell
   Cromwell (with Dialogue
      Highlights).   Capitol ST-640

Georges Delerue
   A Walk with Love and Death.   Citadel CT-6025
   Promise at Dawn.   Polydor 245502
   The Horsemen.   Sunflower SNF 5007
   The Day of the Dolphin.   Avco 11014

Manuel De Sica
   The Garden of the Finzi-Continis.   RCA LSP-4712

Pino Donaggio
   Don't Look Now.   Enterprise ENTF 3003
   Carrie (1976).   United Artists LA716-H

George Duning
   Bell, Book and Candle (Reissue).   Citadel CT-6006

Jerry Fielding
   The Outlaw Josey Wales.   Warner Bros. BS-2956
   The Gauntlet.   Warner Bros. BSK-3144
   Scorpio.   Filmmusic Collection FMC-11

Hugo Friedhofer
   Boy on a Dolphin (Reissue).   MCA 7136
      Conducted by Lionel Newman.
   The Sun Also Rises, Solenelle; The
      Lights of Paris.   RCA ARL1-0912
      Conducted by Charles Gerhardt.
   In Love and War, Main Title and
      Requiem.   Entr'acte ERS 6506
      Conducted by Fred Steiner.
   Private Parts, Orchestral Fantasy;
     and *Richthofen and Brown,*   Delos DEL/F-25420
  Symphonic Suite
      Conducted by Kurt Graunke.

Ernest Gold
   Cross of Iron.   EMI EMA-782 OC

Billy Goldenberg
   Red Sky at Morning.   Decca DL 79180
   The Grasshopper.   National General NG 1001
   Play it Again Sam.   Paramount PAS 1004

Jerry Goldsmith
   Freud.   Citadel CT-6019
      Conducted by Joseph Ger-
  shenson.
   A Patch of Blue (Reissue).   Citadel CT-6028
   The Blue Max (Reissue).   Citadel CT-6008
   Patton.   20th Fox S-4208
   Wild Rovers.   MGM ISE-31ST
      Conducted by Sydney Sax.
   The Last Run.   MGM ISE-30ST
   Chinatown.   ABC ABDP-848
   Papillon.   Capitol ST-11260
   QB VIII (TV Score).   ABC ABCD-822
   Ransom.   Dart ARTS-65376
   The Wind and The Lion.   Artista AL 4048
   Logan's Run.   MGM MG-1-5302
   The Omen.   Tattoo BJL1-1888
      Conducted by Lionel Newman.
   The Cassandra Crossing.   Citadel CT-6020

| *MacArthur.* | MCA 2287 |
| *Coma.* | MGM MG-5403 |

John Green
 Raintree County (Reissue).   Entr'acte ERS 6503 (2 lp set)

Dave Grusin
 3 Days of the Condor.   Capitol SW-11469
 Bobby Deerfield.   Casablanca NBLP 7071

Marvin Hamlisch
 The Way We Were.   Columbia KS 32830
 The Spy Who Loved Me.   United Artists LA774-H

Scott Lee Hart
 The Lighthouse Tone Poem.   Soleil Divin V7012s
  Conducted by Jack Murchison.
 Death Be Not Proud (Crocodylus).   Canadisque RD 207.84
  Conducted by Alain-Charles
   Surais.
 Portrait in Immortality Suite.   Pathe OM-974 006
  Conducted by Marcus Dods.

Bernard Herrmann
 Citizen Kane and The Classic Film   RCA ARL1-0707
  Scores of Bernard Herrmann:
 Suites from *Citizen Kane; White
  Witch Doctor; Beneath the
  Twelve-Mile Reef;*
  Piano Concerto from
  Hangover Square; Death Hunt
  from *On Dangerous Ground.*
  Conducted by Charles Gerhardt.
 Citizen Kane.   United Artists LA372-G
  Conducted by LeRoy Holmes.
 The Ghost and Mrs. Muir.   Filmmusic Collection FMC-4
  Conducted by Elmer Bernstein.
 The Fantasy Film World of Bernard   London SP 44207
  Herrmann: Suites from *Journey to
  the Center of the Earth; The 7th
  Voyage of Sinbad; The Day The
  Earth Stood Still; Fahrenheit 451.*
 King of The Khyber Rifles;   RCA ARL-42005
  The Mountain Pass.
  Conducted by Charles Gerhardt.
 The Kentuckian Suite.   Entr'acte ERS 6506
  Conducted by Fred Steiner.
 A Christmas Carol (TV Score).   Unicorn RHS-850
 The 7th Voyage of Sinbad
  (Reissue).   United Artists UAS 29763
 Vertigo (Reissue).   Mercury Golden Imports SRI-75117
  Conducted by Muir Mathieson.
 The Mysterious Film World of Ber-   London SPC 21137

nard Herrmann: Suites from *The Three Worlds of Gulliver; Mysterious Island; Jason and the Argonauts.*

Psycho.	Unicorn RHS-336
Torn Curtain.	Filmmusic Collection FMC-10
Conducted by Elmer Bernstein.	
Battle of Neretva.	Entr'acte ERS 6501
Sisters.	Entr'acte ERQ 7001ST
Obsession.	London SPC 21160
Taxi Driver.	Arista AL 4079
Conducted by Dave Blume.	

Lee Holdridge

Forever Young, Forever Free	MCA 2093
The Other Side of the Mountain, Part 2.	MCA 2335

Frederick Hollander

Sabrina; Main Theme.	RCA ARL1-0422
Conducted by Charles Gerhardt.	

Maurice Jarre

Doctor Zhivago Suite.	London SP 44173
Conducted by Stanley Black.	
Ryan's Daughter.	MGM ISE-27ST
The Life and Times of Judge Roy Bean.	Columbia S-31948
Island at The Top of The World (with Dramatic Highlights).	Disneyland ST 3814
The Man Who Would Be King.	Capitol SW-11474
Mohammad-Messenger of God.	EMI SLCW-1033
Crossed Swords.	Warner Bros. BSK-3161

Laurie Johnson

The Belston Fox.	Ronco RR 2006

Quincy Jones

They Call Me Mister Tibbs!	United Artists UAS 5214
$ (Dollars).	Reprise RS 2051
The Hot Rock.	Prophecy SD 6055

Bronislau Kaper

The Film Music of Bronislau Kaper: Themes from: *Lili; Mutiny on the Bounty; The Glass Slipper; Auntie Mame; The Chocolate Soldier; The Swan; Green Dolphin Street; Lord Jim; The Brothers Karamazov; San Francisco; Invitation; Butterfield 8.* The Composer at The Piano	Delos DEL/F-25421

Sol Kaplan

Living Free.	RCA LSO-1172

Fred Karlin
  Westworld.   MGM ISE-47ST

Basil Kirchin
  The Abominable Dr. Phibes.   American International A-1040

Erich Wolfgang Korngold
  The Sea Hawk and The Classic Film   RCA LSC-3330
    Scores of Erich Wolfgang
    Korngold: The Sea Hawk, Main
    Title, Reunion, and Finale; *Of*
    Human Bondage, Nora's Theme;
    The Adventures of Robin Hood,
    March of The Merry Men and
    Battle;   *Juarez,* Love Theme;
    The Constant Nymph, Tomorrow
    (Tone Poem); *Captain Blood,*
    Overture; *Anthony Adverse,*
    No Father, No Mother, No
    Name; *Between Two Worlds*
    Suite; *Deception,* Main Title;
    Devotion, The Death of Emily
    Bronte; *Escape Me Never* Suite.
    Conducted by Charles Gerhardt.
  The Adventures of Robin Hood,   Delos DEL/F-25409
    A Symphonic Suite, Conductd
    by the Composer; Narrated by
    Basil Rathbone.
  Elizabeth and Essex and The Classic RCA ARL1-0185
    Film Scores of Erich Wolfgang
    Korngold: The Private Lives of
    Elizabeth and Essex, Overture;
    The Prince and the Pauper Suite;
    Anthony Adverse, In the Forest;
    The Sea Wolf, Suite; *Deception,*
    Cello Concerto in C, Op. 37;
    Another Dawn, Night Scene;
    Of Human Bondage, Suite.
    Conducted by Charles Gerhardt.
  The Sea Hawk, Kings Row, and   Warner Bros. 3XX 2736
    The Adventures of Robin Hood,
    (Sound track excerpts).
  The Sea Hawk Suite.   London SP 44173
    Conducted by Stanley Black.
  Captain Blood, The Classic Film   RCA ARL1-0912
    Scores of Errol Flynn: Captain
    Blood, Ships in the Night; *The*
    Sea Hawk, The Albatross, The
    Throne Roome of Elizabeth I,
    Entrance of the Sea Hawks, The
    Orchid, Panama March, The
    Duel, Strike for the Shores of

Dover; *The Adventures of
Robin Hood,* Suite.
Conducted by Charles Gerhardt.
Die Tote Stadt. An Opera.   RCA ARL3-1199
Neblett, Kollo, Prey, Luxon.
Conducted by Erich Leinsdorf.

Constant Lambert
Anna Karenina (1947) Suite. London SPC 21149
Conducted by Bernard Herr
mann.

Phillip Lambro
Murph The Surf.   Motown M6-839S1

John Lanchbery
Peter Rabbit and Tales of Angel S-36789
Beatrix Potter.

Michel Legrand
The Happy Ending.   United Artists UAS 5203
Ice Station Zebra.   MGM ISE-14ST
Wuthering Heights (1970). American International A-1039
Le Mans.   Columbia S-30891
Summer of '42 and *The Picasso
Summer.*   Warner Bros. S-1925
The Three Musketeers. Bell 1310
Gable and Lombard.   MCA 2091
The Other Side of Midnight. 20th Fox T-542

Raymond Leppard
Alfred the Great.   MGM English 8112

Alan Jay Lerner and Frederick Loewe
The Little Prince.   ABC ABDP-854
Conducted by Angela Morley.

Henry Mancini
Sometimes a Great Notion. Decca DL 79185
Sunflower.   Avco AVE 0-1100
Oklahoma Crude.   RCA ARL1-0271
Visions of Eight.   RCA ABL1-0231
Mancini: Touch of Evil and Citadel CT-6015
The Night Visitor.
Touch of Evil conducted by
Joseph Gershenson.
The Thief Who Came to Dinner. Warner Bros. BS-2700
The Great Waldo Pepper. MCA 2085
The Return of the Pink Panther. RCA ABL1-0968
W. C. Fields and Me (with
Dialogue).   MCA 2092
The White Dawn, Suite. RCA APL1-1379
The Pink Panther Strikes Again! United Artists UA-LA694-G

John Mandel
   M*A*S*H.   Columbia S-32753

Gil Melle
   The Andromeda Strain.   Kapp 5513

Ennio Morricone
   Once Upon a Time in the West.   RCA LSP-4736
   Two Mules for Sister Sara.   Kapp 5512
   The Red Tent.   Paramount PAS 6019
      Conducted by Bruno Nicolai.
   Sacco and Vanzetti.   RCA Italiana OLS-4
   Duck You Sucker.   United Artists LA302-G
   Moses, The Lawgiver (TV Score).   RCA TBL1-1106
   Exorcist II: The Heretic.   Warner Bros. BS-3068
   Novecento.   RCA TBL1-1221

David Munrow
   Henry VIII and His Six Wives.   Angel SFO-36895

Stanley Myers
   Long Ago Tomorrow (The Raging
     Moon).   Odeon-EMI J 062.92.159

Mario Nascimbene
   The First Night of Quiet.   CBS S-65403

John Morris
   Silent Movie.   United Artists LA672-G
   Young Frankenstein (with
     Dialogue).   ABC ABCD-870
   High Anxiety.   Elektra-Asylum 5E-501

Alfred Newman
   Wuthering Heights.   Filmmusic Collection FMC-6
     Conducted by Elmer Bernstein.
   The Prisoner of Zenda.   United Artists LA374-G
     Conducted by LeRoy Holmes.
   Captain from Castile,   Delos DEL/F-25411
     A Symphonic Suite.
   Captain from Castile and The   RCA ARL1-0184
     Classic Film Scores of Alfred
     Newman: Street Scene; Captain
     from Castile, Catana and
     Conquest; *Wuthering Heights,*
     Cathy's Theme; *Down to the Sea*
     in Ships, Hornpipe; *The Song*
     of Bernadette, Prelude and
     The Vision; *The Bravados;*
     Anastasia; The Best of
     Everything, London Calling;
     Airport; The Robe, Suite.
     Conducted by Charles Gerhardt.

Hollywood Maestro: Themes from   Citadel CT-6003
  A Royal Scandal; How Green
Was My Valley; The Song of
Bernadette; The Razor's Edge;
Pinky; A Letter to Three
Wives; All About Eve.
Down to the Sea in Ships, Suite.   Entr'acte ERS 6506
  Conducted by Fred Steiner.
The Egyptian (with Herrmann:
  Reissue).   MCA 2029
Anastasia (Reissue).   MCA 7137
The Diary of Anne Frank (Reissue).   20th Fox GXH-6049
The Greatest Story Ever Told
  (Reissue).   United Artists LA277-G
Airport.   Decca DL 79173

Jack Nitzsche
  One Flew Over the Cuckoo's Nest.   Fantasy F-9500

Alex North
  A Streetcar Named Desire (Reissue).   Angel S-36068
    Conducted by Ray Heindorf.
  Film Music: Themes from *Un-*
    chained;   Citadel CT-6023
    The Racers; Viva Zapata! The
    Bad Seed; A Streetcar Named
    Desire; The Bachelor Party;
    The Thirteenth Letter; Stage
    Struck; I'll Cry Tomorrow;
    Les Miserables (1952);
    The Rose Tattoo; Desiree.
  Viva Zapata! and *Death of a*
    Salesman.   Filmmusic Collection FMC-9
    Conducted by Elmer Bernstein.
  Spartacus (Reissue).   MCA 2068
  A Streetcar Named Desire and   Warner Bros. 3XX 2736
    Who's Afraid of Virginia Woolf?
    (Sound track excerpts).
  Rich Man, Poor Man (TV Score).   MCA 2095

Andre Previn
  The Four Horsemen of the
  Apocalypse (Reissue).   Polydor MGM-Select 2353.125

Robert O. Ragland
  Grizzly.   Truluv GRZ 1119

Alfred Ralston
  Young Winston   Angel SFO-36901

David Raksin
  Laura; The Bad and the Beautiful,   RCA ARL1-1490
    Scenarios: *Forever Amber,* Suite.

Laurence Rosenthal
  The Return of a Man Called Horse.   United Artists LA692-G

Nino Rota
  War and Peace (Reissue).   Columbia ACL 930
    Conducted by Franco Ferrara.
  The Clowns.   Columbia S-30772
  The Godfather.   Paramount PAS 1003
    Conducted by Carlo Savina.
  Fellini's Roma.   United Artists LA052-G
  The Godfather, Part II.   ABC-856
    Conducted by Carmine Coppola.
  Amarcord.   RCA ARL1-0907
    Conducted by Carlo Savina.
  Film Music: Themes from Romeo   Cam SAG 9054
    and Juliet; The Leopard; Rocco
    and His Brothers; The Taming
    of The Shrew; War and Peace;
    The Godfather; Sunset Sunrise;
    White Nights.
    Conducted by Carlo Savina.
  Rota and Fellini: Themes from   Cam SAG 9053
    La Strada; I Vitelloni; The
    Nights of Cabiria; La Dolce
    Vita; Boccaccio '70; Juliet
    of the Spirits; Fellini's
    Satyricon; 8½.
    Conducted by Carlo Savina.

Miklos Rozsa
  The Thief of Bagdad.   Filmmusic Collection FMC-8
    Conducted by Elmer Bernstein.
  Miklos Rozsa Conducts His Great   Polydor 2383.327
    Film Music: The Thief of
    Bagdad, Short Suite; *A Double*
    Life, Prelude; *The Lost*
    Weekend,
    Walk along 4th Avenue; *A*
    Time to Love and a Time
    To Die, Love Scene; *The Naked*
    City, Epilogue-The Song of
    a City; *Knights of the*
    Round Table, Suite; *Diane,*
    Finale; *The Story of Three Loves,*
    Nocturne; *Young Bess,* Brief
    Suite.
  Miklos Rozsa Conducts The Royal   Polydor 2383.384
    Philharmonic Orchestra: Knight
    Without Armour, Suite; *Tribute*
    to A Bad Man, Prelude and
    Finale; *The Asphalt Jungle,*
    Prologue and Epilogue; *Moon-*

fleet, Seascape; *Double Indemni-*
ty, Suite; *Lust for Life,* Suite;
Men of the Fighting Lady,
Blind Flight.

Rozsa Conducts Rozsa: Julius   Polydor 2383.440
Ceasar, Overture; *Lady Hamil-*
ton, Love Theme; *The Killers,*
Prelude; *Lydia,* Love
Theme and Waltz, Four Piano
Improvisations; *The Private Life*
of Sherlock Holmes Fantasy; *5*
Graves to Cairo, Suite; *The Red*
Danube, Prelude, Nocturne (Love
Theme),
Deportation Scene.

Sahara, Main Title.   RCA ARL1-0422
Conducted by Charles Gerhardt.

Jungle Book and *The Thief of*   United Artists UAS 29725
Bagdad Suites (Reissue).

Spellbound (Reissue).   Stanyan SRQ-4021
Conducted by Ray Heindorf.

Spellbound and The Classic Film   RCA ARL1-0911
Scores of Miklos Rozsa: The Red
House, Suite; *The Thief of*
Bagdad, Love of The Princess;
The Lost Weekend, Suite;
The Four Feathers, Suite;
Double Indemnity, Themes;
Knights of the Round Table,
Scherzo; *The Jungle Book,*
Song of The Jungle: *Spellbound,*
Dream Sequence and Mountain
Lodge; *Ivanhoe,* Prelude and
Finale.
Conducted by Charles Gerhardt.

Ivanhoe; Madame Bovary;
Plymouth Adventure, Excerpts   Polydor 2353.095
(Reissue).

Julius Caesar Suite.   London SPC 21132
Conducted by Bernard Herr-
mann.

Young Bess.   Filmmusic Collection FMC-5
Conducted by Elmer Bernstein.

Ben-Hur; Quo Vadis; El Cid; King
of Kings, Themes (Reissue).   Angel S-36063

The Golden Voyage of Sinbad.   United Artists LA308-G
Providence.   Pathe Marconi C 066 14406
Ben-Hur (Newly Recorded).   London SPC 21166
Ben-Hur, Suite.   London SP 44173
Conducted by Stanley Black.

Hans J. Salter
    Maya (TV Score).   Citadel CT-6017
    Wichita Town (TV Score).   Citadel CT-6022
    Horror Rhapsody: Music for   Citadel CT-6026
      Frankenstein, Dracula, The
      Mummy, The Wolf Man, etc.

Walter Scharf
    Harold Lloyd's World of Laughter.   Citadel CT-6018

Lalo Schifrin
    Enter the Dragon.   Warner Bros. BS-2727
    Voyage of the Damned.   Entr'acte ERS 6508
    Rollercoaster.   MCA 2284

Robert B. and Richard M. Sherman
    Charlotte's Web.   Paramount PAS 1008
      Conducted by Irwin Kostal.
    Tom Sawyer.   United Artists LA057-F
      Conducted by John Williams.
    Huckleberry Finn.   United Artists LA229-F
      Conducted by Fred Werner.
    The Slipper and The Rose.   MCA 2097
      Conducted by Angela Morley.

David Shire
    Farewell, My Lovely.   United Artists LA556-G
    The Hindenberg.   MCA 2090

Dmitri Shostakovich
    Zoya and *Pirogov* Suites.   Angel S-40160
      Conducted by M. Shostakovich.
    Hamlet (1964) Suite.   London SPC 21132
      Conducted by Bernard Herr-
      mann.

Stephen Sondheim
    Stavisky.   RCA ARL1-0952
      Conducted by Carlo Savina.

Max Steiner
    King Kong.   Entr'acte ERS 6504
      Conducted by Fred Steiner.
    King Kong.   United Artists LA373-G
      Conducted by LeRoy Holmes.
    A Star Is Born (1937).   United Artists LA375-G
      Conducted by LeRoy Holmes.
    Gone with the Wind.   RCA ARL1-0452
      Conducted by Charles Gerhardt.
    Now, Voyager and The Classic Film   RCA ARL1-0136
      Scores of Max Steiner: Now,
      Voyager Suite; *King Kong* Suite;
      Saratoga Trunk; The Charge of
      The Light Brigade, March; *Four*

Wives, Symphonie Moderne; *The Big Sleep,* Suite; *Johnny Belinda,* Suite; *Since You Went Away,* Main Title; *The Informer,* Suite; *The Fountainhead,* Suite. Conducted by Charles Gerhardt.

Classic Film Scores for Bette Davis: Dark Victory Suite; *A Stolen Life,* Main Title; *In This Our Life; Jezebel,* Waltz; *Beyond The Forest,* Suite; *The Letter,* Main Title; *All This, and Heaven Too,* Suite. Conducted by Charles Gerhardt.　　RCA ARL1-0183

Casablanca, Classic Film Scores for Humphrey Bogart: Casablanca Suite; *Passage to Marseille,* Rescue at Sea; *The Treasure of the Sierra Madre* Suite; *The Big Sleep,* Love Themes; *The Caine Mutiny* March; *Virginia City,* Stagecoach and Love Theme; *Key Largo* Suite. Conducted by Charles Gerhardt.　　RCA ARL1-0422

Classic Film Scores for Errol Flynn: The Adventures of Don Juan, Suite; *They Died with Their Boots On,* Suite; *Dodge City,* Suite. Conducted by Charles Gerhardt.　　RCA ARL1-0912

All This, and Heaven Too; The Treasure of the Sierra Madre; Now, Voyager; and *The Adventures of Don Juan.* (Sound track excerpts).　　Warner Bros. 3XX 2736

Since You Went Away, Now, Voyager and *The Informer,* (Reissue).　　Angel S-36068

A Summer Place and *Helen of Troy.* Conducted by Elmer Berstein.　　Filmmusic Collection FMC-1

Mikis Theodorakis
　State of Siege.　　Columbia S-32352
　Serpico.　　Paramount PAS 1016

Virgil Thomson
　The Plow That Broke the Plains and *The River,* Suites. Conducted by Neville Marriner.　　Angel S-37300

Dimitri Tiomkin
　Lost Horizon and The Classic Film　　RCA ARL1-1669

Scores of Dimitri Tiomkin:
Lost Horizon Suite; *The Guns of*
Navarone, Prelude: *The Big Sky,*
Suite; *The Fourposter* Overture;
Friendly Persuasion; Search for
Paradise, Choral Finale.
Conducted by Charles Gerhardt.

The Alamo, Suite.   London SP 44173
Conducted by Stanley Black.

The Thing from Another World
Suite.   RCA ARL-42005
Conducted by Charles Gerhardt.

Land of the Pharaohs and *The*
High and The Mighty   Warner Bros. 3XX 2736
(Sound track excerpts).

The Old Man and the Sea   Columbia ACS 8013

Ralph Vaughan Williams
The Invaders, The 49th Parallel.   London SPC 21149
Conducted by Bernard Herr-
mann.

Sir William Walton
Escape Me Never (1935) Ballet.   London SPV 21149
Conducted by Bernard Herr-
mann.

Shakesperean Film Music: Music   Seraphim S-60205
from: *Hamlet, Henry V, Richard*
III (Reissue).

Richard III, Prelude.   London SPC 21132
Conducted by Bernard Herr-
mann.

Franz Waxman
Sunset Boulevard and The Classic
Film Scores of Franz Waxman: RCA ARL1-0708
Prince Valiant Suite; *A Place in the*
Sun Suite; *The Bride of Frank-*
enstein, The Creation of the
Monster; *Sunset Boulevard* Suite;
Old Acquaintance, Elegy; *Rebecca*
Suite; *The Philadelphia Story;*
Taras Bulba, The Ride to Dubno.
Conducted by Charles Gerhardt.

Classic Film Scores for Humphrey   RCA ARL1-0422
Bogart: To Have and Have Not,
Main Title and Martinique;
The Two Mrs. Carrolls, Brief
Suite.
Conducted by Charles Gerhardt.

Classic Film Scores for Bette Davis: RCA ARL1-0183

Mr. Skeffington, Forsaken.
  Conducted by Charles Gerhardt.
Classic Film Scores for Errol Flynn: RCA ARL1-0912
  Objective, Burma!, Parachute
  Drop.
  Conducted by Charles Gerhardt.
The Silver Chalice.   Filmmusic Collection FMC-3
  Conducted by Elmer Bernstein.
The Spirit of St. Louis (Reissue).   Entr'acte ERS 6507
Peyton Place, Hilltop Scene.   RCA ARL-42005
  Conducted by Charles Gerhardt.
The Nun's Story (Reissue).   Stanyan SRQ 4022
The Nun's Story and *Sayonara*   Warner Bros. 3XX 2736
  (Sound track excerpts).
Sunrise at Campobello, Brief Suite.   Entr'acte ERS 6506
  Conducted by Fred Steiner.

David Whitaker
Run Wild, Run Free.   SGC/Atco SD 5003

John Williams
Fitzwilly.   United Artists UAS 5173
Jane Eyre (TV Score).   Capitol SW-749
Cinderella Liberty.   20th Fox 100
Earthquake.   MCA 2081
The Towering Inferno.   Warner Bros. BS-2840
The Eiger Sanction.   MCA 2088
Jaws.   MCA 2087
The Missouri Breaks.   United Artists LA623-G
Star Wars.   20th Fox T-541 (2 Lp set)
Close Encounters of the Third
  Kind.   Arista AL 9500
Star Wars and *Close Encounters of*   RCA ARL1-2698
  The Third Kind, Suites.
  Conducted by Charles Gerhardt.

Star Wars and *Close Encounters of*   London ZM 1001
  The Third Kind, Suites.
  Conducted by Zubin Mehta.
The Fury.   Arista AL 4175

Victor Young
For Whom the Bell Tolls (Reissue).   Stanyan SRQ 4013
  Conducted by Ray Heindorf.
For Whom the Bell Tolls, Suite.   London SP 44173
  Conducted by Stanley Black.
Classic Film Scores for Humphrey   RCA ARL1-0422
  Bogart: The Left Hand of God.
  Conducted by Charles Gerhardt.

Motion Picture Music: A Select Bibliography

By Win Sharples, Jr.

Reference and Bibliographic

ASCAP—30 Years of Motion Picture Music. New York: American Society of Composers, Authors and Publishers, 1967.

Harris, Steve, ed. *Recorded Music for Motion Pictures, TV and the Theater*. Los Angeles: A-1 Record Finders, 1976.

Lang, Edith, and West, George. *Musical Accompaniment of Moving Pictures*. Reprint. New York: Arno Press, 1970.

*Limbacher, James. *Film Music: From Violins to Video*. Metuchen, N.J.: Scarecrow Pres, 1974.

McCarty, Clifford. *Film Composers in America: A Checklist of Their Work*, 1953. Reprinted with minor additions and corrections. New York: Da Capo Press, 1972; new edition in progress.

Rapee, Erno. *Encyclopedia of Music for Pictures*, 1925. Reprint. New York: Arno Press, 1970.

———. 1928. *Motion Picture Moods for Pianists and Organists*, Reprint. New York: Arno Press, 1970.

*Basic collections of composers' filmographies, with Limbacher more up to date, but marred by errors. In addition, filmographies for many composers may be found in *Music for the Movies* (Thomas) and *Filmmusic Notebook* (Bernstein).

*Books***

Arnheim, Rudolph. *Film as Art*. Berkeley: University of California Press, 1957.

Baker, Fred, and Firestone, Rose, eds. *Movie People: At Work in the Business of Film*. New York: Douglas Book Corp., 1972. Chapter "Quincy Jones on the Composers.

Bazelon, Irwin. *Knowing the Score*. New York: Van Nostrand Reinhold, 1975.

Berg, Charles Merrell. *An Investigation of the Motive for and the Realization of Music to Accompany the American Silent Film, 1896-1927*. New York: Arno Press, 1976.

Beynon, George. *Musical Presentation of Motion Pictures,* New York and Boston: G. Schirmer, 1921.

Chase, Donald, ed. *Filmmaking: The Collaborative Art*. Boston and Toronto: Little, Brown and Company, 1975. Chapter 9, "The Composer."

Chavez, Carlos. *Toward a New Music: Music and Electricity*. Translated from the Spanish by Herbert Weinstock. New York: W.W. Norton, 1937.

Clair, Rene. *Cinema Yesterday and Today*. Translated from the French by Stanley Applebaum. Edited and with an introduction and annotations, by R.C. Dale. New York: Dover, 1972.

Colpi, Henry. *Defense et illustration de la musique de film*. Paris: Societe d'Etudes, de Recherches et la Documentation Cinematographique, 1963.

Copland, Aaron, *The New Music*. New York: W.W. Norton & Co., 1968. Revision of *Our New Music*, 1941.

———. *What to Listen for in Music*. 1939. Revised edition. New York: McGraw-Hill, 1957.

Davy, Charles, ed. *Footnotes to the Film*. New York: Oxford University Press, 1937. "Music on the Screen," by Maurice Jaubert.

Dolan, Robert Emmett. *Music in Modern Media*. New York and Boston: G. Schirmer, 1967.

Eisler, Hanns. *Composing for the Films*. 1947. Reprint. Plainview, N.Y.: Books for Libraries Press, 1971.

Evans, Mark. *Soundtrack: The Music of the Movies*. New York: Hopkinson and Blake, 1975.

Faulkner, Robert. *Hollywood Studio Musicians: Their Work and Careers in the Recording Industry*. Chicago: Aldine-Atherton, 1971.

**Many of these titles are out of print and not generally available.

Geduld, Harry, ed. *Film Makers on Film Making: Statements on Their Arts by Thirty Directors,* Bloomington, Ind.: Indiana University Press, 1975.

————. *The Birth of the Talkies: From Edison to Jolson.* Bloomington, Ind.: Indiana University Press, 1975.

Gillett, John, and Manvell, Roger. "Music and Film." In *The International Encyclopedia of Film.* Edited by Roger Manvell et al. New York: Crown, 1972.

Hagen, Earle. *Scoring for Films.* Hollywood, Calif.: E.D.J. Music, 1971.

Hamilton, James C. *Leith Stevens: A Critical Analysis of His Work.* D.M.A. dissertation. University of Missouri-Kansas, 1976.

Hofmann, Charles. *Sounds for Silents.* New York: Drama Book Specialists, 1969.

Huntley, John. *British Film Music.* 1947. Reprinted. New York: Arno Press, 1972.

Irving, Ernest, with Hans Keller and Wilfred Mellers. "Film Music." In *Grove's Dictionary of Music and Musicians.* 5th ed., Eric Blom, ed. New York: St. Martin's Press, 1954.

Keller, Hans. *The Need for Competent Film Music Criticism.* London: British Film Institute, 1947.

Kobal, John. *Gotta Sing, Gotta Dance: A Pictorial History of Film Musicals.* London and New York: Hamlyn, 1971.

Kracauer, Siegfried. *Theory of Film.* New York: Oxford University Press, 1960. Chapters 7 and 8, "Dialogue and Sound" and "Music."

Levy, Louis. *Music for the Movies.* London: Sampson Low, 1948.

Limbacher, James. *Four Aspects of the Film.* New York: Russell and Russell, 1968. Part 4, "Sound."

London, Kurt. *Film Music: A Summary of the Characteristic Features of Its History, Aesthetics, Technique; and Its Possible Developments.* Translated by Eric Bensinger. 1936. Reprint. New York: Arno Press, 1970.

Mancini, Henry. *Sounds and Scores.* Northridge Music, 1962.

Manvell, Roger and John Huntley. *The Technique of Film Music.* Revised and enlarged by Richard Arnell and Peter Day. New York: Hastings House, 1975.

Meeker, David. *Jazz in the Movies.* London: Britich Film Institute, 1972.

Naumberg, Nancy, ed. *We Make the Movies.* New York: W.W. Norton, 1937. ("Scoring the Film," by Max Steiner).

Nisbett, Alex. *The Technique of the Sound Studio.* New York: Hastings House, 1962.

Oringel, Robert. *Audio Control Handbook.* New York: Hastings House, 1963.

Palmer, Christopher. *Rozsa*. London: Breitkopf and Hartel, 1975.

Reisz, Karel, and Millar, Gavin. *The Technique of Film Editing*. Enlarged ed. New York: Hastings House, 1968.

Roberts, Kenneth, and Sharples, Win, Jr. *A Primer for Film-Making*. Indianapolis, Ind.: Bobbs-Merrill, 1971. Chapters 10, 11, and 12, "The Aesthetics of Film Sound," "The Sound Cutting Room," and "The Sound Mix."

Ross, Lilian. *Picture*. New York: Avon, Discus Books, 1969. Chapter "Piccolos Under Your Name, Strings Under Mine."

Ross, T.J. *Film and the Liberal Arts*. New York: Holt, Rinehart & Winston, 1970. Section "Film and Music."

Sabaneev, Leonid. *Music for the Films: A Handbook for Composers and Conductors*. Translated by S.W. Pring. London: Pitman, 1935.

Skiles, Marlin. *Music Scoring for TV and Motion Pictures*. Blue Ridge Summit, Pa.: Tab Books, 1976.

Skinner, Frank. *Underscore*. New York: Criterion Music Corp., 1960.

Sternfeld, Frederick. "Film Music." In *Harvard Dictionary of Music*, 2d ed. Edited by Willi Apel. Cambridge, Mass.: Belknap/Harvard University Press, 1969.

Sutak, Ken. *The Great Motion Picture Soundtrack Robbery: An Analysis of Copyright Protection*. Archon Books, 1976.

Thomas, Tony. *Music for the Movies*. South Brunswick, N.J. and New York: A.S. Barnes, 1973.

Thomson, Virgil. *The State of Music*. 2d ed. New York: Random House, 1962.

Ulrich, Allan. *The Art of Film Music: A Tribute to California's Film Composers*. The Oakland Museum, 1976.

Winkler, Max. *A Penny From Heaven*. New York: Appleton-Century-Crofts, 1951.

Articles

*Berstein, Elmer. "The Man with the Golden Arm." *Film Music* 15 (Spring, 1956.)

———. "On Film Music." *Journal of the University Film Association* 28 (Fall 1976): 7-ll.

*———. "The Ten Commandments." *Film/TV Music* 16 (Winter 1956).

Clair, Rene. "The Art of Sound." *Film: A Montage of Theories*, ed. Richard Dyer MacCann, E.P. Dutton, New York.

*Cook, Page. "What's the Matter with Helen." *Films in Review*. 22 October 1971.

*Dahl, Ingolf. "Notes on Cartoon Music." *Film Music* 8 (May-June 1949).

Driscoll, John. "Music is for Beauty." *Journal of the University Film Association* 13 (Fall 1960): 2-4.

*Duning, George. "Salome." *Film/TV Music* 12 (March-April 1953).

Faulkner, Robert R. "Dilemmas in Commercial Work: Hollywood Film Composers and Their Clients." *Urban Life* 5 (April 1976): 3-32.

Fiedel, Robert. "The Beast Goes On." *American Film* (March 1977).

Film Quarterly 22 (1969). The entire issue was devoted to film music.

Geduld, Harry. "Film Music: A Survey." *Quarterly Review of Film Studies* (May 1976).

*Green, John. "Raintree County." *Film/TV Music* 17 (Fall-Winter 1957-58).

*Hamilton, William, "The Bad and the Beautiful." *Film/TV Music* 12 (March-April 1953).

*Huntley, John. "Oliver Twist." *Film/TV Music* 11 (September-October 1951).

Johnson, William. "Face the Music." *Film Quarterly* 22 (Summer 1969).

**Kellog, Edward. "The ABC of Photographic Sound Recording." *Journal of the Society of Motion Picture Engineers* 44, (March 1945).

**———"History of Sound Motion Pictures." *Journal of the Society of Motion Picture and Television Engineers* 64 (June, July, and August 1955).

Lambert, Gavin. "Sight and Sound." *Sequence* (Summer 1950). Reprinted in *Film: A Montage of Theories* by Richard Dyer MacCann, New York: E.P. Dutton, 1966.

Lavastida, Bert, et al. "Music for Motion Pictures." *Journal of the University Film Association* 7 (Winter 1954): 12-17.

**Lewin, Frank. "The Soundtrack in Nontheatrical Motion Pictures." *Journal of the Society of Motion Picture and Television Engineers* 68 (March, June, and July 1959).

Magliozzi, Ron. "Starting a Soundtrack Collection." *The Thousand Eyes Magazine* 2 (February 1977).

Mancini, Henry. *Dialogue on Film*. 3 The American Film Institute.

"Music in Films: A Composer's Symposium." *Films: A Quarterly of Discussion and Analysis* (Winter 1940). Reprint, New York: Arno Press, 1968.

Nelson, Robert and Rubsamen, Walter. "Literature on Music in Film and Radio." *Hollywood Quarterly.* Supplement to vol. 1, 1946. Rubsamen compiled an addendum for vol. 3 1949.

Parker, David and Shapiro, Burton. "The Phonograph Movies." *Journal of the Association for Recorded Sound Collections* 7 (1975).

Raksin, David. "Raksin on Film Music." *Journal of the University Film Association* 26 (1974): 68-71.

———. "Whatever Became of Movie Music?" *Filmmusic Notebook* 1 (Fall-Winter 1974).

*Rozsa, Miklos. "Julius Caesar." *Film/TV Music* 13 (September-October 1953).

*———. "Music From Historical Films." *Film/TV Music* 11 (March-April 1952).

*———. "Quo Vadis." *Film/TV Music* 11 (November-December 1951).

Sharples, Win, Jr. "The Aesthetics of Film Sound." *Filmmakers Newsletter* 8 (March 1975).

———. "Love's Labour Found." *American Film* 1 (March 1976).

Steiner, Fred. "An Examination of Leith Stevens' Use of Jazz in The Wild One." *Filmmusic Notebook* 2 1976).

———. "Herrmann's 'Black and White Music.' " *Filmmusic Notebook* 1 (Fall and Winter 1974).

Stern, Seymour. "Griffith: I. The Birth of a Nation," *Film Culture* 36 (Spring-Summer 1965).

*Stevens, Leith. "The Wild One." *Film Music* 13 (January-February 1954).

*Tiomkin, Dimitri. "Composing for Films." *Films in Review* 2 (November 1951).

*Walton, Sir William. "Music for Shakespearean Films." *Film/TV Music* 15 (Spring 1956).

*Williams, Martin. "Jazz at the Movies." *Saturday Review* 50 (July 15, 1967).

*Winkler, Max. "The Origin of Film Music." *Films in Review* 2 (December 1951).

Winter, Marion Hannal. "The Function of Music in Films." *Musical Quarterly* 27 (1941).

*Articles reprinted in Limbacher, James, *Film Music: From Violins to Video,* Metuchen, N.J.: Scarecrow Press, 1974. These reprints are without their original music examples. They are far more valuable—not to say comprehensible!—in the original form.
**Available in reprint form from SMPTE, 862 Scarsdale Avenue, Scarsdale, N.Y. 10583.

Society Publications, Journals, Columns

American Film. The American Film Institute, John F. Kennedy Center for the Performing Arts, Washington, D.C. 20566. Regular column, various subjects and authors.

L'Ecran sonore. Club Filmusic, 8 Rue Gamby, 75011, Paris, France.

Films In Review. 210 E. 68th St., New York, N.Y. 10021. Regular review column, Page Cook [pseud. for Charles Boyer.]

*Filmmusic Notebook.*Elmer Bernstein's Film Music Collection, P.O. Box 261, Calabasas, Calif. 91302.

Film Music Notes/Film Music/Film and TV Music. Vol I, No. 1, October, 1941 - Vol XVII, No. 1, Fall-Winter, 1957-58.

High Fidelity. 1 Sound Avenue, Marion, Ohio 43302 (Regular review column, Royal Brown).

Journal of the Association for Recorded Sound Collections. Fine Arts Library, University of New Mexico, Albuquerque, N.M. 87131.

Main Title. Entr'acte Recording Society, P.O. Box 2319, Chicago, Ill. 60690.

The Max Steiner Music Society, P.O. Box 45713, Los Angeles, Calif. 90045.

Modern Music. League of Composers, Inc. ed. Minna Lederman. New York, vol. 1, 1924-vol. 23, No. 4, Fall, 1946. Issue 1 in 1924 and issue 2 in April 1925 were published as *League of Composers Review.*

Pro Music Sana. The Miklos Rozsa Society, 303 E. 8th Street., Bloomington, Ind. 47401.

SCN: Soundtrack Collector's Newsletter. Luc Van de Van, Astridlasn 165, 2800 Mechelen, Belgium.

Take One. Box 1778, Station B, Montreal, Canada H3B 3L3. Regular column, Robert Fiedel.

The Thousand Eyes Magazine. 144 Bleeker St., New York, N.Y. 10012. Regular column, various subjects and authors.

Documentary Films on Film Music

Two excellent films on the subject of motion picture music are also available: *Hollywood's Music Moods,* available on rental or purchase from Christian Blackwood, Blackwood Productions Inc., 58 West 58th Street, New York, N.Y. 10019, and *The Score,* available from BMI, Rusell Sanjek, Vice President, Public Relations, Broadcast Music Inc., 40 West 57th Street, New York, N.Y. 10019. Either film can serve as an introduction to the subject for interested groups.